BOXING INTERVIEWS OF A LIFETIME

By

"BAD" BRAD BERKWITT

EDITED BY LENORE AVIN

LAYOUT BY EDWARD TORREGANO, JR

ISBN: 1-4033-6998-4 (e-book)
ISBN: 1-4033-6999-2 (Paperback)
ISBN: 1-4033-7000-1 (Dustjacket)

Library of Congress Control Number: 2002094121

This book is printed on acid free paper.

Printed in the United States of America
Bloomington, IN

1stBooks - rev. 10/28/02

Contents

If you would like to schedule the Author "Bad" Brad Berkwitt for a book signing, TV & radio event, personal appearances or you would like him to personally sign your book, contact him at: **bberkwitt@aol.com**

Book Dedication - Acknowledgements

This book is dedicated to my late Father Alvin Frank Berkwitt. Without his guidance, love, and introduction to the sport of boxing, this book would not be possible for me.

Alvin Frank Berkwitt
April 12, 1928- July 2, 1998

Dad, each breath I take, each fight I make, each interview I create, you are always with me. I will love you for the rest of my life.

I would like to acknowledge the following people who have made this journey to the release of my first book so special for me.

My son, Daniel Elias Berkwitt. Your birth, brought me so much joy and opened my heart to all the wonderful things that have come into it ever since. Daddy will always love you.

My wife, Gwendolyn Berkwitt. You're the most beautiful woman and person, I have ever met. Baby, with you, my dreams have come true.

Uncle's Stan Cooper & Jack Reardon. Your love, support and constant encouragement, of my writing, means the world to me. I love you both dearly.

Casey Dansicker of 10 Kount Productions. You are my brother not by blood, but by choice. I love you.

Arnie and Sam Dansicker. Two gentlemen with a lot of class. Thanks for everything.

My little sister female IBF & UBA Lightweight & IWBF JR Lightweight Champion of the world the "Raging Beauty" Isra Girgrah. Izzy thanks for including me in your career and I know how much you appreciate what I have done for you. I am truly proud of you and from my heart, I love you Lil Sis.

Marty "Martino" Wynn Isra's other half, we had fun in Atlantic City. Thanks for everything.

Dr Eddie Roca and Carmen Roca. The love you have for my father and the true kindness along with the true love you showed him over the years, especially his last year, I will never forget. I love you both for it.

Former IBF JR Middleweight Champion, Paul "The Ultimate" Vaden. I cherish our friendship. Thanks for everything.

NABF Welterweight Champion, Golden "14 Karat" Johnson. Thanks for asking me to carry your belt in the ring on your ESPN2 televised main event fight seen around the world. It was an honor, and thanks for the close and caring friendship you have shown me.

Former IBF Lightweight and WBA JR Middleweight Champion, Vinny Paz. We have spoken many times about our life's and fathers. I know I have made my late father proud, and you my friend, have also made your dad proud. You're a credit to boxing and to the human race. Thanks for everything.

IFBA Lightweight Champion Brenda Vickers-Dudney. I am so proud of you. You know I always said you could do it. Thanks for all the support.

Glenn Harris of the legendary News channel 8 Sports Talk TV show. In your words, "I made you a star, Brad." Thank you for your support and for acting like an older brother to me and yes, you did make me a star in the Washington, DC, Maryland and Virginia areas. Also, thanks to your producer Terry Cornwell.

Norman "Doc" Hayes. Again, a brother not by blood, but by choice. I am so glad I could bring you into the boxing world. Thanks for all the support of your friendship and using your wonderful nightclub, Club Elite, in Temple Hills, MD to support my boxing writing and events. For the remainder of my life, I will always remember the going away party you had for me before I left to Seoul, South Korea for my one year tour of duty with the Navy. Thanks for everything.

Troy Williams and Robert (Bobby) A. Odum, SR., (Club Managers for Club Elite) and true friends. Thanks for all your support.

Lexis Matthews, thanks for also looking out for me in the club.

Henry "Dis-com-bob-u-lating" Jones. We have shared in each others dreams and thanks for all the support and true friendship you have shown me.

Promoter Scott Wagner of the simply put, the best boxing shows on any coast. The Ballroom Boxing shows live from Michael's Eighth Avenue that are now syndicated on TV. Thanks for always having a ringside seat for me and all the support for my writing. "Wildman" Dave Wilkerson Scott's right-hand man. Thank you for all the support.

Earnie Shavers, Teddy Atlas, Angelo Dundee, Kenny Norton, Derrick Gainer, George Foreman, Alvaro "Yaqui" Lopez, Mike Fitzgerald, Ron Lyle, William Guthrie, Joey Bishop, (the only living member of The Rat Pack), Chuck and Linda Wepner and John Scully, thanks for all the support.

Al and Judi Martino. Thanks for all the wonderful words of encouragement. Al, your incredible musical career is well documented and now, so is your love for the sport of boxing.

Aaron Pryor. You have always known you're my favorite fighter of all-time. Thanks for the kindness you have shown me over the years. I

xiv

am so proud of you that, through God, you were able to get your life back. It's an honor to be able to spread the positive word of "The Hawk" and add to the long overdue credit you had coming for your amazing boxing career.

The truly funniest, sweetest and accommodating Vanessa Del Rio. V, thanks from your favorite boxing writer, for all that you have done for me.

Michael and Bruce Buffer, two classy guys. Thanks to both of you for your support.

Gary "Digital" Williams. I have enjoyed your company as we have sat side by side at the many fights we have covered. You're a welcomed positive addition to the sport of boxing. Thanks for the support.

Edward "The Eye" Torregano, JR. We had a ball in Korea with David Chung and Moon covering countless numbers of boxing matches. Thanks for all the great pictures to accompany my fight reports from South, Korea. Also, the technical support on the computer and helping with the layout of my book. Your help enabled me to fulfill my dream of putting this book out. From this moment on, no longer call me friend, call me brother.

Lenore Avin, who is already credited as my Editor of this book. L, if not for you, it would have taken a lot longer to fulfill this dream of putting my book together. You are a kindred spirit to me and I cherish our friendship. Thanks for everything.

Steve Vance and Lee Groves. Thanks for all the amazing boxing tapes you took the time to make for me over the years. From my heart, thank you.

To my many editors over the years Greg Maldonado (Boxing Briefcase), Karl Freitag (www.fightnews.com), Chris Cozzone (www.insidewomensboxing.com) Daniel Grimaldi, (3615 Boxing Ave www.boxing-records-com whose also given credit for all the fight records used in my book.), David Dylis (www.boxinghelp.com) and Paul Rosetti along with the late Ace Alanga (The Italian Tribune Newspaper). Thank you.

To the man who made my stay in Korea a sheer delight, while accepting me into the Korean boxing community, and assisting me in everything I needed while doing it, WBC Boxing Judge and Referee, David Chung. I cherish our friendship and look forward to the many wonderful things in the years to come between us. Thank you.

Gwi-Jung Moon, Editor in Chief and designer Ji-Youn Kim, of the number one Korean boxing magazine, Cross Counter. Your magazine adds class to the world of boxing. Thanks for honoring me with the interview you did of me for the June issue of Cross Counter. I cherish our friendship. Thanks for everything.

Alfred "Leo" Halpin III, CTACS, USN (RET). Uncle Leo, thanks for always being in my corner and the never ending support. I love you.

Ken Hawk, thanks for the many kind gestures you have shown me over the years.

Edmond Smoot III. You have always been an older brother since we proudly served together at the Defense Intelligence Agency in 1992. Where did 10 years go? Thanks for all your support.

Beverly Corso. Your friendship and true love throughout my life, has enabled me to make this journey. I love you.

Aimee Benedict. We made a great team in our office and I watched you grow up into a fine young lady. You made the separation from my family a lot easier to deal with by always making me laugh. From your Big Brother, I am very proud of you.

Aida Hawkins-Vindiola. Thanks for being a good friend and helping me while we both served in Seoul, Korea.

Finally, to the countless readers of my various columns in the last four years who took the time to email, call or write with some of the most heartfelt and wonderful compliments. Each one of you, made this journey even more special to me. God Bless each and every one of you.

Forewords by

The "Raging Beauty" Isra Girgrah

I can remember the first time I met "Bad" Brad Berkwitt. It was only two years ago (year 2000), however, it seems like I have known him forever. "Big Bro" is what I call him because he is more than a great writer and a great boxing enthusiast. He is, to me, a great friend and someone to confide in - the big brother I never had at my side following my career, and who gives me great, unbiased advice (sometimes not wanting it when it is negative!!). I don't always listen....but what are sisters for???

Brad has taken my career and made me known throughout the boxing circuit and for that, I am grateful and appreciative. Every time I speak to Brad, he is interviewing someone new or old and allowing them to tell their story - something a lot of writers don't do. He cares that people in the sport of boxing get a chance to be heard. Brad is always looking for new material to write about, which sets him apart from the rest. That is why they have given him the nickname "BAD".

I remember the first interview I had with Brad! It was a phone interview and not knowing he was tape recording the conversation, he caught me cheating on an answer while he went to answer the door. (BUSTED!!) Oh well, the interview was interesting because "Bad" Brad doesn't ask you typical questions. His questions require time and thought to respond to, which also make him a unique asset to boxing.

Brad has been to every fight of mine since we met and has covered each fight, from a few days before, to a few days after the event. He has walked that dreadful (but exciting) walk to the ring before every fight with me. I hope to be accompanied by this great friend and great feature boxing writer, at many more of my fights. I am glad to have been on this path and am proud to be fortunate to have met this great, Influential man.

The "Raging Beauty" Isra Girgrah, Female IBF & UBA Lightweight and IWBF JR Lightweight Champion

Al Martino

I first heard about "Bad" Brad Berkwitt through fellow singer Jerry Vale. Brad had interviewed Jerry on the sport of boxing and he enjoyed it so much, he gave me Brad's number to call him to do an interview on boxing. Brad was more than willing to conduct the interview and from the first moment, I could hear in his voice, a passion we both shared for boxing.

In my fifty plus years of being in the entertainment industry, I have been blessed to be involved with some amazing fighters and it has allowed me great insight into the sport. Brad brought that out in our interview by asking intelligent, well researched and compassionate questions, which is quite evident by his deep concern for a mandatory retirement fund for all boxers.

In the years since our interview, Brad has sent my wife and me many positive boxing interviews and fight reports that we enjoy reading. With such an extensive knowledge on the sport of boxing, positive writing style and true concern for not just boxers, but the entire sport of boxing, I have no doubt that Brad will succeed in any facet of boxing he decides to go into when he retires from the United States Navy.

Al Martino, Legendary Singer and actor who played singer Johnny Fontane in The Godfather

Paul "THE ULTIMATE" Vaden

I was privileged with the opportunity of being exposed to "Bad" Brad Berkwitt while reading an article he wrote on former Light Heavyweight Champion William Guthrie, a couple years back. Anyone who knows my friend Guthrie, is fully aware of his past controversial lifestyle. But, what struck me most, was the rhythm of the story that Brad displayed to the readers, as it did not dwell on William's past, but celebrated his triumph in defying the odds in life and the ring. I was so floored, that I instantly felt compelled to email this writer and reveal to him how overjoyed I was to see a writer render such a positive piece. This led me to allow Brad to interview me at a time when I wasn't doing interviews.

Now, I've experienced several highlights in my career, but I've also met torrential times that would eventually create my competitive exit from boxing. Brad was so sensitive and sensible in his questions, which led me to open up a plethora of things that I'd normally not discuss with anyone, let alone a writer.

An immediate, trusting, friendship took place from our very first interview back in late 2000. What I admire most about Brad, is his push for the betterment for boxers, and for being so vocal in trying to institute a pension plan for all the boxers who put their life's on the line each and every time they step in a ring.

What's most unique about our friendship is that we've never met face-to-face. All I can say is, that Brad's writings are a welcome sight to the boxing fraternity which is clustered with negativity and evil and I'm honored to call him a friend.

In Peace,

Paul "THE ULTIMATE" Vaden
Former IBF Junior Middleweight Champion

Quotes about the Author by

Teddy Atlas

"If boxing is to continue to serve as a farm system for rehabilitated youth, then more people must learn how and why the sport helps young boys find dignity and direction, which it does through discipline and understanding of what is truth, and what are only excuses. A portal into this world is provided by boxing writer, "Bad" Brad Berkwitt as he shows more than black eyes, but the bright light of hope and future for those who live in this world."

Legendary boxing trainer and current ESPN2 Friday Night Fights Boxing Commentator, Teddy Atlas

Michael Buffer

"It was a pleasure to be interviewed by a fine boxing writer such as "Bad" Brad Berkwitt. I consider him to be amongst the best of the boxing press active today."

Michael Buffer, legendary ring announcer who made the words, "Let's Get Ready To Rumble" part of boxing history

Kathy "Wildcat" Collins

""Bad" Brad Berkwitt has been a great supporter of the women's boxing game; a game that needs as much coverage as it can get. He has taken a brave stand, and has come to the forefront as a reporter in the world of boxing - not just women's boxing. He is a man with integrity and stands for what he believes in."

Four time Women's Boxing Champion, Kathy "Wildcat" Collins

Vanessa Del Rio

"I really enjoyed being interviewed by Mr. "Bad" Brad Berkwitt! I usually get asked typical sex questions, but with "Bad" Brad, I was able to talk about my long standing interest in boxing and how much I love the sport. His questions were focused and intelligent. It's about time someone is doing for boxing what he has, and should have been done long ago, especially the retirement fund issue. Too many Boxers are left in the dust once their celebrity has faded and everyone has taken their share of the money."

Vanessa Del Rio, Legendary adult movie star and true boxing fan

Derrick "Smoke" Gainer

"I was first interviewed by "Bad" Brad Berkwitt in late 2000. From the very first moment we started talking, I knew he was different from other writers I had dealt with. You could hear the passion in his voice when he spoke about the sport of boxing, which may be unmatched by anyone, I have ever met.

His questions are ones that the fans like to hear and allow fighters a chance to answer - not your everyday type of boxing questions. He never took what I said out of context and since I am an avid reader of his column, I see that he doesn't do it with any of the fighters he has interviewed.

I have no doubt, other fighters feel comfortable talking to him as I did, because as I said earlier, they will be heard in their own words. This is something we don't see that much of throughout our careers. The boxing scene needs more writers like "Bad" Brad."

WBA Featherweight Champion, Derrick "Smoke" Gainer

Glenn Harris

""Bad" Brad Berkwitt is honest and tough. He makes the boxers feel comfortable with his ability to relate to them on a personal basis. He gets to the core of the soul of his subject, and in· the next few years, he will get his just due as one of the top boxing journalists in the world. When Brad does my TV show, the lines light up because the fans know that he really knows his stuff."

Glenn Harris, Sports Talk TV host for News Channel 8 in Virginia, Washington, DC and Maryland

Golden "14 Karat" Johnson

""Bad" Brad Berkwitt is one of the easiest boxing writers to talk to because he's one of us. He started out as an amateur boxer many years ago and it has given him great insight into our world. Brad's respect for fighters and what we go through is something I admire about him. This has turned into a close friendship between us. He is without a doubt, one of the few positives in boxing."

Golden "14 Karat" Johnson, former NABF Lightweight and current NABF Welterweight Champion

Roy Jones, JR.

"I liked the interview with "Bad" Brad Berkwitt, because his interview didn't misquote me, and it was in my own words, for a change. He stuck to intelligent questions and remained positive throughout the interview. It was refreshing to have a writer do such a positive story on me."

Roy Jones, JR., World Light Heavyweight Champion

Alvaro "Yaqui" Lopez

"I thought my interview with "Bad" Brad Berkwitt was very good and it was an honor to be remembered in such a way. I truly appreciate the fact that he thinks I was a first class fighter. During our interview, he asked very interesting and straight forward questions. It's great that he does recognize honest efforts in the ring. I deeply feel that a positive writing style such as his, will be a major factor in continuing to keep boxing alive."

Alvaro "Yaqui" Lopez, former 1970s – early 80s, top ranked Light Heavyweight and Cruiserweight, who fought for the world championship five times

Greg Page

"During my career which has spanned 30 + years, I have been interviewed by many writers. Being interviewed by "Bad" Brad Berkwitt was a refreshing change. Brad is very savvy and also extremely knowledgeable about the sport. It is apparent in his writings that boxing is his passion."

Greg Page, Former WBA Heavyweight Champion of the World

Vinny Paz

"In order for boxing to be raised to the next level of sport, we need more positive, boxing writers like "Bad" Brad Berkwitt. With a flair for writing and an insiders knowledge of the game, he brings out the good, bad, ugly and passion of the interviewee. "Bad" Brad gets two thumbs up from the PAZMAN."

Vinny PAZ, 5X World Champion, The PAZMANIAN DEVIL

Aaron "The Hawk" Pryor

""Bad" Brad Berkwitt is one of the most knowledgeable sports writers I know. He always brings something new and fresh to the world of boxing. The personal stories, stats and little known facts, just keep coming. Anything from Brad is a must read."

Aaron "The Hawk" Pryor, former WBA and IBF JR Welterweight Champion

Brenda Vickers-Dudney

"I always consider it a privilege to be interviewed. "Bad" Brad Berkwitt took the time and interest to interview me and expressed his confidence in my ability, even though I had not proven myself at that time. He has always said, "He could hear it in my voice during our first interview that I was destined to be a champion." That was almost two years before I won my IFBA Lightweight Championship Belt.

"Bad" Brad has kept in touch with my husband and I over the past couple of years mostly through e-mails, giving us solicited advice and encouragement towards my then title quest.

Even though we have never met in person, I consider Brad a good friend. His interviews, articles, and positive publicity for female boxers will help all of us in our careers."

IFBA Women's Lightweight Champion, Brenda Vickers-Dudney

Chuck Wepner

"My interview with "Bad" Brad Berkwitt was thoroughly enjoyable because he was so easy to talk to. He asked very interesting questions and his knowledge on the sport of boxing comes through. One question in particular that is hardly asked if ever, is about a mandatory retirement fund for all boxers. I am glad he asked that question and it shows his true dedication to the sport of boxing. I have always felt there must be some type of retirement plan for boxers and by asking this question, he is constantly putting it to the forefront of the sport, where it needs to be.

I feel in the years to come, "Bad" Brad's positive writing style along with his dedication to the sport of boxing, will initiate changes for the betterment of not just the boxers, but the entire sport."

Chuck Wepner, former Heavyweight Title Challenger who the movie Rocky is based on

Views That Count...

Up Close and Personal with ESPN2 Boxing Commentator, and World Class Trainer, Teddy Atlas

In life, I have always admired those who speak their minds from experience, and who "paid their dues", as we say in any profession. Teddy Atlas has done both in the many years I have seen him in boxing circles.

His ideas are fresh, come from the heart, and whether you agree with him or not, you must respect him for what he has accomplished in boxing. I happen to be one who agrees with him on many issues in boxing.

Most importantly, talking with Teddy as I recently did from my home office, I now have no doubt how sincere this man is and how much he cares about the sport of boxing. For this fact alone, he has earned my respect.

Both Teddy and I are strong believers in the mere fact that, in boxing you need to see things instituted for the good of the fighters, as well as, the whole state of boxing, instead of giving lip service to doing it.

How long have you been involved in boxing?

I have trained fighters for the last 25 years. Very early in my amateur career, I got the opportunity to go up to the Catskills in upstate New York and work with Cus D' Amato. While up there, I won the 139 LB amateur championship.

The plan at the time was for me to stay up there for a year and work with Cus, eventually turning professional. I had an injury that ended my boxing career but, Cus thought I had a born ability to teach, at a very young age. He asked me to become a trainer and at that early age, I had the opportunity to work with the many fighters that Jim Jacobs would send up to train. One of the first name fighters I worked with was, Wilfred Benitez. I also got a lot of experience developing a team of amateur fighters.

Now that you mentioned you fought in the amateurs many years ago, do you think there is a difference in the quality of fighters coming out now?

Yes, I do feel that there is a difference. There is not as much activity in the amateurs as there was in my days to really develop a young fighter. This is especially evident on the East Coast. One problem today is, there are less amateur programs than when I was involved in them.

Obviously, with less programs, there are not as many chances for a young man to learn his skill. In my day, there were more subsidized programs such as Kronk Gym that had lots of amateur fighters and boxing cards for them to fight on.

It was not unusual for a young man of only 14 or 15, to have over one hundred amateur fights which allowed him to really perfect his skills. Today, there are just not as many amateur places to fight outside of the tournament level.

Bottom Line: I would have to say that because of circumstances, the amateur fighters of old were more skilled then they are today.

Who is the first professional fighter you trained and how did he turn out?

As I said earlier, I was training fighters very young and probably guys that I had no right to train at the time. I did, in time, gain the right through working very hard with Cus and, paying my dues. One of the first fighters that I can recall, was Rafael Solis who lost his Bantamweight Title to Jeff Chandler.

Being close to Cus D' Amato as you were for many years, what qualities did you take from him and use as a trainer?

Brad, I worked with him for about 8 years, so he really taught me the many building blocks that a trainer must have in order to be successful. One of the most important things he taught me was a way to articulate to a fighter, the plan that is needed to achieve what we both are working towards.

I have watched many of your telecasts on ESPN2 and it seems that you have made the transition from trainer to commentator pretty easily. For those other trainers out there, can you give any words of wisdom on how to do this?

Well first of all, let me talk a little bit about the trainer side. One of the things that bothers me about this business from a training aspect is, that too many people get into it without paying any dues. It's the only business I know that people come in, throw towels on their shoulders, and call themselves a trainer. It insults me, and it's not fair to the other real trainers around who have worked very hard in this profession.

I feel that you must work in an apprentice program to learn the skills required to be a boxing trainer. I will give you an analogy. I love football, but I could not show up next week at the New York Jets training camp and be working the sidelines as an assistant coach. You must invest time to become a trainer with first, practical experience and then, in an apprentice role. When you feel totally comfortable from the bottom to the top, it should come out in your training methods.

With the commentary side of the house, you must remember I have been around boxing since I was kid. I never did anything else, but boxing and if you're half way successful as a trainer, one thing that you have to do, is talk to the public on a regular basis. I always felt comfortable doing this so when I got in front of the camera, it was an easy transition. One thing I try to always do Brad, when I talk to the audience, is teach them about boxing same as I would a fighter.

Who are you three favorite fighters of all-time and why?

First of all, Michael Moorer. We won two Heavyweight Titles together. I had a true bond with him and we took each other to the top. Second would be, Muhammad Ali. I have seen lots of tape on him before his layoff and he was a tremendous talent. I have always felt he was a pioneer in the sport and as I got older, I was able to see it for myself. When he made a stance he stuck to it unlike many who talk about and never do it.

Finally, Roberto Duran as a Lightweight. I used to see all those great fights he was in. One thing he really impressed me with, was he could be smart and appealing at the same time. He was a very solid fighter in all aspects and being a trainer, you had to admire that.

What is the greatest fight you have ever seen and why?

Bobby Chacon vs Cornelius Boza-Edwards I, back on May 30, 1981. Boza was defending his Lightweight Title and I can just remember that he was down early in the fight and cut. He came back in that fight and knocked out Bobby in the 14th round. It showed a fighter's will to win!

If you could personally change any factors in the ranking systems, what would that be?

You have to get rid of these organizations. For about thirty or so years, there was speculation that they were corrupt. Now it has been proven that promoters have paid bribes to get their fighters ranked, beyond a doubt. Don't just go after the IBF. You need to go after the WBA and WBC and the only reason they don't, is that they are located outside of the United States.

These organizations make 99% of their money in this country and the politicians can go after them if they really wanted to. They don't, because it's boxing! If it was football or baseball, there would be no doubt that it would have been handled long ago. We need a national commission that institutes the same rules in each state where boxing is concerned.

One of my suggestions for a more worthy and legit ranking system would be, to put a panel of respected boxing writers across the country who could rank the fighters. Also, a panel of boxing historians who could compliment the boxing writers who would take part.

Finally, you could have the local state boxing commissioners that see the fighters in the ring which would allow them to help in the ranking of them.

Do you favor a mandatory retirement fund for all boxers and if so, how would you like to see it accomplished?

They really need one, but it has to be worked out very closely. I think it should be done like this, you always have three or four huge fights a year that generate a lot of money. One thing with getting rid of these corrupt sanctioning bodies would be doing away with the sanctioning fees. They could take that money and put that in a retirement fund. Promoters have been paying it for years, so it's not like they are not use to giving it up. From there, have the commission monitor it. Fighters who met all the requirements, could get a pension from it.

In addition, I would add a simple one percent boxing tax on maybe, the three largest bouts of the year. The tax revenue would be put into the pension pool.

Do you feel that the comparison of fighters of yesteryear to today is a fair comparison to make?

I don't think you can do it because of things such as training techniques like diet doctors, conditioning specialists, etc. fighters are just different. I do feel that the fighters of old were mentally tougher because of circumstances in society.

There were less options for them in the old days to make the money that they do today. Back then, you had more clubs for a fighter to learn their trade than there are today. By fighting more, they just were better rounded because of the vast amount of experience. Finally, there was a true pride back then being a fighter and it didn't matter if a fighter lost a fight.

Today, they put too much emphasis on a glossy record instead of getting them the fights they need to develop. If they lose, they feel they will not put me on say, an HBO card. In the old days, if someone lost in a big fight, but put up a great effort, he could come back another day because of so many clubs for him to fight at. Fans always remembered the effort you put up and when you gave a good effort, they would always come back to see you.

Would you like to see boxing go back to the 15 round championship fights vs. 12 that it is today?

There is no doubt that those last three rounds separated a fighter from what they could do physically and what they could not do

21

mentally. You see a fight today, that if there were the extra rounds, it would have a different outcome. You could always test a fighter's character and will when the 10th round came, and they had five rounds instead of two, to finish.

For that reason, I would like to see them back because I want to reward a fighter who worked his whole career to be mentally better where he was not physically better than his opponent. I think with the old rounds reinstated, it would do just this.

Now with all that said, because of the safety issue, I don't think it will ever come back.

Being a true boxing enthusiast as you are, do you feel that staging fights with man against woman does anything for the sport of boxing?

Yes it does do something for boxing, it hurts it! It brings it to a WWF level and takes away the legitimacy from the sport.

When you finally hang up your microphone and trainers hat, how do you want your many fans to remember you?

That I never sold myself out and always had good standards.

Finally, what is the saying you live your life by?

"No matter what a man says, it's what he does in the end, that he intended to do all along"!

Writers closing comments:

As you have read, Teddy has many thoughts about boxing and with his outstanding career;

I feel he has earned the right to be heard. I only hope that the powers that be, will listen and take him on as an advisor. With someone like him, you can't lose.

As always fight fans, keep reaching for the stars, and all your dreams can be fulfilled.

Interview conducted May 2000

Photo Courtesy of Roger Williams

Going Back in Time...

Up Close and Personal with Former WBA Bantamweight Champion Paulie Ayala

Many may remember the old Friday Night Fights that were sponsored by Gillette many years back. I know from seeing tapes that there were some wars in that series and meeting many from that era, they have verified this to me. Well, the subject of this piece is Going Back in Time. This is what the boxing fans get every time Paulie Ayala steps into a boxing ring.

Ayala would have been perfect for Friday Night Fights and in two fights with Johnny Tapia and Bones Adams, he has cemented a lasting impression on many boxing fans as "MR Excitement" when he fights on TV. In this interview, I found him to be very down to earth, willing to discuss his boxing career,

24

and someone who has deep rooted values, which has always been a very admirable quality to me.

First of all, what is on the horizon for you in your boxing career?
Next on the horizon for me is a change in weight to the featherweight class where I can make some bigger paydays.

Reviewing your fight record, you have fought many times in front of your hometown. For the young fighter who hasn't done that yet in their career, explain how special that must be?
Fighting in front of my hometown is very nice, but I feel like Las Vegas is my home away from home. While I was coming up, many great talents fought on my under cards such as, Jesus Chavez, Ike Ibeabuchi along with former world champs Junior Jones and Genaro Hernandez who fought on one of my cards in FT. Worth, Texas.

In your first fight with Johnny Tapia, did you ever think it would turn out to be remembered as one of the best fights in the last several years?
No, I never would have imagined that the first Tapia fight would have been remembered as a great fight. I'm glad to have been part of such a memorable fight.

You faced Bones Adams twice in the ring and defeated him both times. The first time around many thought he won, but in the rematch, you won easily and left nothing up for debate. What was different in your fight plan the second time around?

25

My fight plan for the second fight with Bones Adams was to take his heart out of the fight early. I wanted to continue what I was doing in the first two rounds in our first meeting in the ring.

Who are your three favorite fighters of all-time and why?

I really have no specific favorites. I just appreciate good boxing.

What is the greatest fight you have ever seen and why?

That's a hard one because I have seen some really great ones. I enjoyed Michael Carbajal vs Humberto Gonzalez I, Julio Cesar Chavez vs Meldrick Taylor I, Mickey Ward vs Arturo Gatti, Mickey Ward vs Emmanuel Burton and finally, Evander Holyfield vs Mike Tyson I. As you can see, it's hard to name just one.

Do you favor a mandatory retirement fund for all boxers and if so, how would you like to see it accomplished?

Yes, I think the mandatory retirement plan would be great for the fighters. I would just like to see it set up separate from boxing and when the fighter retires, there will be a set amount of money in a foundation for him.

What are your words of wisdom to the young fighters just turning professional and trying to get to your level?

I just think young fighters should first, put Christ in their lives. They need to be smart outside the ring as well as in the ring. ALWAYS do your best and never give up.

Is there any venue that to date, you have not fought at, but you would really like to?

I've fought everywhere I wanted to. Madison Square Garden, the top Vegas Casino's, Yokohama Arena in Japan, and in front of my hometown.

When you finally hang up the gloves, how would you like your fans to remember you?

I want to be remembered as a fighter who loved the LORD and always did his best.

Finally, what is the saying you live your life by?

"No weapon formed against me will prosper. Greater is "HE" that is in me, than he that is in the world, and I can do all things in Christ who strengthens me."

Paulie has a neat website boxing fans can check out at:

http://www.paulieayala.com/ (Tell him "Bad" Brad sent you).

Paulie AYALA

Weight class: Super Bantamweight/122 LBS

Professional record : 35 fights; 34+ (12 KO), 1-
1995-1997: North America Bantamweight
1999-2001: W.B.A. Bantamweight

- **1992 -**
+ (Nov-27-1992, Dallas) Jaime OLVERA 6

- **1993 -**
+ (Mar-5-1993, Dallas) Jesse MAGANA kot 4
+ (Apr-2-1993, Dallas) Manuel ROBLES kot 2

+ (Jun-24-1993, New York) Evgueni Novocelov 6
+ (Aug-28-1993, Fort Worth) Marcos Flores ko 1
+ (Oct-13-1993, Dallas) Arturo ESTRADA 6
+ (Nov-11-1993, Fort Worth) Enrique Gomez kot 1
+ (Dec-9-1993, New York) George Acevedo 6

- **1994** -
+ (Feb-17-1994, Fort Worth) Javier DIAZ 8
+ (Apr-16-1994, Moore) Lee CARGLE kot 3
+ (Aug-23-1994, Fort Worth) Julian FLORES 10
+ (Dec-2-1994, Fort Worth) Juan Francisco SOTO 8

- **1995** -
+ (Jan-26-1995, Shreveport) Juan MENDOZA 8
+ (Mar-10-1995, Fort Worth) Mike Espinoza kot 3 (North America, Bantamweight)
+ (Jun-20-1995, Fort Worth) Mario DIAZ 12 (North America, Bantamweight)
+ (Sep-9-1995, Fort Worth) Sergio MILLAN 12 (North America, Bantamweight)
+ (Dec-6-1995, Fort Worth) Lupe Jose RANGEL kot 4

- **1996** -
+ (Feb-22-1996, Corpus Christi) Roland GOMEZ kot 7 (North America, Bantamweight)
+ (Sep-28-1996, Fort Worth) Ivan ALVAREZ 12 (North America, Bantamweight)

- **1997** -
+ (Jan-11-1997, Las Vegas) Famosito GOMEZ 12 (North America, Bantamweight)
+ (Apr-12-1997, Las Vegas) Nestor LOPEZ 10
+ (Aug-8-1997, Las Vegas) Roberto LOPEZ kot 5 (North America, Bantamweight)

+ (Sep-13-1997, Las Vegas) Ricardo MEDINA 10

- **1998 -**
+ (Feb-11-1998, Fort Worth) Elias PAULIN ko 4
+ (May-16-1998, Indio) Antonio RAMIREZ kot 7
-     (Aug-23-1998,   Yokohama)   Joichiro TATSUYOSHI injury 7 (W.B.C., Bantamweight)
+ (Nov-14-1998, El Paso) Ivan SALAZAR ko 4

   1999
+ (Feb-20-1999, Fort Worth) David Vasquez 10
+ (Jun-26-1999, Las Vegas) Johnny TAPIA 12 (W.B.A., Bantamweight)
+   (Oct-23-1999,   Fort   Worth)   Saohin SORTHANIKUL 12 (W.B.A., Bantamweight)
- 2000 -
+ (Mar-4-2000, Las Vegas) Johnny BREDAHL 12 (W.B.A., Bantamweight)
+ (Oct-7-2000, Las Vegas) Johnny TAPIA 12

- **2001 -**
+ (Mar-30-2001, Fort Worth) Hugo DIANZO 12 (W.B.A., Bantamweight)

+ (Aug-4-2001, Las Vegas) Clarence ADAMS 12
2002 -
+ (Feb-23-2002, Las Vegas) Clarence ADAMS 12

As always fight fans, keep reaching for the stars, and all your dreams can be fulfilled.

Interview conducted July 2002

The Professor...

Up Close and Personal with Legendary Comedian and Rat Pack Member, Joey Bishop

Joey Bishop has been on the top of his game for many years as a comedian, talk show host and 1/5 of the legendary Rat Pack that included Frank Sinatra, Dean Martin, Sammy Davis, JR., Peter Lawford and yours truly, Joey Bishop. I thought it would be really neat to bring in a new idea of interviewing celebrities who love the sport of boxing. I am here to tell you, they come no bigger than Joey. He knows his stuff about the sport, and was a true pleasure to interview for my very first column with a celebrity boxing fan.

Tell me about the different fighters you have met and how you were involved with them?
You better sit down so I can tell you this, or otherwise you're going to faint. I did Rocky Marciano's eulogy, and I sparred with Jack Dempsey back in 1938 when I did a show

with him. These are the some of the guys I put the gloves on for my talk show: George Foreman, Rocky Marciano and Muhammad Ali. A few years ago, I did a benefit show for handicapped children at a nearby hotel with Sugar Ray Robinson. I won a Senior Welterweight Title, which they now call Junior Middleweight, when I was in the Army. I also sparred with Barney Ross, Tony Canzoneri and Joe Louis.

How long have you followed boxing?
Since the age of 15 (68 years ago,) when I ushered at the fights in Philadelphia. I was paid a dollar to show people to their seats.

Whom have you seen in your lifetime that you consider the greatest fighter who ever lived?
Well you have to go by records. They do everything by records, such as when the guy wins the homerun hitting championship, they say he is the greatest hitter. Rocky Marciano has the greatest record.

Do you feel that boxing is more corrupt now or back in the old days?
No. I think it's more divided today. If a guy is pronounced World Champion he better be of all the boxing organizations.

Then you like back in the day when you had only one belt?
I don't mind more than one belt, but if you're proclaimed World champion, it better be one belt.

What is the nicest venue you have ever watched a fight in?

It's not so much the nicest place, but a place that was laid out best for a fight and that was Madison Square Garden.

What era do you feel had the best fighters and why?

Well first of all do you know who my coach was? Joey replied, "Fritzie Zivic". He then asked me who did he beat for the title? I had no clue and he told me Henry Armstrong. He then asked, "What was his claim to fame?" I replied he was the first one to win four different titles in three different weight classes. Joey, being the boxing fan he is, corrected me and said three. "Fritzie and I go back to 1938 and served in the service together." Joey felt the fighters of old were the best fighters.

How long did you serve in the Army?

3 years, 9 months and 17 days. (I laughed at his response because he remembered all these years later that exact time down to the days).

Who are your top three favorite fighters of all-time?

Sugar Ray Robinson, Rocky Marciano and Joe Louis.

Since you are in the entertainment business and have been for many years, do you have any funny stories about any of the fighters you ever met?

I boxed Danny "Little Red" Lopez a few years back for a local handicapped children's benefit. We got three of the LA Rams' cheerleaders to escort Danny into the ring and then I got three · women wearing the same outfits to escort me into the ring, with the youngest one being 78 years old. We had to help them up the stairs to escort me in the ring. My cornerman was the late Archie Moore. We asked Jerry Quarry who was the referee, if we could, at the end of the fight, both hit him and knock him out. Jerry Quarry turned to me and said, "I have never been knocked out and will not even do it in fun." Jerry's mom was my number one fan and I sat with her when he faced Muhammad Ali.

I am going to tell you another very funny story of something Jerry Quarry did on my live talk show. Jerry and I laced up the gloves and he was going to show me how he was going to knock Muhammad Ali out. Jerry said, "I am going to faint him and hit him with a hook." Well as I said, we had the gloves on, Brad and we were on LIVE TV for my talk show. As he went to faint with the hook, I caught him - not hard but, I caught him. You know what he said? Jerry said, "Nobody hits me in the fucking face not even in fun." Brad can you imagine LIVE TV? I ran out of the ring with the camera following me running down Sunset Boulevard

In today's boxing, are there any fighters that remind you of fighters from the old days?
Oscar Delahoya. The only thing I don't like is that, recently he changed his style, which I don't appreciate, because he seems to be more careful.

Do you prefer 15 round championship rounds instead of the current 12 rounds in championship fights?
I don't think it's necessary because if a fighter is going to show what he needs to do, it doesn't have to take 15 rounds.

What is the greatest fight you have ever seen and why?

Well the biggest disappointment was Max Schmeling beating Joe Louis. The greatest fight to me is when I guy goes down in the first round and then in the 13th round, knocks his opponent out. He also could hardly see because his opponent was using some type of salve that got into his eyes and they almost stopped the fight.

"Do you know who that was Joey asked?" He then told me Rocky Marciano vs. Jersey Joe Walcott. Rocky knocked Walcott out stiff and Walcott's arm was over the rope. They had a hard time bending it back to his body. This is the greatest fight I have ever seen. Joey then went on to tell me that Rocky used to duck walk thirty flights of stairs and then would get in the pool at the low end and punch under water for an hour and a half. "I used to workout with him in those days."

Finally, in all your years as a boxing fan, what was the most brutal knockout you have ever seen in the ring?

To me, a knockout that kills the opponent, like Ray Robinson did against Jimmy Doyle in their fight that took place in Cleveland back in 1947. That is the most brutal. Do you know that back in the old days when a fighter killed an opponent, the fighter gave his purse to the wife. Sugar Ray Robinson did that.

Joey closed with telling me one more very funny story of when he and Frank Sinatra were at the first Muhammad Ali vs. Joe Frazier fight at Madison Square Garden. The old ring announcer for the Garden, Teddy Brenner announced, "Ladies and gentlemen in our

34

audience tonight is a former amateur boxer, Joey Bishop who had 13 fights with 13 knockouts. Who ever fought him knocked him out."

As always fight fans, keep reaching for the stars, and all your dreams can be fulfilled.

Interview conducted April 2000

Sounding Off...

Up Close and Personal with Ring Announcer Michael Buffer

"Lets Get Ready to Rumble" are the words that he has made famous for more than a decade. Yes, it's the one and only, Michael Buffer. He has excited fight crowds throughout the world and always adds excitement to any fight he covers. I had the chance to interview Michael, a man who I think has even a busier work schedule than I, the Navy Recruiter. Mike was very gracious and allowed me to get some insight from a non-fighter on the sport of boxing.

In all your years of announcing fights, which one are you most proud of and why?
The night George Foreman, at age 44, knocked out Michael Moorer to win the Heavyweight Championship. My final announcement began

with, "Ladies and Gentlemen, the impossible dream has come true."

Do you have any other interests in boxing besides for announcing?
I am strictly a fan of boxing.

How did you get your start in boxing?
In 1982, just for fun. Then, it just took off from there.

Being in boxing as long as you have, what changes would you like to see to the current state of boxing?
The adoption of the Muhammad Ali bill, now in Congress, for protection of boxers (medically and financially) would be a great start. (I have been telling lots of my readers and boxing people I have met about this bill and enjoyed hearing this answer from Mike.)

Do you have a "funniest" story of an event in boxing that you were involved in that you would like to share?
Most outrageous moment has to be when the Fan Man dropped out of the sky at the Holyfield vs. Bowe II.

What inspired you to get into announcing?
The poor job being done by others.

Do you have a favorite fighter?
Without hesitation, Muhammad Ali and at 1B, Sugar Ray Robinson.

What is your favorite match of all-time?
Yvonne Durelle vs. Archie Moore.

As always fight fans, keep reaching for the stars, and all your dreams can be fulfilled.

Interview conducted April 2001

(L) Injin Chi and photographer Ed "The Eye"
Torregano match power punches

Don't Let the Quiet Demeanor Fool You...

Up Close and Personal with WBC Number One Ranked Featherweight Contender Injin Chi

In boxing, you have personalities, some more
flamboyant than others, and some who are very
quiet. One such fighter who is quiet, yet is
heard around the world when he steps into the
ring, is current WBC number one ranked
featherweight contender, Injin Chi, from
Seoul, South Korea.

Chi, who I recently reported on in my first
fight, which I covered in Korea, knocked out
former title challenger, Samuel Duran with a
body shot, and he certainly wasn't quiet in
the ring on that night. Since then, I have
been with him on two occasions and both times,
he showed true respect to his many fans. Chi
is a huge star in Korea, but one would never
know it by his quiet, unassuming demeanor when
he is at the fights. This is a quality amongst

many fighters I have met over the years and truly admire them for it.

Both Ed "The Eye" Torregano and I, think that Chi is destined to become a world champion. And if he does, he will represent the sport of boxing in a positive light in my opinion.

What inspired you to get into boxing?

I got into boxing because I have always loved it since I was very young.

If you had to pick one fight in your career to date, which would you say the fans saw the best performance from Injin Chi?

My fight in which I won the Korean Boxing Championship on March 26, 1994. I beat Han-Kil Cho by an eighth round knockout. Fighting in front of my hometown in Seoul, Korea was an honor and I think I looked best in this fight.

What differences do you see with fighting in the United States instead of Korea?

Brad, I really don't see any differences. Either one is fine with me. I just like to fight.

There was a time when Korean boxing was very strong. Why do you feel there is not as much boxing in Korea today, as there was in the early 80's to mid 90's?

I feel boxing has been pushed away by other professional sports which have been prospering because of it.

What do you think could be done to fix the problem of a lack of boxing in Korea?

I think three factors are the cause of this. First, you need good fighting. Second, good boxers. Finally, good promoters. Currently, promoters KU-Sung Lee and Dong-Ahn Park are really working hard to put on quality shows that will highlight many of the talented fighters we have here in Seoul, Korea.

What are your words of wisdom to the young Korean and American fighters just starting out?

I would like to advise them not to try and knockout your competitor every time, but to learn how to box, using your brain. A knockout is not going to come each time you fight and if you are only trying to do that, you're going to be in trouble, if the fight goes the distance.

Are there any fighters in today's boxing, you would like to emulate?

Just one, Oscar Delahoya

How would you judge your attempt for the WBC Featherweight Title against current champion Erik Morales?

Simply put, if we fight again, I will not repeat my failure the second time around.

What do you consider your best weapon in the ring at this point of your career?

My best weapon in the ring is taking control of a situation when I have my opponent hurt. I like to finish hard.

Who are your three favorite fighters of all-time and why?

First would be Yu-Myong-Woo, Mike Tyson and Julio Cesar Chavez. They're all warriors and I have always enjoyed their fights.

Do you favor a mandatory retirement fund for all boxers and if so, how would you like to see it accomplished?

Yes, I think it's needed throughout boxing. However, I am not the right person to ask about how it should be done.

When you finally retire from boxing, what do you want your fans to remember you for?

I would like all my fans to remember me as a good ring technician.

Finally, what is the saying you live your life by?

"Do your best at anything you attempt".

In-Jin CHI

Weight class: Featherweight/126 lbs

Professional record: 27 fights; 25+ (15 KO),
2-
1994: South Korea Bantamweight
1995: Orient Bantamweight

- **1991** -
- (Nov-20-1991) Tae-Sun Park 4

- **1992** -
+ (Jan-18-1992) Jae-Yun Chang 4
+ (Mar-24-1992) Ho-Nam Choi 4
+ (Jul-7-1992) Kap-Yong Lee ko 5
+ (Sep-26-1992) Kap-Yong Lee 8

- **1993** -
+ (Feb-6-1993, Cuneta) Ronnie Belaro 10
+ (Jul-25-1993, Seoul) Jesse MACA 10

- **1994** -

+ (Mar-26-1994, Seoul) Han-Kil Cho ko 8 (KBC Championship, Bantamweight)

- **1995** -
+ (Feb-8-1995, Seoul) Junjun Gigataras kot 1
+ (Apr-23-1995, Seoul) Jesse MACA 12 (Orient, Bantamweight)
+ (Sep-6-1995, Kwangmyong) Ric RAMIREZ ko 6

- **1996** -
+ (Jan-13-1996, Inchon) Alexander PAK 10
+ (May-8-1996, Seoul) Eddy PENASO ko 4

- **1997** -
+ (Feb-5-1997, Kwangyang) Colin GRAHAM ko 1
+ (Aug-21-1997, Seungnam) Praw SUKMUANGKLAENG ko 4
+ (Nov-7-1997, Kuri) Wichit CHUVATANA 10

- **1998** -
+ (May-8-1998, Kuri) Akarat KHOTKAENAN ko 2
+ (Aug-29-1998, Seoul) Joe ESCRIBER 10

- **1999** -
+ (Jan-10-1999, Seoul) Sammy SURDILLA kot 3
+ (Mar-26-1999, Chunan) Teofilo TUNACAO ko 4
+ (Jun-13-1999, Seoul) Siengthipya SITHSYASEI kot 5
+ (Oct-20-1999, Chungnam) Rungsurin LOOKLONGCHAN ko 5

- **2000** -
+ (Jan-2-2000, Seoul) Andy ALAGENIO ko 3
+ (May-14-2000, Seoul) Baby LORONA 10
+ (Dec-8-2000) Dino OLIVETTI ko 9

- **2001** -
- (Jul-28-2001, Los Angeles) Erik MORALES 12 (W.B.C., Featherweight)

- 2002 -
+ (Mar-30-2002, Seoul) Samuel DURAN ko 3

As always fight fans, keep reaching for the stars, and all your dreams can be fulfilled.

Interview conducted April 2002

(L) "Bad" Brad mixing it up with David Chung

Making A Difference...

Up Close and Personal with World Boxing Council (WBC) Boxing Judge and Referee David Chung

"David Chung is one of the WBC's most distinguished and preferred ring officials because of his competency, his impartiality and his sense of responsibility, as well as his participation through the years, in all the congresses, clinics and training programs for ring officials of the WBC.

He is one of the leading ring officials of the Oriental Pacific Boxing Federation (OPBF). I respect him as a gentleman, a man of integrity, a man of service and, a very good friend. I am proud of our friendship." —-***Jose Sulaiman World Boxing Council President (WBC)***

In boxing, I have had the opportunity to meet some incredible people who have made great strides in their areas of the sport. Well, one such person is World Boxing Council (WBC) boxing judge and referee, David Chung of Seoul, Korea. Upon my arrival to Seoul, Korea for my one year tour of duty with the Navy, I

45

was introduced to Mr. Chung, who would be my liaison into Korean boxing, while stationed here.

Chung has been more than a liaison, but a teacher, and more importantly, a friend who I truly respect. Chung brings to the sport of boxing, over 35 years of experience.

As a young man, Chung fought as an amateur while serving in the Korean Army around 1963. During this time, he had over 100 fights, winning many military belts to include a Silver Medal in the Military games. Chung stopped boxing in 1970, but continued to be involved in several facets of the sport.

He has been with the World Boxing Council (WBC) since the early 1980's as a boxing judge and referee. During that time, he has earned the respect of his colleagues, boxing media and now this writer, for the professional manner in which he carries out his duties at the fights.

When did you first become involved in boxing?

I thought that boxing was a very competitive one-on-one sport that made a man out of a young boy. I had many friends who encouraged me to box. With their encouragement, I began boxing as a hobby back in 1963. Once I got up to speed in the sport, I started competing as an amateur boxer.

What led you to become a boxing judge and a referee?

After I stopped boxing, I wanted to continue my friendships in boxing and build new ones. With that said, I stayed in the sport on many different levels.

For the readers, explain the criteria you are looking for when judging a fight?

My judging criteria is based on the cleaner punches, power shots and overall ring generalship as the main factors.

Have you ever had the decision for a fighter, and when the cards were announced, you were surprised that the other two judges had the fight scored completely different from how you saw it?

Brad, on three occasions I was surprised by the outcome of my fellow judges. This is not a bad thing because each judge sees the fight from a different angle and it is quite possible to see a different version of a boxing match.

What was the first championship fight that you judged?

The first fight I judged was the WBC Flyweight Championship held in Kuwait, back in 1986 between Sot Chitalada of Thailand and Freddie Castillo of Mexico.

What was the first championship fight you ever refereed?

The first fight I refereed was an IBF title match in Seoul, Korea back in 1983 between Kwan Soon-Chun and Rena Busa-Young. I don't remember if it was a vacant title or who the champion was at the time.

Which do you enjoy more, being a referee or judge, and why?

I prefer being a referee because I am right in the middle of the action and, I love the exercise you can get if you go the full ten rounds.

Do you think the referee should be involved with scoring a fight like it used to be?

No, the referee should be concerned about the operation of the boxing match only and save the scoring for the judges

Who are your three favorite fighters of all-time and why?

First Muhammad Ali. Second, Julio Cesar Chavez. Finally, Oscar DeLahoya. Each one of these fighters were' great technicians in the ring and added a legacy to the sport that will carry on for many years.

What is the greatest fight you have ever seen and why?

Sugar Ray Leonard vs. Tommy Hearns I. In this fight, you had a tremendous boxer vs. a heavy hitting puncher. It lived up to every bit of hype and gave the boxing fans a fight memory that will last a lifetime.

Do you favor a mandatory retirement fund for all boxers and if so, how would you like to see it accomplished?

Yes, but I really don't know how to set it up. It is needed for all boxers and I would like to see the proposals to create one throughout boxing.

What are you words of wisdom to the young man or woman who wants to become a boxing judge or referee?

If you want to be a judge or referee in the sport of boxing, you should always study boxing matches thoroughly which will give you great insight into the sport. From there, work at the bottom level which will give you experience to move up. Finally, always have perseverance because without that, you cannot succeed.

What are the differences that you see from boxing in Korea vs. the United States?
I really don't think there is any difference between the two.

When you finally hang up your judging pen and boxing shoes, how you would you like to be remembered within the boxing world?
I want to be remembered as fair referee and judge who was respected by the Korean boxing community.

Finally, what is the saying you live your life by?
"Throughout life, you must have diligence and integrity to truly succeed".

As always fight fans, keep reaching for the stars, and all your dreams can be fulfilled.

Interview conducted May 2002

Kathy Collins "Wildcat"
"Four Time" World Champion

Holding Nothing Back...

Up Close and Personal with Four Time Women's Champion Kathy "Wildcat" Collins

Many months ago I made a commitment to interview ladies who could fight and represented the sport in a positive fashion. My goal then and now, is to try to continue to move female boxing forward, helping to earn the respect for the ladies who can fight.

With that said, four time world champion Kathy "Wildcat" Collins is my latest interview and yet another example of a lady who can fight. From start to finish, I found Collins very honest, straight to the point and someone who wants to back up everything she says in the ring.

In fact, Kathy was very excited about her upcoming match against Christy Martin on the undercard of Felix Trinidad vs William Joppy at Madison Square Garden on May 12, 2001. This fight will be the largest in female boxing and the most lucrative. Collins has dreamed about this fight for many years and to have it finally signed, is a dream come true for her.

What inspired you to get into boxing?

When I first started boxing in 1994, I weighed 240 LBS. I was always a jock during my high school years, but once out, I gained a lot of weight. Boxing was like a divine intervention for me and a means to get myself really in shape. It really saved my life, and I love it.

What are your words of wisdom to a young female that wants to lace up the gloves?

Work hard and be very patient with yourself, all the while having a good time with it.

If you could emulate any fighter who would it be and why?

I don't think I would emulate any one fighter. It would be better to take the best from various fighters so I can be the best I can be.

For example, I would take Sugar Shane Mosley's speed and footwork. Roy Jones, JR's anticipation of his opponent's movement blows my mind. Evander Holyfield's willingness to never give up. Finally, Dora Webber who was a female fighter before the sport really took off. I credit her with a lot of things she showed me to make me a better fighter.

How long have you followed boxing?

Only for the seven years I have been it.

Who are your top three favorite fighters of all-time and why?

First, Muhammad Ali. I loved the way he dropped a right hand which was perfect. He could fight backing up and just everything he did in and out of the ring was great. Second, Sugar Ray Robinson. He was the original speed demon. Finally, Roberto Duran. He was just mean in there.

What is the greatest fight you have ever seen and why?

George Foreman vs Ron Lyle. They both would get knocked down and showed so much heart by continuing to get back up.

Do you favor a mandatory retirement fund for all boxers and if so, how would you like to see it accomplished?

I really think it needs to be done. You see so many fighters who have come back because of the money and gotten hurt. If there was a retirement fund, it may have helped avoid some potentially dangerous situations when an older fighter came back for the money.

You could take a percent of the fighter's purse and stick it in a 401k and the promoter also would put some money into it. The fighter could not touch it until he is totally retired from boxing.

What do you think of the female ranking systems, and if you had control of them, what changes would you make?

I think we should just pistol-whip all these ranking bodies. The whole ranking system needs to be revamped, and it just blows mind.

What went through your mind the first time you stepped in the ring as a professional?

"I almost feinted" Cathy said with a chuckle. I can remember looking down at my now husband, and saying, "I don't feel too good". The whole event was just overwhelming to me. I made it through the fight, and it ended in a draw.

Even though you don't have the chance to fight in 15 rounds today, would you like to see it reinstated?

No I wouldn't like to see it brought back. I feel you can get just as much in 12 rounds and more accidents happen between the 13th - 15th to fighters.

Being a female fighter, what is your take on the age-old complaint that female fighters are only for entertainment purposes and not equal to their male counter parts?

We aren't equal to our male counter parts in strength and speed. But on a whole, I think all of boxing is for entertainment. With that said, I just want to give the boxing fans the best Kathy Collins I can give them when I step into the ring. At no time do I ever compare myself to Zab Judah who is one of the male champions in my weight class. (I really liked Kathy's answer on this and shows the honesty I talked about earlier in the interview.)

Do you have a particular location to fight at one day and why?

I would love to fight in Las Vegas.

When you finally hang up the gloves for good, what would you like your fans to remember you for?

First off, that I was God fearing. Without HIM, nothing would have happened in my career. That I was really a hard worker and gave boxing everything I have within me. Finally, that I was cute.

Finally, what is the saying that you live your life by?

"Do unto others as you would have done unto you".

Kathy COLLINS
Nickname: "Wildcat"

Weight class: Super Lightweight/140 lbs

Professional record: 18 fights; 14+ (3 KO), 3=, 1-

- 1995 -
= (Apr-28-1995, Westbury) Leslie Howe 4
+ (Aug-28-1995, Westbury) Laurie Bischoff 4

- 1996 -
+ (Apr-26-1996, Westbury) Erica Schmidlin 4
+ (Aug-20-1996) Andrea Deshong 6
+ (Sep-18-1996) Angela Buchanan kot 2
= (Oct-15-1996) Helga Risoy 6

- 1997 -
= (Mar-7-1997) Dora Webber 6
+ (Jun-20-1997) Leah Mellinger 6
+ (Aug-2-1997) Christina Berry kot 2
+ (Oct-24-1997) Helga Risoy kot 3

- 1998 -

54

+ (Jan-10-1998, Atlantic City) Andrea Deshong 10

+ (Mar-27-1998) Glenda Watkins 8

+ (May-24-1998, Atlantic City) Maruscha Sjauw 10

+ (Jul-31-1998, Atlantic City) Olivia Gerula 10

- (Sep-11-1998, Atlantic City) Leah Mellinger 10

- 1999 -

+ (Apr-17-1999, Atlantic City) Olivia Gerula 8

- 2000 -

+ (May-13-2000, Tulsa) Denise Moraetes 10

+ (Aug-11-2000, Atlantic City) Cheryl Nance 6

As always fight fans, keep reaching for the stars, and all your dreams can be fulfilled.

Interview conducted May 2001

WBC Heavyweight Champion Larry Holmes takes it on the chin from challenger Gerry Cooney.

Giving Back...

Up Close and Personal with Former Heavyweight Title Challenger "Gentleman" Gerry Cooney

I don't think there was a more suited nickname in the history of boxing than Gerry Cooney's. He was nicknamed the "Gentleman" and he is, truly that. Gerry is a man of such admirable qualities, and you will see just what I mean in the following interview.

Cooney's rise to the top of the heavyweight ranks in the late 1970's came fast and secured him a shot at then Heavyweight Champion, Larry Holmes, on June 11, 1982. In a fight that was action packed throughout, Cooney would come out the loser for the first time in his career by TKO in the 13th round. Cooney would only fight sporadically for the next five years.

Since Cooney's retirement from boxing after being stopped by George Foreman in 1990, he has worked very hard on the behalf of ex-fighters. I hope that when you come away from reading our interview, that you are as moved

56

by Cooney's dedication to his organization and what it's doing to help ex-fighters, as I was. People like Cooney, can be called the true heroes of boxing for making the difference in an ex-fighters life's, who badly needs it.

I can't tell you how many countless readers of my column and boxing fans I know, are always bringing up your name when we talk about boxing. They all are wondering what you're up to today?

"Well Brad, they got some nerve," Gerry said with a chuckle. You know I have a very busy, hectic life. I am married and have two beautiful children. I still am in the fight game and spar about 30 - 40 rounds a week in New Jersey at a gym called Rocky Marciano's.

I am involved in minor league baseball. I go around the country speaking to troubled youths, trying to help them understand that whatever path they choose, they'll need to really pay attention to it - telling them, that by the time you're 30 years old, you can be on a nowhere street, if you're not careful. I just try to get kids to look at themselves in a good light.

I also have my F.I.S.T. Foundation which stands for, Fighters Institution for Support & Training. What we do is help bring in retired prize fighters who are unemployed. They are usually in dire need of assistance. You see Brad, all of the sports have a safety net, but boxing is the only sport that has none. So when the fighter is through, he is through. While he was fighting his management was very excited for him, but now that he is done, that management team is moving on.

We help them with things like aptitude testing to find out where their strengths lie.

From there we direct them to job training and put them into jobs. This is a tough goal, due to the fact that these guys are not used to working a 9-5 job, because all they did was train and fight.

Where is your organization out of?

We are basically out of the tri-state area of NY, NJ and CT. In the next 18-24 months, we are taking it nationwide. We are in the learning stages of my organization, so we are taking it slow, to be able to help the fighters with the best options we have out there.

What can we the fans of boxing and boxers do to help your foundation?

Well, pretty soon we are going to be up on the web page. We are a non-profit organization with a Federal Tax ID number. Donations are always welcome. Once we get our web page up, everybody will be able to hook up to the F.I.S.T. Foundation online and they'll be able to communicate with each other. We are currently in the process of putting together a big charity function at Bob Guiciones mansion in Manhattan. He has donated his place for a charity event to support the foundation.

We will be doing this in October of this year. HBO, Showtime, and ESPN to name a few, are all involved. It's very exciting because we started from the ground up.

How does an ex-fighter get in touch with your foundation?

Well Brad, you know boxers are a tight-knit group of people. They have been beat up so bad that they are very leery of others. But through word of mouth, you hear someone's story about coming into F.I.S.T. and filling out an application for help. We send the application up to Albany and process it.

Then what happens is they say to other ex-fighters that Cooney is doing a good job and this is how word spreads. You know that life is a series of going from one room to the next. For that period of time though, when you have to stand in the hallway, it's a scary place. Bottom line is, I want them to know that, "you are not alone and we are going to continue to fight for you guys."

Who or what inspired you to get into boxing?
Well, I grew up in a big Irish, Catholic family. My dad was a pretty rough guy. So one of my brothers left home when he was 15 and found his way to the gym. It gave me the opportunity to go and spend some time with him and workout in the gym. But actually, prior to that, my father had always had a heavybag in the basement. I used to work out on it regularly and thought I was pretty good at it. So, when I use to go and see my brother at the gym, I finally told him that I wanted to box with someone there.

They put me in with this little Italian guy who was half my size and he punched me around that gym. I said to myself, that this is not for me. So, I went home and had a different perspective on boxing, realizing that with hitting the heavybag, it was not going to hit me back like that kid did. About three months down the road, I went back to the gym and asked to box that kid again. I knew then that I really wanted to pursue boxing.

Since you fought in the days of 15 rounds, would you like to see them come back or do you favor 12 instead?

Well, in my fight with Larry Holmes it was a 15 round fight. That night in the ring it was 115 degrees under the lights. So, even if it was 12 rounds it was pretty hot out there, no matter what you did. I think the benefit of 12 rounds is they found that most people get hurt from the 13th round to the 15th round. By cutting it down, it made you pick up the pace during the fight and the fans get a better paced, more competitive fight.

What did you consider your best weapon in the ring?

I was a left hooker, and I loved hooking. I also really liked to jab and mix it up right away.

What big fights were you approached for, but never materialized?

John Tate was one, but he was on the decline at that time. Mike Weaver was another instead of Larry Holmes. My management chose to go to Larry instead. In fact, Larry and I are really good friends right now. We are currently working on some projects together.

What are you words of wisdom to the young fighter who is just turning professional?

You know I just left the gym tonight and they had this young amateur kid who is 19-0. He sparred with another guy who is ranked 5th in the world. They boxed four rounds and had a good workout. When they got out of the ring, the kid who was ranked 5th in the world, continued to train. The 19-0 amateur kid picked up the telephone and started talking to this one and that one, taking off his wraps. He stopped training. You have a small period of time when you can perfect your career and become good at it. A lot of guys get distracted, which only hurts them. You must stay focused and work very hard at boxing.

Who are you three favorite fighters of all-time and why?

First, Muhammad Ali. He was the kind of guy you either loved or hated, but you wanted to see him. I happen to really love him. He brought boxing to another level and always made you laugh. Second, Roberto Duran when he was a lightweight. He was the kind of guy who was a true fighter and you hardly see guys like that anymore. Finally, Aaron Pryor. I spend time with him every year and he is just a great man.

What do you consider the greatest fight you have ever seen and why?

Well Brad, there have been so many great fight's that I have seen over the years. I really loved all the Ali Vs Frazier fights because, here were two guys who just gave you their all in there. Evander Holyfield has given us some great fights and you can't go without mentioning Hearns Vs Leonard and Duran Vs Leonard.

What was it like being up there fighting for the heavyweight Championship of the World?

It was great and scary at the same time. I was a small kid from Huntington, Long Island. I never imagined that anything like that would happen to me. It's one of the most impressive things when they come to your dressing room and say "hey Cooney you're up." You take that walk from the dressing room to the ring and that's when the real man comes out. Then you climb up those four stairs and into the ring. Then finally, you can't wait for the bell to ring.

In my opinion, you gave a good account of yourself when you challenged Larry Holmes for the title. In hindsight, would you have fought him differently?

Yes! I would have fought my fight instead of being concerned with going the distance. I would have come out to swarm him instead.

The one thing that I remember after that fight was when you addressed the fans. It moved me how sincere you were and felt that you had let them down. I don't think you did, but explain what you were trying to get across to them when you spoke to them.

I have always been a people person. I was also disappointed for not succeeding in my attempt to win the title against Holmes. I had never lost a fight before that. But back to the people side of it. Growing up training, I use to get up so early I would wave to the garbage men going by. So, I had this relationship with Blue Collar America and I really liked it. I felt that lots of those people looked forward to me winning that night for nothing other than they just liked me.

What do you think of females in boxing?

I have seen some women who can fight, but I don't think there is a place for me to see women in there getting punched around.

If you could have chosen any other profession besides boxing, what would it have been?

Boxing really was it for me. I started at the young age of 15. I liked it very much and went into the Golden Gloves at 16. There, I won the Middleweight Title. After every fight, I saw my picture on the back of the Daily News, one of the largest papers in New York. I really liked that.

I feel the current Heavyweight division lacks the excitement of when you were in it. What do you think of the Heavyweight division today?

Right now it's kind of at a mixed up state, but I think it's getting itself worked out.

With all the hype and big bucks heavyweights are getting today, how do you feel they would have faired against the fighters of your era?

That's a good question. If you really want to talk to someone about that, you should ask Larry Holmes, who said these guys really couldn't have shined our shoes. That is the one thing about boxing that people have tried to do - compare fighters throughout history.

It's like the track stars from years ago couldn't really compete with the runners of today, because training is so different. Today, they are adding weight training which is making their muscles compete better. It's just too hard to say who would beat who.

Who nicknamed you the "Gentleman"?

When I got out of High School I worked at a gas station. There was a fellow I worked for named Harry, God rest his soul. I worked for him for awhile and he told me that I reminded him of Gentleman Jim Corbett.

Have you stayed friendly with any of the fighters from your era?

Yes. In fact, I just spoke today with Eddie "The Animal" Lopez. I am seeing all the guys, like Earnie Shavers, Tex Cobb, and Larry Holmes all the time.

Do you have any funny stories about boxing that you were involved in or have been around?

Yes, when I fought Jimmy Young in Atlantic City. If you know anything about Jimmy it was that he always made you look bad in there. He was a true spoiler, who was always in shape and came on strong. This was my first nationally televised bout. I was thinking this guy is going to kill me.

When I trained I used to knock myself down and build myself back up by hard training. So, it was kind of a funny thing. I was on the third floor of the hotel in Atlantic City and thinking to myself, 'what am I going to do here tonight? I am fighting on national TV and this guy is going to make me look terrible.' I was thinking, 'maybe I should just jump out of this window here' Gerry said with a chuckle. I finally get in the ring with Young and the fight was easier than I thought it would be. Young was so worried about my left hook, that every time I threw a hook, he bent forward. I caught on to this, stepped to my right and threw a left uppercut. This opened a big gash on his nose and I was able to take him out in four.

When I was fighting Kenny Norton I thought he was unbelievable. I had remembered how big he was in Mandingo. I did a Warner Wolfe show in New York a few days before the bout and he asked me how did I feel? I looked Kenny right in the eyes and told him I wished we were fighting right now. I assure you though that I could wait the time. Finally I get into the ring with him and realize he really is not that big. I had built him up to be this big guy, but in reality, he was not bigger than me.

One more story I want to tell you. One time in Detroit I went to see Larry Holmes fight Leon Spinks. We both were sitting with Howard Cosell and Larry knocked off Howard's wig. I thought to myself 'this is getting serious now.'

After the Holmes fight you were very inconsistent in your getting into the ring. Why was that?

I was mixed up and not happy with the people I was with at the time. Boxing was not the sport that I thought is was due to all the politics. If you look at my career, towards the end you will see I was fighting like once a year. I was not part of the Don King top heavyweights, so I was kind of kept out. His guys were getting three to four fights a year and I could only get one. It's hard to build your skills like this and on top of that, I was catching lots of bad press for it.

The bad press came because they thought I should fight more. I couldn't get the fights because if I would sign to fight one of King's guys I would be signed to him. I chose not to do that. It's a free country and I did not want that. In hindsight, that might have been a mistake. I should have found some other way around it.

Going into the Michael Spinks fight, what did you think the outcome would be?

Going into that fight, I was at the worse point in my life. I was drinking heavily and taking some kind of drugs. The fight was on and off several times and I didn't think it was going to happen. I went into that fight drinking heavily. I am ashamed about that fight to this day. I lost three times in my career. Losing to Holmes I could deal with, because I lost to a true champion.

In the Foreman fight I caught George in the first round and had him hurt. I thought I hurt him and wanted to take him out. Gil Clancy wanted me to move around for six or seven rounds. I hadn't fought for awhile and got excited with trying to take him out of there and got caught with a shot. I have no shame in that fight with George, because I picked up myself and dusted off my pants. I said to myself 'it's time to move on to something else.'

But in the fight with Spinks, he did not belong in the ring with me, in my estimation.

Finally now that you are retired from the ring, what would you like your fans to remember you for?

That I always fought from my heart. When that bell rang, I wanted to go out there and do my thing. I want them to know that I always have time to say hello to that person who is walking down the street, sees me and says "is that Gerry Cooney?" They usually are uncomfortable to approach me, so I approach them and say hello. I am spending lots of time with the youth of America, like I told you earlier, and only wish when I was a kid, that I had someone to talk too.

In closing, Gerry asked me to let all the folks out there know that his foundation is not ever going to give up on these ex-fighters who have fought, sweat and bled their hearts out in the ring, for the boxing fans around the world. He says, "they need help, and I mean great champions, who need to get their dignity back and enjoy what they did in the ring. I am in this fight and any help is greatly appreciated it."

Gerry COONEY
Nickname: "Gentleman"

Weight class: Heavyweight/Unlimited

Professional record: 31 fights; 28+ (24 KO), 3-

- **1977** -
+ (Feb-15-1977, New York) Bill Jackson ko 1
+ (Mar-2-1977, New York) Jimmy Robertson ko 2
+ (Mar-20-1977, Louisville) Jose Rosario ko 2
+ (Aug-3-1977, New York) Matt Robinson 4
+ (Nov-18-1977, New York) Joe Maye ko 4
+ (Nov-30-1977, White Plains) Quentin Locklear ko 1
+ (Dec-21-1977, Brooklyn) Jimmy Sykes ko 1

- **1978** -
+ (Jan-14-1978, Hauppauge) Terry Lee Kidd ko 1
+ (Jan-27-1978, Hempstead) Austin Johnson ko 1
+ (Feb-11-1978, Las Vegas) Gary Bates ko 4
+ (Mar-17-1978, Las Vegas) S.t. Gordon disq.4
+ (Jun-22-1978, New York) Geo Maldonado ko 8

+ (Oct-4-1978, Westchester) Charlie Polite ko 4
+ (Nov-1-1978, White Plains) Sam Mc Gill 8
+ (Dec-15-1978, New York) Grady Daniels ko 5

- 1979 -
+ (Jan-13-1979, Miami Beach) Eddie Lopez 8
+ (Feb-26-1979, New York) Charlie Johnson ko 1
+ (Jun-29-1979, New York) Tom Prater kot 2
+ (Aug-22-1979, New York) Broderick Mason ko 4
+ (Oct-19-1979, Commack) Mali Dozier ko 6
+ (Nov-9-1979, New York) Dino Dennis kot 3
+ (Dec-14-1979, Atlantic City) Leroy Boone kot 6

- 1980 -
+ (May-25-1980, Atlantic City) Jimmy Young kot 4
+ (Oct-24-1980, Uniondale) Ron Lyle ko 1

- 1981 -
+ (May-10-1981, New York) Ken Norton ko 1

- 1982 -
- (Jun-11-1982, Las Vegas) Larry Holmes kot 13 (W.B.C., Heavyweight)

- 1983: inactive -

- 1984 -
+ (Sep-29-1984, Anchorage) Philipp Brown kot 4
+ (Dec-8-1984, Phoenix) George Chaplin kot 2

- 1985: inactive -

- 1986 -

+ (May-31-1986, San Francisco) Eddie Gregg ko 1

- 1987 -
- (Jun-15-1987, Atlantic City) Michael Spinks kot 5

- 1988-1989: inactive -

- 1990 -
- (Jan-15-1990, Atlantic City) George Foreman kot 2

As always fight fans, keep reaching for the stars, and all your dreams can be fulfilled.

Interview conducted April 2000

From left to right: The "Raging Beauty" Isra
Girgrah, Jr Middleweight Ishmail Arvin
(managed by 10 Kount Productions) and boxing
manager, Casey Dansicker
Photo courtesy of Mike Greenhill

Setting the Standard...

Up Close and Personal with Boxing Manager Casey Dansicker

"What Casey Dansicker has done for current female IBF & UBA Lightweight and IWBF Junior Lightweight Champion, the "Raging Beauty" Isra Girgrah, is truly what a manager is supposed to do. Not only has he moved her career inside the ring in great fashion, but more importantly, the marketing effort that he has provided her outside, is something that most fighters lack. This is quite evident by the tremendous sponsorship deal with Kutskova Vodka.

Marketing fighters outside the ring is something the sport and the fighters need more of. As Girgrah becomes a recognizable name in the sport, that recognition will be for her skill and performances in the ring, her charm and beauty, and the hard work of her manager.

From a promoters standpoint, Dansicker is tops because he takes care of all the last minute details and works with us not against us. With that said, he is a promoter's dream and he can't have enough boxers."—Scott Wagner, Promoter and owner of the highly rated syndicated Ballroom Boxing Shows from Glen Burnie, Maryland.

Anyone involved with boxing on the East Coast will say, without any reservations when the name Casey Dansicker is mentioned, he is a true delight to work with and a superb boxing manager, who cares about his fighters not just in the ring, but out. This is quite evident with his most famous boxer, current female IBF & UBA Lightweight and IWBF JR Lightweight Champion, The "Raging Beauty" Isra Girgrah.

In only two years, Dansicker has guided her into two title belt wins and a huge endorsement deal. He treats his champion not as a fighter, but as a partner who he is constantly mentoring into areas that she will be able to enter once she hangs up the gloves.

Finally, look for him to be voted Manager of the Year in the Virginia, Washington, DC, and Maryland areas, very soon.

How did you first become involved in boxing?
Four years ago my brother Arnie Dansicker was approached by a local promoter to invest in a professional boxing show. After discussing this with our family, we agreed to do it, with his guidance. Shortly after, we put on two of our own shows which did very well. This success created the birth of 10 Kount Productions

How did this involvement lead to you becoming a full-time boxing manager?

After having a family meeting, we broke up the duties we felt that we were best suited for in our new company, 10 Kount Productions. Arnie became the promoter, my brother Sam handled all of the legal matters, my father Stanley handled the public relations for the company and finally, I became the manager of our fighters.

We base our success on two simple things. First, we work as a team, succeed as a team and if we make a mistake, we fix it as a team. Second, our fighters are not just clients, but family. When you treat someone with respect, encouragement, and concern for them to succeed not only in the ring, but in life, you have a much better chance to tap all of their potential in the ring.

You have guided current female UBA & IBF Lightweight and IWBF JR Lightweight Champion, The "Raging Beauty" Isra Girgrah to two world titles. When you first signed her, what did you envision for her and are you surprised at the success you have had in only two plus years?

I am not suprised one bit by Isra's recent successes. When I first met Isra, I knew she had it all. She could already fight, had a great personality, a concern to better the sport of women's boxing and, she wanted to use her fame to better her community, especially towards the children.

Her community service really endeared me to her because she is just amazing with the children - speaking to them about the importance of staying off drugs and staying in school.

Our team had hoped to set her up with a big endorsement deal that would help her when she finally hangs up the boxing gloves to pursue other interests.

When we landed her the Kutskova Vodka deal, we did just that.

From all accounts, you are more than just a manager to Girgrah, but a mentor and business partner, as well. Why is that we see so many manager/boxers relationships sour, but yours continues to grow?

In my opinion, too many managers think about just making money. With that said, I realize this is a business and you have to make money to stay afloat. But, if you think you're going to make it right away, you may be in for a shock. Our relationship continues to blossom because she is like my little sister and not just a boxer who I book fights and endorsement deals for. Isra and I will be together when she hangs up the gloves. That is why we are working on joint business ventures outside of boxing.

Isra is not the only fighter in our group, and we treat each one with respect, and dignity, and truly want them all to become world champions.

Before Girgrah retires, what do you want too see in her growing career as a true female World Champion?

Before Isra retires, I would like her to be known as "The Best Female Fighter in the World" because of her hard work and dedication to the sport.

What do you see in the future of 10 Kount Productions?

Everyday, we continue to grow, with boxing
on an upswing in the state of Maryland,
through shows such as Scott Wagner's
syndicated Ballroom Boxing. We want to
continue to move it forward by putting on top
notch boxing shows, that in the years to come,
will leave fans with a boxing memory that was
created by 10 Kount Productions.

**What are your words of wisdom to the young
man or woman just breaking into boxing and
wanting to become a manager?**

It seems like everyone wants to become a
boxing manager these days because of the fame
and fortune, but they need to make a
commitment to it, which is dedication, hard
work, and showing your fighters that you care
about them in and out of the ring. Don't
expect success right away. It takes time and
you have to invest quality time to your
fighter or fighters. Encourage input from
them, because if you have a close and
professional relationship, you will work
better with them and not against them. Bottom
line: Be smart in all your dealings, read the
fine print and always think about the big
picture. Harsh actions or quick actions now,
can cause huge problems in the future.

**What do you think the current state of
women's boxing is in?**

I think the current state of women's boxing
is getting better. With more and more talent
being talked about and having the fans
screaming to see them on mainstream
television, I am hoping more of the ladies who
can fight, get the time slots. We are trying
to match Isra in tough title defenses that the
fans will appreciate.

We want to face anyone in her division and we're throwing out an open invitation to all the top ranked women fighters, to step in the ring.

What is the greatest fight you have ever seen and why?

Lennox Lewis vs Hasim Rahman I. I am little bit biased on this selection because Rahman is a friend of our family. The boxing world gave him no chance, but we truly felt he could do it. When he knocked out Lennox and shocked the world, we couldn't have been happier for him.

Who are your three favorite fighter's of all-time and why?

First, Sugar Ray Leonard. Second, Muhammad Ali. Finally, Joe Frazier. Each time one of these great fighters stepped into the ring, you knew that a war would be waged. Also, each one brought the sport of boxing forward and they have earned my respect for that.

Do you favor a mandatory retirement for all boxers and if so, how would you like to see it accomplished?

At this time, I don't believe it should be mandatory. A fighter should have the choice if he wants to pay into one or not.

When you finally hang up the contracts, managers pen and hat, how do you want to be remembered in the boxing world?

I would like to be remembered as a manager who helped his fighters become world champions in and out of the ring.

Finally, what is the saying you live your life by?

"Dedication to your family and friends is a must. Also, always keep the faith and all good things will happen".

***** I would like to thank Sam Dansicker of 10 Kount Productions for assisting me in this interview.

As always fight fans, keep reaching for the stars, and all your dreams can be fulfilled.

Interview conducted May 2002

A True Boxing Fan...

Up Close and Personal with Legendary Adult Movie Star Vanessa Del Rio

When the name Vanessa Del Rio is mentioned, I have no doubt that many thoughts come to the reader's mind. I'm sure that over half of the male population have seen her many adult movies in the late 1970's and early 80's. She gained her success in the many movies that she made, and still to this day, they generate a huge revenue for the adult movie industry which she retired from in December 1985/January 1986.

Well, as you know, I don't do the obvious interviews. I have interviewed many celebrities, and Vanessa now joins that elite group that I had the pleasure to interview about their love for the sport of boxing.

77

As you will read, Vanessa has many good points that she makes. I feel that anyone who has positive things to say about a sport that always seems to get more negative press for the small fraction that is bad, is someone I enjoy interviewing.

How long have you followed boxing?

I can remember when I was like in the sixth grade going to Catholic School and we had this Franciscan Black Nun who was crazy about Cassius Clay. I can remember her bringing all the news clippings to class and she would be so very excited reading to us about him.

In addition to this, I really followed it when I was dating an ex-fighter back in the early 1970's named, John Rotondo. He trained up in the Catskill Mountains with the legendary, Cus D'Amato. After that timeframe, I was on and off with watching boxing. However, I always kept up with it through the news.

Who are your top three favorite fighters of all-time and why?

Number one hands down is, Muhammad Ali for the obvious reasons. His confidence was unlike anyone's I have ever seen. I looked at him as a role model because everything he set his mind to do he always did. He exemplifies what you can do when you put your mind to it and for that, I truly respect him.

I really like Prince Naseem Hamed. He is so cocky with his pre-fight act and the funny thing is, he pulls it off. I like the skills and showmanship he provides in the ring.

Finally, Lennox Lewis. At first, I was like United States all the way, but after he got truly robbed in the first Holyfield match, I admired how calmly he handled himself. Since then, I have watched how he acts in and out of the ring, and I like the class in which he carries himself.

I know you only said three, but I have to add one more. Sugar Ray Leonard. He was just so fast and schooled in the ring. Each time you would see him fight you got your fill of excitement.

Did you watch the recent Oscar Delahoya vs Sugar Shane Mosley fight, and what did you think about it?

I felt looking at both fighters that they were evenly matched in there. It was a fantastic fight and one that boxing needs more of. They should be applauded for the efforts they both gave in that fight.

Being a fan of boxing for many years, what changes have you seen in the sport?

I think at one point in the late 1980s through the early 1990s, it kind of went down. It now seems to be getting back to when I first started watching it. As of late, there have been so many great matches that I have watched. Brad, you should hear me rooting for the fighters. The neighbors probably think I am nuts, especially when the fight comes on late and they can hear my yelling.

What divisions today do you find the most exciting?

The Heavyweights and the Middleweights.

Would you like to see boxing go back to the days when you had 15-round championship fights vs. the 12 they have today?

I would have to say yes because watching the Mosley vs Delahoya fight, which had that great 12th round, makes me wonder what 13-15 would have brought us. I think we would have seen some really great action in there.

What fighters excite you enough as a paying customer to order their PPV matches?

To be honest Brad, I pay to see them all the time. I was taken a little back when they charged $50.00 dollars for the Mosley vs Delahoya fight, but after seeing it, I think it was worth every dime.

Do you think fighters should have a mandatory retirement fund and if so, how would you like to see it accomplished?

Yes I do. Actors have their unions that take care of them when they get older. Boxers put so much into the sport and should have some type of fund when they finally hang up the gloves.

What is the greatest fight you have ever seen and why?

Hands down, The Thrilla in Manilla. I love watching it time and time again, which they show on the Sports Classic TV show here. In this legendary match, you had two men who fought with every ounce of energy they could muster up.

It was a back and forth war, and when I saw Frazier at the end unable to come out for the 15th round, I saw the greatness of Muhammad Ali. He persevered throughout a fight that almost saw him retire in his corner, as well. You have to respect a man like Ali for not giving up in a true rumble, such as this was.

What do you think of females in boxing?

It's ok as long as they get in there and fight. I think it would be neat to see Ali vs Frazier's daughter fight. I actually made a documentary movie in the 1970s about a female fighter named Cathy "Cat" Davis.

They filmed me in the ring boxing and I wasn't bad with my fists because as I told you earlier, I was friends with that boxer and he taught me a couple of moves.

Finally, what is the saying you live your life by?

"Never give up and never take no for an answer".

Vanessa has an official website at: www.vanessadelrio.com In addition, she encourages fans to write her fan club at:

Vanessa Del Rio
285 5th Avenue
#234
Brooklyn, NY 11215

***This site is for Adults over the age of 18, so please be responsible.

As always fight fans, keep reaching for the stars, and all your dreams can be fulfilled.

Interview conducted July 2000

Photo Courtesy of Roger Williams
The Legend...

Up Close and Personal with Legendary Corner Man Angelo Dundee

The phone rings, and on the other end, a woman says "Hello Angelo Dundee's Office." I tell her who I am she says, "Hold on Brad I will tell Angelo you're on the phone". There is a short pause and then, Angelo picks up and without hesitation says, "Brad, How are you doing?" I replied, "good" and then he said, "There ain't no fad when you talk to Brad".

This is the kind of man Angelo is. A man of humor, warmth, honor and above all, loyalty - a loyalty he has shown his fighters over so many years. I had the pleasure of meeting Angelo several times in the early 80's at the gym I used to train at in North Miami Beach Florida named Allen Park.

Many years later, while home on leave from Desert Shield/Desert Storm, I would again run into Angelo with my late father, at the famous Lorenzo's Italian Restaurant in North Miami Beach Florida. The event was the closed circuit fight between Tommy Hearns and Virgil Hill. My dad, who knew Angelo over the years, took me to his table and asked if he would take a picture with us. Angelo didn't hesitate. To this day, the picture hangs in my office at home.

In my opinion, Angelo is to boxing what Frank Sinatra is to music. Both legends who moved their respectful industries in a positive manner, adding CLASS, and a body of work to admire, for many years to come. If you ever have the chance to meet Angelo, you will know what I did in about 30 seconds of talking with this sweet man.

In your 50 plus years of boxing, what is the greatest fight you have ever seen?

I have seen so many great fights. When you think back in your memory, you don't want to be like the old Over-the Hill-Gang that gives you some BS about some old-time fights. Fact is, we see some great fights coming on now, and I have been personally involved in them by working the corner.

You have to say Muhammad Ali Vs Sonny Liston I, Willie Pastrano Vs Harold Johnson, where the impossible happened. Finally, how can you top the Thrilla in Manilla and the first Frazier Vs Ali at the Garden? It's hard to name just one.

In all your years of boxing, what fighter do you feel had the total package?

83

It had to be Muhammad Ali. Muhammad changed the whole gist of boxing where the media got to talk to the superstar. I pride myself with that because I pushed Ali to them, because I knew if you get the proper media and you don't beat on each other, this would cultivate a romance. This is what Muhammad created. The first superstar available of our era was Muhammad Ali. He could handle it inside and outside the ring with his talent. Bottom line: He changed the whole sport of boxing.

Who inspired you to be a trainer?

Nothing actually inspired me. I was in England during World War II. My brother Jimmy and I were there. At that time I was in what was called the Air Corp and with the 459 Service Squadron, 318th Service Group. We naturally were in Europe and my brother Chris knew these guys with the USO.

They had boxing tournaments over there or boxing exhibitions ala Joe Louis. They needed guys for those inner military tournaments, so Jim and I, low and behold, used to second them. God help those fighters if they really needed something. They were in deep stuff. I didn't even know how to hold a bucket back then. When my time was up I came back to the states. I was an aircraft inspector with a place in Philly, but the types of planes I inspected had changed and I wanted to move on.

I called my brother Chris who was stationed in New York at the time and asked him if I could come there and give boxing a shot. I took it all in by listening, watching and learning from the best in those days, with guys such as Charley Goldman and Ray Arcel. I was the bucket guy in the corner. I used to watch these guys in the gym and noticed that each guy was a different study.

I admired these guys because they truly gave of themselves. I had so many wonderful teachers and got one heck of an education.

Do you favor a mandatory retirement fund for all boxers and if so, how would you like to see it accomplished?

YES! We need to find a way to do this maybe like a slush fund for these kids. I am all for it. Take the money off the purse, promoter, or any place you can. It will line up if you do it from the start. They did that in California for awhile. (We both agreed deeply that fighters should have something afterwards when they retire, because accolades do not put food on their families' tables).

What qualities must a boxer possess in order for you to train him or her?

First of all, I must feel that they have a future. There is no tougher profession than being a fighter. It's tough, due to the simple reason that the managerial end of it has been taken away, because what's happening is the promoters are handling the fighters. I feel that the personal touch is the thing you need with each other. I always have a personal touch with a fighter.

By doing this, it allows you to get out of each other what's there. So when you get a fighter, he needs to respect you and vice versa. If they have the talent to exploit, then you have a party, yet you must still bring up the talent gradually.

I am known for being a slow guy. I like to take my time and allow my fighter to have every advantage. I don't want to give away too much in a learning experience. In other words, when I have a young kid, I don't want to give away too much maturity, punch, and want my guy to have the edge where he can win. So with that said, the qualities are that the kid has got to want it.

What are your words of wisdom to the young man or woman that wants to become a trainer?

If you have the talent and the quality, then it's a tremendous adventure. But you must have the talent and the quality to do it. You must persevere because it's not going to come easy.

What was your favorite Ali fight that you were involved in and why?

First of all I must say that Muhammad was so much fun and this is what you need in the profession to excel at it. Brad, I had fun since day one with him and still to this day, when we see each other, it's so much fun. I would say my favorite was the Thrilla in Manilla.

It's my favorite because it brought back that these guys have a way of sucking it up, which is a mark of greatness. Here was Muhammad who in the 11th round looked like he could have tossed it in, but he sucked it up and dominated Frazier, causing him to throw it in. This was Muhammad!

Do you think it's fair to say that the years Muhammad was out because of the War issue would have been his best years?

I don't think Muhammad lost, I think the public did. They didn't see him at his greatest. When he came back he did lose some of the magic he had before the layoff.

What was your favorite Sugar Ray Leonard fight that you were involved in and why?

Marvin Hagler because everyone figured no chance that Ray could win. I would also have to say the Hearns fight, as well.

What do you think of each division having three titles?

I think it's nuts. We should have one title because too many champions mix up the fans. They don't know who is around and the real McCoy in there. You don't want to mix up a fight fan.

Is there any profession besides for boxing that you wanted to pursue?

Brad I have been doing this since 1948 and have known about boxing from way before that.

Who was your first fighter to challenge for a title and what was the outcome?

Carmen Basilo was my first. He knocked out Tony Demarco in the 12th round to win the Welterweight Championship.

If you could put together the perfect fighter, what qualities would you pull and from what fighter?

Boxing style would have to be Willie Pep because of the quickness of the jab and the mobility. Willie Pastrano would feint you out of your socks and hit you with a shot and wouldn't be there. Willie was the original hit and doesn't get hit.

This is something you got to have because it gives you longevity. I would take the left hook of a Carmen Basilo. As I said early, for the jab Pep, but would throw Muhammad's jab in too. For defense, Luis Rodriguez. Footwork

Willie Pastrano and Ali. Right hand, Joe Louis.

Of all the honors bestowed upon you, which one are you most proud of?
Brad, listen I am proud of anything. I once got an award from a guy in Ohio that said, GOOD GUYS WIND UP FIRST! I loved that Angelo said that with such a wonderful, honest laugh. Look, I am very happy that people acknowledge my presence on this earth.

Finally, how would you like your legions of fans to remember you?
Not for anything special, just as a guy who enjoyed what he did.

As always fight fans, keep reaching for the stars, and all your dreams can be fulfilled.

Interview conducted March 2000

The Big Man...

Up Close and Personal with Former Two Time Heavyweight Champion George Foreman

Recently I interviewed legendary boxing announcer, Michael Buffer. I asked Mike what single moment in all his years of announcing was he most proud of? He replied, "The night George Foreman, at age 45, knocked out Michael Moorer to win the Heavyweight Championship of the World. My final announcement began with, Ladies and Gentleman, the impossible dream has come true."

Well, I saw that fight and always said I really would like to do an interview with Big George because I always felt he really had a wonderful career and deserved all the good things that came his way.

That day finally came and I found George more than willing to talk about boxing along with his legendary career. He is a very funny

89

man and if you get the chance to meet him at a fight one day, you will probably be in stitches. He has a wonderful sense of humor and I think that is what endears him to so many people.

What inspired you to get into boxing?

I went into boxing at the age of 17 to lose weight and become a great street fighter. I left California and went back to Houston, Texas. Next thing I know, I was fighting as a Golden Glover. It basically all happened as an accident.

You came from the era of legendary heavyweights such as Muhammad Ali, Joe Frazier, Earnie Shavers, Larry Holmes and of course, yourself. How do you rate the overall heavyweight division today compared to the days when you first came into it?

I think what has happened, and it's really a shame, is this. Muhammad Ali defined the heavyweight division for a long time with his pre-draft and after fight career, winning the heavyweight title three times and fighting Joe Frazier and myself.

I think people compare the heavyweights of then and now just too much. The heavyweights today are very good and should not be compared to the ones of the past. They are very competitive today and like I said earlier, just as good.

What big fights were you approached with that never materialized?

The fight that should have happened and we were on the steps so close was Mike Tyson. For some reason, Mike never wanted to fight me and it could have been for good reasons, probably for my benefit as well.

How about in your first career?

I was supposed to face Jerry Quarry. He was very strong and always drew a good crowd. Brad, he was a real good counterpuncher and they kept me away from him.

Out of all the tough opposition you faced in the ring, who do you feel was the toughest opponent and why?

Toughest has to be Muhammad Ali. He just took everything I had and gave me back something just as equally devastating. However, he was not the hardest hitter. That award goes to Ron Lyle who I faced in 1976 and who hit me harder than any other fighter I ever faced.

Your achievement of winning the title at the age of 45 is unprecedented in the sport of boxing and quite an accomplishment. You have several other accomplishments including, winning the Gold Medal in the '68 Olympics and the Heavyweight Championship, twice. What event do you cherish the most?

There will never be anything to top my athletic career like winning the Gold Medal in the Olympics back in 1968. To stand on that platform as a 19 year old boy, who till that point, had never accomplished anything, was a day I will never forget. (To my young readers, read this answer very closely because when I asked George this particular question, I could tell the answer came from deep in his heart. It shows you what all of you have the capability to do if you put your mind to it.)

What aspects of announcing do you enjoy the most?

When I really get to sit there and watch the boxer, then turn around and explain to the fans what is going on from a boxer standpoint, is a joy to me. I can explain things that the ordinary fan may overlook and I have the opportunity to point it out to them.

What fighter in the last 30 years do you feel moved the sport of boxing forward the most?

I would have to say Mike Tyson. He had a lot to do with the sustaining of the heavyweight Pay-Per-View fights. He brought the cable and PPV back which enabled a lot of us fighters to get the big bucks for these fights.

With all your knowledge of boxing and skills, are we going to see George Foreman the trainer?

Not at all. My big hope, is and I am trying to convince my wife of it is this, is at the age of 55, I want to make one more comeback

What is the greatest fight you have ever seen and why?

Marvin Hagler vs. Sugar Ray Leonard. I think it's the greatest fight I have ever seen at anytime. It was a fight of science and Sugar Ray doing the improbable. So many people talked about it and I can remember commercials about it. I do feel Sugar Ray won that fight and executed the perfect game plan.

Recently I interviewed Earnie Shavers, who you are compared to when it comes to the level of power in your punches. Earnie told me that his power came from the days when he worked on

a farm chopping trees and throwing bales of hay. What do you attribute your punching power to?

FEAR! I always had the fear that if I did not get my opponent out of there early, I would not be able to go past four rounds. I had this tremendous amount of fear and it enabled me to hit very hard.

I know we both support a retirement fund for all boxers. How would you like to see it accomplished?

I totally agree with you Brad, that we need one. I think it should be handled like this. Every time there is a boxing event a certain percentage of each ticket sold and each fighter's purse should go into a pension fund.

I retired with money and you will see on my record, so and so, and only say that guy fought George Foreman. Well, those guys need a retirement fund just like the bigger guys do.

When you finally walk away from boxing, if you haven't already, what do you want your legion of fans to remember you for?

That George Foreman had a lot of fun with his boxing career. I am even having more fun with the broadcasting career.

Finally, what is the saying you live your life by?

"Evil lurks where disappointment lodges".

George FOREMAN
Nickname: "Big"

Weight Class: Heavyweight/Unlimited

Amateur record: 25 fights; 22+, 3-

1968: America Heavyweight:
+ Henry Crump points
1968: Olympic Games Mexico Heavyweight:
+ Lucjan Trela (Pol) points
+ Ion Alexe (Rou) ko 3
+ Giorgio Bambini (Ita) ko 2
+ Ionas Chepulis (URSS) kot 2
Professional record: 81 fights; 76+ (68 KO),
5-
1971: North America Heavyweight
1973-1974: World Heavyweight
1976: North America Heavyweight
1994-1995: World Heavyweight
1995: I.B.F. Heavyweight

- **1969** -
+ (Jun-23-1969, New York) Donald Waldheim ko 3
+ (Jun-30-1969, Houston) Fred Askew ko 1
+ (Jul-14-1969, Washington) Sylvester Dulaire ko 1
+ (Aug-18-1969, New York) Chuck Wepner kot 3
+ (Sep-18-1969, Seattle) John Carroll ko 3
+ (Sep-23-1969, Houston) Cookie Wallace ko 2
+ (Oct-7-1969, Houston) Vernon Clay ko 2
+ (Oct-31-1969, New York) Roberto Davila 8
+ (Nov-5-1969, Scranton) Leo Peterson ko 4
+ (Nov-18-1969, Houston) Max Martinez ko 2
+ (Dec-6-1969, Las Vegas) Bob Hazelton ko 1
+ (Dec-16-1969, Miami Beach) Levi Forte 10
+ (Dec-18-1969, Seattle) Gary Wiler ko 1

- **1970** -
+ (Jan-6-1970, Houston) Charlie Polite ko 4
+ (Jan-26-1970, New York) Jack O'Halloran ko 5
+ (Feb-16-1970, New York) Gregorio Peralta 10
+ (Mar-30-1970, Houston) Rufus Brassell ko 1

+ (Apr-17-1970, New York) James J. Woody ko 3

+ (Apr-29-1970, Cleveland) Aaron Eastling ko 4

+ (May-16-1970, Los Angeles) George Johnson kot 7

+ (Jul-20-1970, Philadelphia) Roger Russell ko 1

+ (Aug-4-1970, New York) George Chuvalo ko 3

+ (Nov-3-1970, Oklahoma City) Lou Bailey ko 3

+ (Nov-18-1970, New York) Boone Kirkman ko 2

+ (Dec-18-1970, Seattle) Mel Turnbow kot 1

- **1971** -

+ (Feb-8-1971, Saint-Paul) Charlie Boston ko 1

+ (Apr-3-1971, Lake Geneva) Stanford Harris ko 2

+ (May-8-1971, Oakland) Gregorio Peralta kot 10 (North America, Heavyweight)

+ (Sep-14-1971, El Paso) Vic Scott ko 1

+ (Sep-21-1971, Beaumont) Leroy Caldwell ko 2

+ (Oct-8-1971, San Antonio) Ollie Wilson ko 2

+ (Oct-29-1971, New York) Luis Faustino Pires kot 4

- **1972** -

+ (Feb-29-1972, Austin) Murphy Goodwin ko 2

+ (Mar-7-1972, Beaumont) Clarence Boone ko 2

+ (Apr-10-1972, Inglewood) Ted Gullick ko 2

+ (May-11-1972, Oakland) Miguel Angel Paez ko 2

+ (Oct-10-1972, Salt Lake City) Terry Sorrels ko 2

- **1973** -

+ (Jan-22-1973, Kingston) Joe Frazier ko 2 (World, Heavyweight)
+ (Sep-1-1973, Tokyo) Jose Roman ko 1 (World, Heavyweight)

- 1974 -
+ (Mar-25-1974, Caracas) Ken Norton kot 2 (World, Heavyweight)
- (Oct-30-1974, Kinshasa) Muhammad Ali ko by 8 (Loses World, Heavyweight)

- 1975: inactive -

- 1976 -
+ (Jan-24-1976, Las Vegas) Ron Lyle ko 4 (North America, Heavyweight)
+ (Jun-14-1976, Uniondale) Joe Frazier ko 5 (North America, Heavyweight)
+ (Aug-14-1976, Utica) Scott Ledoux ko 3
+ (Oct-15-1976, Hollywood) Dino Dennis kot 4

- 1977 -
+ (Jan-22-1977, Pensacola) Pedro Agosto ko 4
- (Mar-17-1977, San Juan) Jimmy Young 12

- 1978-1986: inactive -

- 1987 -
+ (Mar-9-1987, Sacramento) Steve Zouski kot 4
+ (Jul-9-1987, Oakland) Charles Hostetter ko 3
+ (Sep-15-1987, Springfield) Bobby Crabtree kot 6
+ (Nov-21-1987, Orlando) Tim Anderson kot 4
+ (Dec-18-1987, Las Vegas) Rocky Sekorski kot 3

- 1988 -

+ (Jan-23-1988, Orlando) Tom Trim ko 1
+ (Feb-5-1988, Las Vegas) Guido Trane kot 5
+ (Mar-19-1988, Las Vegas) Dwight Braxton kot 7
+ (May-21-1988, Anchorage) Frank Lux kot 3
+ (Jun-26-1988, Atlantic City) Carlos Hernandez ko 4
+ (Aug-25-1988, Fort Myers) Ladislao Mijangos kot 2
+ (Sep-10-1988, Auburn Hills) Bobby Hitz ko 1
+ (Oct-27-1988, Marshall) Tony Fulilangi ko 2
+ (Dec-28-1988, Bakersfield) David Jaco ko 1

- **1989** -
+ (Jan-26-1989, Rochester) Mark Young kot 7
+ (Feb-16-1989, Orlando) Manuel Clay De Almeida kot 3
+ (Apr-29-1989, Galveston) J.B. Williamson kot 5
+ (Jun-1-1989, Phoenix) Bert Cooper kot 3
+ (Jul-20-1989, Tucson) Everett Martin 10

- **1990** -
+ (Jan-15-1990, Atlantic City) Gerry Cooney kot 2
+ (Apr-17-1990, Lake Tahoe) Mike Jameson kot 4
+ (Jun-16-1990, Las Vegas) Adilson Rodrigues ko 2
+ (Jul-31-1990, Edmonton) Ken Lakusta ko 3
+ (Sep-25-1990, London) Terry Anderson ko 1

- **1991** -
- (Apr-19-1991, Atlantic City) Evander Holyfield 12 (World, Heavyweight)
+ (Dec-7-1991, Reno) Jimmy Ellis kot 3

97

- **1992** -
+ (Apr-11-1992, Las Vegas) Alex Stewart 10

- **1993** -
+ (Jan-16-1993, Reno) Pierre Coetzer kot 8
- (Jun-7-1993, Las Vegas) Tommy Morrison 12
(W.B.O., Heavyweight)

- **1994** -
+ (Nov-5-1994, Las Vegas) Michael Moorer ko 10 (World, Heavyweight)

- **1995** -
+ (Apr-22-1995, Las Vegas) Axel Schulz 12 (I.B.F., Heavyweight)

- **1996** -
+ (Nov-3-1996, Tokyo) Crawford Grimsley 12

- **1997** -
+ (Apr-26-1997, Atlantic City) Lou Savarese 12
- (Nov-22-1997, Atlantic City) Shannon Briggs 12

As always fight fans, keep reaching for the stars, and all your dreams can be fulfilled.

Interview conducted October 2000

True Champion...

Up Close and Personal with Former Middleweight Champion Gene Fullmer

When the name Gene Fullmer is mentioned, a boxing historian automatically will say, he comes from the era of the great middleweights that include, Robinson, Lamotta, and Basilo, to name just a few. Gene was not only a true gentleman, but enjoyed talking about his legendary career, which saw his induction into the International Boxing Hall of Fame in 1991.

I found it a true honor to interview a man who has always been respected in boxing circles and now I can see why.

First of all, for the many boxing fans who speak of you as one of the great middleweights of your day, what are you doing today?

I basically have a few quarter horses that I race. I also chase around my wonderful grandkids, and work in a boxing gym with children. Other than that, I am pretty much retired.

What inspired you get into boxing?

I think my father and my mother. My mother named me Gene after former Heavyweight Champion, Gene Tunney. My father's nickname was, "Tough". So, with heritage like that, you almost have got to end up in boxing.

How do you compare the fight game of today, to the days when you fought?

Personally, I think today they are paying too much money for what they are getting from the fighters. When I was fighting I had to fight the number one contender, no matter who he was. I could not go down the rankings and fight someone, say 2 -10 in the rankings. Nowadays, they fight whoever they think will pay the most. It seems like it's basically about the money today.

Who do you see in the middleweight division today, that impresses you?

Well, any man that goes out there and fights is impressive. I don't have any one favorite over another. Who ever goes out and fights hard for the sake of fighting are the ones I like.

Looking at your record, which is quite impressive at (55-6-3, 24 Ko's), you fought the legendary, Sugar Ray Robinson four times and were victorious in two bouts, with one loss and one draw. In all four fights, which fight do you feel Sugar Ray Robinson was at his best and why?

I don't really know. Maybe in the first fight, he was at his best. I sure had to fight hard in that one. In the second bout, I was beating him pretty good for five rounds, when somebody turned the lights out on me. I found out later that it was Ray who turned my lights out, Brad.

I can't really say that was his best in the second fight, because when I watched it again on TV, I saw that he was very lucky with that big punch. A matter of fact Brad, that punch was in Ring Magazine's 75th anniversary issue. They gave it the honor of being the best left hook ever thrown, and I happen to be the one who caught it. (Gene said this with such a warm chuckle.)

Bottom line: The first one had Ray at his best.

Who do you feel was your toughest opponent and why?

I don't really know. They were all tough and they hit back pretty hard. When I think back, I can remember an opponent I defended against, named Florentino Fernandez. It was a very tough fight and he broke my right arm with a left hook in the 13th round. I had to fight the last two rounds with one arm. That wasn't too easy. He picked up on something was wrong with my arm because I couldn't throw it and that made for a much tougher fight.

Who are your three favorite fighters of all-time and why?

I really liked Joe Louis because he was fighting when I was growing up, and then I actually fought on the undercard when he fought Cesar Brion back on August 1, 1951. That was a true thrill. Jersey Joe Walcott was another. He really moved around very well and it seems the heavyweights were very dominant in my mind, back then. Tony Zale would be my third. I liked him as a person and as a fighter who fought very well.

What is the greatest fight you have ever seen and why?

That's a tough one Brad. There were so many. I can tell you the greatest knockout and that's when Robinson knocked me out. Brad, I had to watch that on television to see what really happened. I had no clue what happened and can remember my manager holding on to me in the ring.

I turned to· him and asked, "How come Robinson is exercising between rounds?" He said, "What do you mean?" I said, "he is over there jumping up and down." I was then informed that the referee gave me a ten count. The funny thing Brad, I never heard it. So in my lifetime, that was probably the greatest fight.

Do you prefer 15 rounds vs.12 in the championship fights of today?

I always did well in 15 round fights because I always trained hard. It always seemed that I had just as much stamina in the early rounds as the late ones. Today though, working in a gym with kids, 12 rounds is adequate for a fighter's stamina. After 12, it can be very hard.

Were there any fights that you wanted to have but, couldn't get the fighter to the negotiating table?

Not that I remember. I never really had anything to do with who I fought next. This was left up to my manager. I had a brave manager named Marv Jenson and he felt I could whip anybody out there. He made me feel like that too, which I would say was a good attribute to have.

Do you favor a mandatory retirement fund for all boxers and if so, how would you like to see it accomplished?

I think they should have one, for the amounts of money they are making today such as millions vs. thousands, when I was fighting. I think there should be a fund set up for the fighters in the future who are not as lucky or good enough to fight for these million dollar purses.

What do you think of all these organizations in boxing vs. when you fought and there was only one belt with one true world champion?

Well, it wasn't as hard to keep track of all the champions. Nowadays, you can watch three or four fights in a week and everyone is for a championship belt from all these different organizations, which is a little more confusing. It does, however, pay more money to the fighters and that's what it's all about.

What are your words of wisdom to the young fighter just turning professional?

Getting in condition is the number one, single, most important thing. Roadwork is probably as important as any other thing along with, sparring. You need someone sharp enough to make sure you are doing the rights things. I feel these are the best words I can give them.

Have you stayed friendly with any of the fighters of your day and if so, who?

I have been very friendly with Carmen Basilo and see him every year up at the Hall of Fame up in Canastota, New York. I remain very friendly with all the guys that go up there.

Do you have any funny stories involving any of the fights or maybe behind the scenes of a fight?

It may not be funny, but it's true. I was fighting Spider Webb in Salt Lake City, Utah on September 11, 1958. I came back to the corner in about the third or fourth round and told my manager, "I hate to tell you this, but I think I am getting the flu." He asked me why I thought I was getting the flu? I told him I didn't feel good. He then asked me, "You don't think it's because he is beating the hell out of you?" I never thought about that and went out, got over the flu, and won most of the last rounds, to give me the victory.

Finally, what is the saying you live your life by?

"Try to be honest and fair".

In closing, Gene would like to say the following:

I would like to say something about my promoter, the late Norm Rothchild. He promoted most of my fights after I beat Ray Robinson. After Carmen Baslio won and then lost to Robinson, they let Carmen and I fight for the title. Norm Rothchild was the promoter from Syracuse, New York very close to where Carmen was from. He also promoted many of Carmen's fights at that time.

My camp thought we were taking a little chance on having him promote the fight because he was a big fan of Carmen Basilo's. I can remember before the fight, he came into my dressing room and he said, "I want you to know Fullmer, Basilo is my favorite fighter and I have been promoting him for a longtime."

He then said, "That has nothing to do with who wins the fight. If you win the fight, then you will win the fight, and I am not doing anything to take that away from you". I have always thought from that day on, he gave me a great tribute by saying that to me, which eased my mind. He truly was a great gentleman.

I would also like to thank my manager, Marv Jenson who really treated me great and always told me how to live right. I was very satisfied with him as my manager and a man. We still stay in touch to this day.

Gene FULLMER

Weight class: Middleweight/160 lbs

Amateur record:
1948: Olympic Trials
Professional record: 64 fights; 55+ (24 KO), 3=, 6-
1957: World Middleweight
1959-1962: N.B.A. Middleweight

- 1951 -

+ (Jun-9-1951, Logan) Glen Peck ko 1
+ (Jun-16-1951, West Jordan) Andy Jackson ko 1
+ (Jun-23-1951, Midvale) Gary Carr ko 3
+ (Jul-2-1951, Vernal) Eddie Duffy ko 1
+ (Jul-9-1951, Salt Lake City) Eddie Duffy ko 2
+ (Jul-16-1951, West Jordan) Lamar Peterson ko 1
+ (Aug-1-1951, San Francisco) Carlos Martinez ko 1
+ (Aug-24-1951, Hurricane) Sam Healy ko 1
+ (Aug-25-1951, Hurricane) Buddy Sloane ko 2
+ (Sep-7-1951, West Jordan) Charley Cato ko 4
+ (Sep-14-1951, Vernal) Sam Healy ko 4
+ (Sep-25-1951, Salt Lake City) Garth Panter 10
+ (Oct-3-1951, West Jordan) Gary Hanley ko 1
+ (Oct-10-1951, Pittsburgh) Rudy Zadell 6
+ (Oct-17-1951, Vernal) Ray Jones ko 1

-1952 –
+ (Aug-8-1952, Ogden) Mickey Rhodes ko 6
+ (Sep-20-1952, Hollywood) Armando Cotero 6

- 1953: inactive -

- 1954 -
+ (Feb-6-1954, West Jordan) Kid Leon ko 1
+ (Apr-26-1954, Salt Lake City) Charley Cato ko 1
+ (May-17-1954, Salt Lake City) Andy Anderson kot 7
+ (Jun-5-1954, Salt Lake City) Kid Rico kot 1
+ (Jul-12-1954, Salt Lake City) Govan Small 10

+ (Jul-29-1954, West Jordan) Reno Abellira 10
+ (Aug-16-1954, West Jordan) Dick Wolfe ko 4
+ (Nov-8-1954, New York) Jackie La Bua 10
+ (Nov-15-1954, New York) Peter Muller 10

- 1955 -
+ (Jan-31-1955, New York) Marcel Assire 10
+ (Feb-14-1955, New York) Paul Pender 10
+ (Mar-21-1955, Salt Lake City) Govan Small 10
- (Apr-4-1955, New York) Gil Turner 10
+ (Jun-20-1955, Salt Lake City) Gil Turner 10
+ (Jul-26-1955, Butte) Del Flanagan 10
+ (Sep-12-1955, Ogden) Al Andrews 10
- (Sep-28-1955, Chicago) Bobby Boyd 10
- (Nov-25-1955, New York) Eduardo Lausse 10

- 1956 -
+ (Jan-4-1956, Cleveland) Rocky Castellani 10
+ (Feb-17-1956, New York) Gil Turner 10
+ (Apr-20-1956, Cleveland) Ralph Jones 10
+ (May-25-1956, New York) Charles Humez 10
+ (Sep-22-1956, West Jordan) Moses Ward ko 3

- 1957 -
+ (Jan-2-1957, New York) Ray Robinson 15 (World, Middleweight)
+ (Jan-28-1957, Salt Lake City) Wilfred Greaves 10
+ (Feb-18-1957, Denver) Ernie Durando 10
- (May-1-1957, Chicago) Ray Robinson ko 5 (World, Middleweight)
+ (Jun-7-1957, Chicago) Ralph Jones 10
+ (Sep-4-1957, Salt Lake City) Chico Vejar 10
+ (Nov-15-1957, New York) Neal Rivers 10

- 1958 -
+ (Mar-3-1958, Salt Lake City) Milo Savage 10
+ (Jul-7-1958, West Jordan) Jim Hegerle 10
+ (Sep-11-1958, Salt Lake City) Spider Webb 10
+ (Nov-10-1958, Salt Lake City) Joe Miceli ko 2

- 1959 -
+ (Jan-9-1959, San Antonio) Milo Savage 10
+ (Feb-20-1959, New York) Wilfred Greaves 10
+ (Aug-28-1959, San Francisco) Carmen Basilio kot 14 (N.B.A., Middleweight)
+ (Dec-4-1959, Logan) Spider Webb 15 (N.B.A., Middleweight)

- 1960 -
= (Apr-20-1960, Bozeman) Joey Giardello 15 (N.B.A., Middleweight)
+ (Jun-29-1960, Salt Lake City) Carmen Basilio kot 12 (N.B.A., Middleweight)
= (Dec-3-1960, Los Angeles) Ray Robinson 15 (N.B.A., Middleweight)

- 1961 -
+ (Mar-4-1961, Las Vegas) Ray Robinson 15 (N.B.A., Middleweight)
+ (Aug-5-1961, Ogden) Florentino Fernandez 15 (N.B.A., Middleweight)
+ (Dec-9-1961, Las Vegas) Benny Paret ko 10 (N.B.A., Middleweight)

- 1962 -
- (Oct-28-1962, San Francisco) Dick Tiger 15 (W.B.A., Middleweight)

- 1963 -

= (Feb-23-1963, Las Vegas) Dick Tiger 15 (World, Middleweight)

- (Aug-10-1963, Ibadan) Dick Tiger retiring 7 (World, Middleweight)

- 1964 -
23.7.1964: Fullmer announces retirement.

As always fight fans, keep reaching for the stars, and all your dreams can be fulfilled.

Interview conducted July 2000

Photo Courtesy of Donna Balkum

Making Moves...

Up Close and Personal with WBA Featherweight Champion Derrick "Smoke" Gainer

As of late, I have really had the chance to interview some truly tremendous fighters, whose talents far exceed those they display in the many rings that they fight in. Derrick Gainer is one of those fighters. Derrick has made tremendous strides in helping out the children of Pensacola, Florida. He does this by going around to every function imaginable, to spread a positive word about what you can do with your life.

In addition, Gainer has opened and owns, an alternative High School in Pensacola, Florida that is named after his Grandmother. It's called, DR RUBY J GAINER SCHOOL FOR REACHING YOUR DREAM. Gainer is the Principal of the school which gives young people a second chance when others have given up on them.

Gainer, I feel has been knocked far too much in recent years for his true friendship with undisputed, Light Heavyweight Champion, Roy Jones, JR. He endures comments such as "If it wasn't for Roy, you would not be where you're at." More recently, you hear, "You would not have gotten the World Title shots if it were not for Roy."

Well, I have heard these comments for far too long and now I'm going to add my two cents. First of all, I was raised that a true friend will go to the ends of the earth for the other. Gainer and Jones, JR. have done this for each other, time and time again.

With that said, if Roy did have something to do with a title shot that took Derrick nine years - yes NINE YEARS - to get, then all he was doing is what a true friend does for another, and don't forget, he is his manager. I then ask, "Did Roy fight for Derrick?" The answer is NO! Derrick is the one who took the punches against Deigo Corrales, eventually being stopped prematurely in his first title attempt.

He bounced back from that loss when many others might have quit. Eventually, he won his share of the Gold on September 9, 2000, stopping Freddy Norwoood for the WBA Featherweight Belt.

I want to go back a little in his career before he won his title. On June 15, 1996, Gainer had what I consider to be his career defining fight against Kevin Kelley. Gainer was well ahead on points and got caught by a good punch which led to a knockout loss. At that point, he could have quit, but chose to go on, and I feel, become a better fighter because of it.

111

It's about time that the boxing world gave him his fair credit as a fighter, World Champion, and a decent man.

Finally, this writer wants to say to Derrick Gainer and Roy Jones, JR., that I commend you both for the true friendship you have shown each other over many years. May others be so lucky to have such a friendship, one which I have witnessed with my own two eyes.

What inspired you to get into boxing?

When I was a little kid, I saw Roy Jones, JR. in the local Pensacola, Florida newspaper, that highlighted his winning the Junior Olympic Nationals in 1984. I was so moved by this, I went down to the gym with two of my cousins and started boxing. They eventually quit, but I went on, because I truly love the competition of the sport.

Now that you have struck Gold, winning the WBA Featherweight Championship of the World, what changes do you feel came with the belt?

Brad, the only changes really are, that people are going to be hunting for me now, versus me hunting them. I want to get right back in there and defend my title. I am the same Derrick Gainer, because I always had faith that this day was finally going to come.

Tell the readers how it felt and what went through your mind when you heard them announce, "And the New World Champion......"

It felt so great that I immediately starting crying because I was finally a World Champion.

In my opening of this interview, I referred to the constant criticism of one; your friendship with Roy, where people say that if

not for him, you would not be where your are, and most recently; you would not have gotten the title shots. I want to give you the chance to address these statements.

Brad, first of all thanks for allowing me to get my side out. When I beat Freddy Norwood, that was for the media which always said Roy led me to this title fight, which is what a true friend is supposed to do. Brad, like you said earlier in our interview, Roy did not, one time, fight for me in that ring. Give me the credit for getting in that ring and beating the guys I beat, when you look at my boxing record.

With that said, give Roy Jones Jr. credit for being a wonderful best friend, mentor, and one heck of a manager. He is the greatest fighter in the world and used his God-given talent to help his best friend out. Now, let's talk about the commentary strictly from HBO when I fought Diego Corrales. I went down from a good shot and the referee stopped the fight prematurely, in my opinion. No one from HBO once said, "Derrick "Smoke" Gainer deserved an opportunity." All they wanted to talk about is, Roy did this and Roy did that. I love Roy, and as you know, he is my best friend. He paved the way for me. Diego Corrales recently fought Angel Manfredy, which was a huge mismatch. The first thing Jim Lampley and Larry Merchant said was, "We hope to see him again." Angel almost got killed in there.

But those same guys did not give Derrick "Smoke" Gainer any type of credit. You will always hear certain people in boxing circles talk bad about Roy and I, because we refuse to sell out on one another. At times, some of the commentators out there need to get into the ring, so they can have a better understanding of boxing by taking the blows.

Case in point, Larry Merchant. When I fought Norwood, he made it seem I was the one fighting dirty, but to everyone else, it was Norwood. That's why I say Larry Merchant needs to get in the ring. When he sees me off camera he constantly smiles in my face. The very moment when we are on the camera, he offers ridiculous remarks. Brad, I feel if you are going to be against me, then be against me all the time. I don't know why he would do that to me, because I am not a bad guy and on the most important night of my life, he tried to take away from the special moment. Larry's comments have always tried to belittle me and I don't appreciate it, or deserve it.

What is the difference in the Derrick we saw against Diego Corrales and the Derrick fans saw against Freddy Norwood?

I moved down to the true weight I should have been fighting at when I faced Norwood. When I fought Diego Corrales, I hit him with one of the hardest left hands I have ever hit someone with in my life, and he kept coming. Now, in the Norwood fight, I hit him with that same punch in the second round and he went down. I was more focused in the Norwood fight and boxed him.

Who are your three favorite fighters of all-time and why?

First, is Roy Jones, JR. because he is a complete fighter. He can beat you inside and out with knockout power. His training is top notch and he always possesses the will to win. Second, Salvador Sanchez. I am so happy that he is not a featherweight right now. I watch a tape of him before every one of my fights. I really loved the fights against Danny "Little Red" Lopez and Azumah Nelson. Finally, Muhammad Ali. He really opened the doors for boxers even today, to make the big amounts of money we do.

What is the greatest fight you have ever seen and why?
Marvin Hagler vs John "The Beast" Mugabi. I pick this one because neither guy would give. Hagler showed so much heart and determination in that fight. I feel that Hagler does not get the fair amount of credit that he deserves.

Your career has gone on now for more than 10 years. Do you feel boxing has gone forward in those years, or backward?
I think it's better. With the passing of the Muhammad Ali Act and the FBI cracking down on the sport, eyes are being focused more on things now, than in the past.

Where does the nickname "Smoke" come from?
It came from Roy Jones, Sr. I was in an amateur fight one time with a guy who had over 100 fights and obviously lots more experience than I. Every time I came back to the corner, they would say, "You are smoking him". It stuck from that day on.

Do you favor a mandatory retirement fund for all boxers and if so, how would you like to see it accomplished?
I really feel they need one Brad, and along with it, health benefits, as well. There should be a requirement in place that you have to be in boxing for a certain amount of years and with fights, to draw a pension. In

addition, the promoters should put funds into
the pension as well. I feel that the promoters
should take it upon themselves to pay in and
the pension should help out fighters who are
not currently fighting, but are down on their
luck needing assistance.

**When you finally retire from boxing what do
you want your fans to remember you for?**
That I was knocked out twice in my career
and never quit. I never gave up on myself and
always had the heart of a champion. If I were
to lose 37 fights in a row, in my 38th fight, I
am still trying to win.

Derrick GAINER
Nickname: "Smoke"

Weight Class: Featherweight/126 lbs

Professional record: 41 fights; 36+ (23 KO),
5-
1995-1996: North America Featherweight
1999: United States Junior Lightweight
2000: W.B.A. Featherweight

- 1990 -
+ (Jul-14-1990, Pensacola) Andres Francisco
kot 1
+ (Sep-25-1990, Pensacola) Albert Lara 4
- (Nov-8-1990, Pensacola) Scott Phillips 6

- 1991 -
+ (Aug-3-1991, Pensacola) Donald Gomez kot 1
+ (Aug-31-1991, Pensacola) Outhei Soundara
kot 4
+ (Dec-17-1991, Pensacola) Willie Richardson
6

- 1992 -
+ (Apr-2-1992, Reno) Rudy Bradley kot 3
+ (Jun-30-1992, Pensacola) Carlos Vergara ko 1

- 1993 -
+ (Jan-10-1993, Atlantic City) Runnell Doll 6
+ (Nov-30-1993, Pensacola) Julian Flores 12

- 1994 -
+ (Mar-22-1994, Pensacola) Roy Simpson kot 1
+ (May-27-1994, Las Vegas) Marcello Rodriguez 8
+ (Sep-20-1994, Pensacola) Darren Mc Grew 6
- (Oct-5-1994, Atlantic City) Greg Torres 10
- (Nov-18-1994, Las Vegas) Roberto Garcia 10

- 1995 -
+ (Mar-18-1995, Pensacola) Feliciano Correa kot 1
+ (Jun-24-1995, Atlantic City) Harold Warren 12 (North America, Featherweight)
+ (Sep-30-1995, Pensacola) Roberto Villareal ko 5 (North America, Featherweight)

- 1996 -
+ (Jan-12-1996, New York) James Crayton kot 10
+ (May-9-1996, Pensacola) Javier Diaz kot 6
- (Jun-15-1996, Jacksonville) Kevin Kelley ko 8
+ (Oct-4-1996, New York) Pat Simeon ko 2
+ (Nov-22-1996, Tampa) Shane Gannon kot 2

- 1997 -
+ (Mar-21-1997, Atlantic City) Aldrich Johnson kot 12
+ (Aug-7-1997, Ledyard) Manuel Medina ko 9

- 1998 -
+ (Apr-25-1998, Biloxi) Wilson Santos ko 3
+ (Jun-9-1998, Biloxi) Orlando Soto kot 5
+ (Jul-18-1998, New York) Kevin Kelley 10
+ (Aug-18-1998, Tunica) Bernard Harris 10
+ (Nov-14-1998, Ledyard) Luis Leija kot 6

- 1999 -
+ (Jan-9-1999, Pensacola) Harold Warren 12
(United States, Junior Lightweight)
+ (Jun-5-1999, Biloxi) Donovan Carey kot 6
+ (Jul-30-1999, Biloxi) Freddy Cruz 10
+ (Aug-20-1999, Temecula) Javier Lucas kot 2
+ (Sep-10-1999, Biloxi) Jay Cantu ko 1
+ (Oct-15-1999, Pensacola) Sergio Reyes kot
5
+ (Nov-19-1999, Tunica) Sergio Liendo 10

- 2000 -
- (Mar-18-2000, Las Vegas) Diego Corrales
kot 3 (I.B.F., Junior Lightweight)
+ (May-13-2000, Indianapolis) Sean Fletcher
10
+ (Jul-15-2000, Biloxi) Richard Carrillo kot
8
+ (Sep-9-2000, Nouvelle-Orleans) Fred
Norwood ko 11 (W.B.A., Featherweight)

**As always fight fans, keep reaching for the
stars, and all your dreams can be fulfilled.**

Interview conducted September 2000

Heart and Soul...

Up Close and Personal with Female Boxer Fredia "Queen Cheetah" Gibbs

Look up the word "dedicated" in Webster's dictionary and without a doubt, there will be a picture of Gibbs. This lady is the role model for ladies out there trying to get ahead, not just in boxing, but in life

I have always said, one thing that cannot be faked is sincerity, and Gibbs showed it throughout our interview. This is my last interview before I leave for Seoul, South Korea, for a one year tour of duty with the Navy, and I am happy to leave out on this one.

What inspired you to become a boxer?

I was born a fighter. My whole life has been a fight and a challenge, to be honest. Brad, fear truly inspired me to fight at a young age. As a young child, I was very thin and quite smart in school. The bullies would chase me home from school and at times, I would bust out the emergency door of the bus to get home faster. I used to scare the heck out of my mother, busting through our door.

My uncle, on my father's side, named William Gross, was a martial arts instructor at the time, who learned about my situation, and that my self esteem was low.

He encouraged me to come to his class three times a week to rebuild my self confidence. From there, I learned to fight, which inspired me down the road to get into boxing.

What went through your mind when you heard the bell ring for your first professional boxing match?

It's time to go. You have to knock her out.

What are you words of wisdom to the young lady who wants to lace up the gloves as a professional for the very first time?

In order to do your best, you have to train hard, dedicate yourself, and have a vision. I feel all girls are born to be champions, too.

Having talent, do you find it hard for your people to set up matches for you?

Unfortunately, yes I do.

In 1998, you faced former champion, Leah Mellinger. Give the readers an insight into that fight?

At that time, I had signed a contract to take four months off to shoot the female boxing movie, "KNOCKOUT". What happened is, right after I signed on for the movie, the chance for a world championship fight came up. I thought I could do both. I tried, and my last few days of the movie were 18-hour days.

We flew to New Jersey and I called myself resting up. The smoke from the shoot and the water they would throw on me for the boxing scenes caused me to catch a cold. I still went on and fought. During the fight, there were times when I would ask my coach, what were my lines? My mind was not right for the fight.

What do you say, to the boxing people out there who feel women's boxing is not legit but a sideshow?

Some people have a problem with dealing with women in sports. But what they fail to realize is boxing, basketball, soccer, and any other sport that women compete in, they too, are born to be champions just like the males.

I feel that if women's boxing, was shown and marketed with the best ladies on TV who can fight, like they usually do with the males, it could be a great, worldwide sport. Women from Europe would come to the United States to be a part of it, as well.

It could blow up like women's basketball and soccer has. Finally, the people putting on those fluke female matches should step back and let the real people, who are willing to put on legitimate female boxing shows, be in the forefront.

Currently, you are into acting. Did your boxing career lead you in that direction?

Pretty much it did along with my kickboxing career. I was a three-time world champion and had taken the kickboxing as far as I could.

To date, what do you feel is your career highlight in the ring?

I can't say a career highlight yet, but I did have a slight one in the tenth round of my last fight against Sumya Anani. In the tenth round, I had realized that I didn't give her my best. She only met "Cheetah" then. In the rematch, "Queen Cheetah" will come out.

What is the greatest fight you have ever seen and why?

I have to say my fight against Valarie Henning billed as the "Most Dangerous Woman in the World". She was from France and we were fighting for the ISKA World Title. Her record was 25 and something at the time, and came to America to major fanfare.

They chose me to be her easy opponent, not knowing a thing about me. I knocked her out at 8:16 of the round. It was also my Grandmother's birthday - August 16, which was the same time as the knockout and I feel that was destiny.

Who are your three favorite fighters of all-time and why?

First of all, Muhammad Ali. I loved his confidence, his ability to market himself and back up the things he said. Second, Roy Jones, JR. I love his left hook and the way he can break off his left uppercut. Also, his rooster attitude in the ring which is, do or die. Finally, Me "The Queen Cheetah" the best kept secret in my division!

Do you favor a mandatory retirement fund for all boxers and if so, how would you personally like to see it accomplished?

Yes, I do. I feel every fighter who has participated in the sport over maybe, three years, and made a career in it, should have an open retirement fund. In addition, they also should have medical and dental benefits. They have it in the other professional sports. It really has to be implemented for all boxers.

Is there anyone in women's boxing you would like to call out?
Brad, I just want to fight the best period! I have always felt to be the best, you must fight the best.

When your boxing career is over, how would you like your fans to remember you?
FAST, DEADLY and SEXY!

Finally, what is the saying that you live your life by?
"Tough times never last, tough people do! Which one are you"?

Fredia wanted added the following to our interview:
I just wish all people in sports understand the sacrifices that world class athletes have to make and take, to reach the pinnacle of their dreams. I feel the emphasis should be on females, since males have always been in the spotlight. Finally, little girls need role models just as little boys do.

Fredia GIBBS
Nickname: "Queen Cheetah"
Weight class: Super Lightweight/140 lbs

Professional record: 10 fights; 8+ (2 KO), 1- 1=

- 1997 -
+ (Jan-23-1997) Maria Recinos 4
+ (Apr-16-1997) Daniele Doobenen 4
+ (Aug-2-1997) Gail Grandchamp kot 1
+ (Oct-24-1997) Anneliese Kolan kot 2

- 1998 -
- (Mar-21-1998, Atlantic City) Leah Mellinger 10
+ (Sep-17-1998, Biloxi) Olivia Gerula 6

- 1999 -
+ (Jan-15-1999, Las Vegas) Hannah Fox 6
+ (Nov-5-1999, Temecula) Michelle Vidales 6

- 2000: inactive -

- 2001 -
+ (Jun-8-2001, Inglewood) Suzanne Howard 4
= (Nov-16-2001, Austin) Sumya Anani 10

As always fight fans, keep reaching for the stars, and all your dreams can be fulfilled.

Interview conducted November 2001

Time of our
interview

Two more title belts
added

Lataiya Gray ("Bad" Brad's granddaughter), Gwen Berkwitt ("Bad" Brad's wife), and Isra Girgrah at the Make A Wish Foundation bowling charity event March 2001.

Champion In and Out of the Ring...

Up Close and Personal with International Boxing Federation Women's Lightweight Champion The "Raging Beauty" Isra Girgrah

This is the first time I have had the chance to interview a female fighter and I could not have picked a better lady to conduct an in-depth interview with. Girgrah is very outspoken, dedicated, and a warm person, who takes her craft very seriously.

When this lady steps into the ring, she brings a fighting spirit that is seldom seen among female fighters today, with the exception of a few. In her match a couple of years back with then highly touted, Christy Martin, she not only put up one hell of a fight, but many felt she beat Martin along with this writer, who scored it 6-2 in rounds for Girgrah.

Girgrah not only brings brawn into the ring, but brains, which is quite evident from her studies at Queens University in Kingston, Ontario where she majored in biology. She must have really learned plenty in her lab classes, because she has the formula for success both in and out of the ring.

I have no doubt, that in the years to come, this lady will go on to win more titles and make a difference in this world based on her positive outlook, caring demeanor and love for children.

What inspired you to get into boxing?

A friend of mine who I went to high school with was doing it to get into shape. She told me I would like it. I decided to try it so I could stay in shape, as well. From that point, I fell in love with it.

What are your observations of the fight game such as contract negotiations and getting fights?

Contract negotiations are very difficult. You really need to know how to go into signing a contract, and need a lawyer, as well. You need to understand the fine print, because I have been through two or three contracts that have always been one-sided. The contracts were always more promoter or manager biased, which don't look out for the fighter's interest. It's very difficult getting fights as a female.

There are lots of female fighters out there, but they do not have a lot of experience. Fighters such as Tracy Byrd, Chirsty Martin, and myself are having a hard time getting fights. Casey Dansicker, my manager, has tried several times to get me fights, but we constantly get turned down.

The whole boxing scene at times is a very shady business. Bottom line: Fighters just need to be very careful.

What are your words of wisdom to the young female fighter just lacing up the gloves?

Make sure you are giving it 110%. It's a brutal sport and you can get hurt at anytime in the gym sparring or in a fight. You have to know inside that you want to do this and never just go in there half way.

If you could emulate any fighter, who would it be and why?

Sugar Ray Robinson or Muhammad Ali. They both were true champions who fought everybody and anybody out there. Their skills, such as movement and defense, to name just a few, made them great fighters.

How long have you followed boxing?

I have followed it for six years. Before that, I used to watch a couple fights here and there. When I turned professional, I really started watching them all.

Who are your three favorite fighters of all-time and why?

First, Sugar Ray Robinson. He was just a true champion and had imminent skills. Second, Muhammad Ali. He was just like Sugar, he never worried about who he was going to fight and just had those great skills in the ring. Finally, Roy Jones, JR. He is just unbeatable in the ring.

What is the greatest fight you have ever seen and why?

Marvelous Marvin Hagler vs Sugar Ray Leonard. They just went toe-to-toe.

Do you favor a mandatory retirement fund for all boxers and if so, how would you like to see it accomplished?

Yes, I definitely agree with it. Managers and promoters putting money into a retirement fund becomes difficult because, if I am not signed with say, America Presents, and I fight on one of their cards, will they put money into it?

I totally agree with you Brad that it should be paid into from day one, but also a lot of fighters walking around broke today, can blame themselves for it.

What do you think of the ranking systems for female fighters and if you had control of them, what changes would you make to them?

The organizations that do the rankings are just like the men's except we don't have mandatory defenses all the time. I think they should make us have mandatory defenses in a certain time frame, just like the men. There are a lot of female champions out there that are not allowing others a chance to fight for their belts.

What went through your mind the first time you stepped into the ring as a professional?

"What am I doing?" I was very nervous and the girl that I fought was ranked and established in boxing. My manager at that time had set me up because he knew her as well. They were just trying to get her a win.

My manager also told me the fight would be just an exhibition match. I went in there having just gotten over the flu. It was a six round fight and for three rounds I went toe to toe with her. When I came back to my corner, I said to myself that I am not properly trained and not going to get hurt in there. I told my corner to stop the fight.

After that fight, I went all out, making sure that each time I stepped into the ring, I was properly trained.

Being a female fighter what is your take on the age old complaint that female fighters are only for entertainment purposes and not equal to their male counterparts?

My opinion that we are just sideshows is one that I totally disagree on. Many women out there, do fight like they're a sideshow because they do not have skills nor try to perfect them. There are women out there such as Christy Martin, Lucia Rijker, and myself, that fight just like the men do!

We have the technique and we give 100% in there and half the time, give better shows than the men do. Once again, I don't appreciate men stereotyping all women fighters as a sideshow. (I like Isra's honesty on this answer. I do agree that some of the women fighters out there are just as good if not better, then the men when it comes to excitement).

Do you have any particular location you want to fight at and why?

I already fought in Madison Square Garden which is something I always wanted to do. I would love to fight there again. Madison Square Garden just has so much magic to it and of course it being New York City, just adds to it. It was such a wonderful feeling to fight there Brad.

After you achieved or attempted to achieve all your goals in boxing. How would you like your fans to remember you?

That I made a stand for women to step up and do what they want to do. When I started, I don't think Christy had been on her first Showtime Card yet. I was one of the pioneers in bringing female boxing forward.

Finally, what is the saying that you to live your life by?
"If you're happy doing it, then do it".

Isra GIRGRAH
Nickname: "The Raging Beauty"

Weight class: Junior Lightweight/130 lbs

Professional record: 17 fights; 12+ (7 KO's), 2=, 3-

- **1995** -
- (Feb-14-1995) Deirdre GOGARTY kot 3
+ (Nov-2-1995, Austin) Melinda ROBINSON 6

- **1996** -
+ (Jan-19-1996, Philadelphia) Amy SHERRALD kot 1
+ (Feb-22-1996, Corpus Christi) Melinda ROBINSON 6
+ (Feb-24-1996) Angela Thomas kot 2
+ (Aug-2-1996, Northport) Tennile DAVIS kot 3
+ (Aug-30-1996, Atlanta) Stephanie Osborne kot 3
= (Oct-10-1996, Washington) Andrea DESHONG 4
+ (Oct-25-1996, Atlanta) Norma Mosley ko 2

- **1997** -
+ (Jan-31-1997, Atlanta) Bethany PAYNE 4
+ (Jul-19-1997, Nashville) Tennile DAVIS 4
- (Aug-23-1997, New York) Christy MARTIN 8

- **1998** -
+ (Apr-11-1998, Columbia) Angela BUCHANAN kot 3

+ (Nov-20-1998, Stone Mountain) <u>Bethany PAYNE</u> 8

- 1999 -
+ (Sep-2-1999, Tunica) <u>Karen RAMOS</u> kot 1
- (Oct-23-1999, Las Vegas) <u>Marischa SJAUW</u> 4

- 2000 -
= (Feb-16-2000, Miami) <u>Britt VAN BUSKIRK</u> 4
***Two career defining milestones came since this interview. First, Girgrah won the Universal Boxing Association (UBA) Lightweight Title on January 12, 2001. On June 1st, 2001, she added the International Women's Boxing Federation (IWBF) JR Lightweight Title to her collection.

As always fight fans, keep reaching for the stars, and all your dreams can be fulfilled.

Interview conducted May 2000

Frankie "G" and his number one fan, daughter Sarah

Pride Runs Deep

Up Close and Personal with International Women's Boxing Federation (IWBF) President Frankie Globschutz

Webster's Dictionary defines PRIDE as the following, [quality or state of being proud]. This word truly defines the feelings of the President of the International Women's Boxing Federation (IWBF), Frankie Globuschutz, better known as Frankie G. During our interview, Frankie talked about the IWBF as a proud parent talks about his child making the Honor Roll.

This interview is one that I have wanted to conduct for about three months because, as I have gotten more involved with women's boxing, Frankie's name constantly came up, and each time, as a person with loads of integrity and knowledge on the sport of women's boxing.

How did you first become involved in boxing?

I started boxing back when I was seven years old. My amateur boxing career went to about the age of 18. Most of my fights were fought as a junior and I won the Junior Olympics two times. Basically, around the age of 17, I was done with boxing. I really didn't feel I was good enough to be a promising professional fighter.

How did that involvement lead to women's boxing?

The way I became involved was to open a gym. The name of the Gym was, and still is, the Academy of Boxing for Women. Back then, it turned a lot of heads. My master plan was to get this gym off the ground and to have it coincide with the (IWBF).

Back in 1992, women's boxing was not at the level it is today. Women were really being used as sideshows. Many women were not getting fair paydays and the female stars back then were really being placated. What we did is go and develop a rule book along with regulations, that followed women's boxing. From that point, we submitted it to the commission without asking them, but I was more in the mind of telling them this is what needed to be done.

I coincided the gym with women's boxing so we had a home for them. Since then, we have had women from all over the world train at our gym from world champions to women just looking to get started in female boxing.

The first couple of years we didn't have any title fights. We really started gaining popularity out there, and word traveled fast. Many promoters called in the early days and thought we were matchmakers. We informed them we were not, but assisted in giving them information on ladies that they could use for their cards.

As long as they were following our rules and regulations that we put forth, we would continue to help them out. It really worked well, and we were working along with everyone else to help, not hinder. Whenever we felt we had to settle something with a promoter or commission, we did it on a good basis.

We did not take them to court to fix problems. Instead, we informed them that the sport is growing, and that we had to follow certain rules. Case in point, the two minute round is something the IWBF instated, as well as the pregnancy testing and OB/GYN exams along with many other medical exams to protect the women.

We submitted this to the New York State Athletic Commission around 1993/1994. They pretty much followed our guidelines. In fact it was funny, they came out like they had discovered, for example, that women needed pregnancy tests. When in fact, we did, but to be honest Brad, it's not all about ego with us. Instead, we looked at it as, hey now it's getting done.

Do you feel the IWBF is where it should be since you first started it?

Yes, I do. I would have liked to see us not have the lull last year, year-and-a-half, that we did. I think what happened is it really peaked in about 1998 with us helping to put together an enormous amount of fights with, what I think, was a record 14 world title fights that year. Bottom line: The lull came, and now it's gaining back plenty the other way. We are going to even hit a higher plateau.

What top three things would you like all participants and the fans of women's boxing to know about the IWBF?

First, we are the sanctioning body that has integrity. Were not biased to certain fighters and give everyone out there a fair chance. Second, we feel safety is a very big issue. Safety has always been an issue, not only in women's boxing but, men's. I feel very secure about our safety precautions.

Finally, that we have our own judges and referees who can feel confident within a title fight, and that they are not being railroaded by anyone. Our judges are very objective, and don't favor one fighter over another.

What can the hard working, legitimate, woman boxer expect from the IWBF when it comes to being ranked and getting a world title shot?

Funny thing Brad, people condemned me because we came up with the term vacated vs. stripped. We will stand on that, and will make a fighter vacate their title if they don't do what they are supposed to do according to our bylaws.

A lady can feel confident that when she gets in the top ten or say top five, that she can feel confident enough that it's not all for nothing, and will eventually get a title shot.

Our champions are not going to sit on their titles and watch fighters in their division's careers run out because they don't want to defend against them.

Other organizations have women champions who have not defended their titles in three years and that is not going to ever happen with us.

How do you reply to the complaint that women's boxing will never really take off?

Ten years ago when I started the Academy of Women's Boxing and the IWBF, I heard the same thing. Well, I am proud to say ten years later, the gym is flourishing and so is the organization.

Many out there may not know that your wife is four time World Champion Kathy "Wildcat" Collins. With that said, how does it effect your organization?

In the beginning, I was under a lot of fire when we started the organization. Today, I hardly get any heat because we made Kathy do far more than any of the other organizations would have done.

I was very hard on Kathy when she held my JR Welterweight Title by making her defend it six times in an eighteen month period. She didn't have to defend that many times, but because of me, she did. We didn't let Kathy fight for an IWBF Title until she was recognized by the other organizations in their rankings first. She actually won a world title in another organization before she won ours.

If you look at my rankings right now, Kathy is not ranked number one in her division. Christy Martin has that ranking and rightfully so.

In your opinion what can the fans of women's boxing do to help lift the sport?

The main thing is to remain loyal fans and don't get frustrated. When they don't get to see their fighters on TV because the networks decided against it. Just hang in there it will change.

Finally, why do you feel the mainstream networks are not showing more women's fighting, and yet when they do, they only seem to put on the Daughters of Legends, or women who really can't fight?

Brad, that is an excellent question. I really believe the networks put these ladies on who can't fight to show the public, hey this is women's boxing. Very rarely do you see a quality women's fight on TV. What I urge ESPN, HBO, Showtime, Fox Sports and any other network to do, is to call me. I will tell you what women's fights to air and I will do this free of CHARGE!

Don't show the public a Mia St. John who is 19-0 fighting a girl 2-3. What are the other ladies in her division going to think? I am not trying to be mean to Mia, but I have to criticize her because this is a joke. I can't believe that any commission in the world would approve a 2-3 fighter against Mia. The fans are not dumb and when you keep giving them mismatches they are going to turn it off. Mia is not the only one out there that commissions are doing this with and it has to stop.

As always fight fans, keep reaching for the stars, and all your dreams can be fulfilled.

Interview conducted May 2001

(L) WBC Super Middleweight Champion Eric Lucas
and photographer Mike Greenhill

Lights Camera Action...

Up Close and Personal with Boxing Photographer Mike Greenhill

Throughout boxing, you can find many people with a passion for the sport, that is unmatched. One such person is boxing photographer, Mike Greenhill.

In the three years I have had the wonderful privilege of covering fights throughout the United States, I have watched Greenhill in action. He is a respected photographer up and down the East Coast, known for his professionalism and truly caring nature which he shows to the boxers, through his lens. Greenhill has taken some fantastic shots, while being involved in boxing for many years. In this interview, I wanted to provide some informative information to all the would-be, young photographers out there who want to get to Greenhill's level.

Greenhill was more than willing to discuss inside tips, which can only come from vast experience. Finally, I have many of Mike's photos amongst my cherished boxing memorabilia and I can say without any reservations, his work really is great.

How did you first become involved in boxing?

I was doing mostly team sports photography since 1981 (baseball, football, soccer, basketball, hockey) and wanted to branch out into boxing. I loved the sport and saw photographing it as another challenge.

How did your love for boxing lead you to shooting pictures of boxing matches?

I started shooting local Baltimore club shows for Eric Bottjer, who had a small publication called Punch. Eric is now the matchmaker for Cedric Kushner Promotions. Then, at the Boxing Hall of Fame in 1996, I met Tom Huff across the street in Graziano's Lounge. It turned out he had a boxing website out of Cleveland, and I started doing photos and articles for him.

Shortly after, Tom turned it into a print magazine called Boxing World. I shot photos and wrote articles for it, and started sending photos to all the major boxing magazines such as Ring, Fight Game (now defunct), Boxing Digest, USA Boxing News, British Boxing News, Uppercut, and Guantes & Seidman Productions.

Your work is featured in many publications. If you had to pick one shot to date that you were most proud of, which photo would it be?

I would have to say it is my shot of Derrick Jefferson knocking out Maurice Harris in their November 1999 bout in Atlantic City. Harris was out cold on his back, arms bent at the elbow, gloves pointing to the sky as Jefferson walks by and referee Steve Smoger counts him out. I got a lot of mileage out of that one.

Also, Sharmba Mitchell's left glove on Pedro Saiz's nose in Washington, D.C. in February 1999. Sharmba was so fast, I was late shooting his right, but accidentally timed his left perfectly. Sometimes luck is involved.

What do you feel was the most exciting boxing match you have covered from a photographer's standpoint?

It was the first Arturo Gatti - Ivan Robinson bout in Atlantic City, in August 1998. I was ringside for the non-stop action in every round. The crowd gave a standing ovation after every round. The Jefferson - Harris heavyweight bout and Gatti - Gabe Ruelas were close seconds.

What is your favorite fight of all time and why?

Muhammad Ali vs Joe Frazier I. I was an 11-year-old Long Islander at the time, and all we talked about in school for the 3 months before, was that fight. It lived up to the hype, was at Madison Square Garden, and thus is to me, the greatest sporting event of all time. One of my schoolmate's fathers went to the fight. I saw his ticket stub later and thought it was gold.

Who are your three favorite fighters of all time and why?

I always liked Thomas Hearns —- his nicknames, his being from

Detroit, his early 80's hairdo, and his power. You always sensed he was excitement about to happen. I also love Arturo Gatti. His fights leave me amazed. As both fighter and person, I love Bernard Hopkins. Mentally, he is the toughest athlete I've ever seen. I admire his drive, his independence, and his principles. He may be my favorite athlete, period!

What are your words of wisdom to the young man or woman that wants to try and break into your profession?

Get good equipment. Various length lenses to cover any situation, from ringside to high up. Do the local shows; get to know local promoters and managers so you can get ringside credentials. Send your photos to as many publications as you can. Be persistent. Watch and play as many sports as you can. I feel the best way to shoot sports is to have played them, because you have a feel for what will happen in a match and when. Anticipation is very important.

Do you favor a mandatory retirement fund for all boxers and if so, how would you like to see it accomplished?

Absolutely. The main problem is enforcing it; who's going to mind the store? The IBF had a policy where 1 or 2% of purses went to a pension, but not much has been heard about it since the IBF was indicted last year. I think a small percentage should come out of all purses. I also think a percentage of site fees should go toward the fund. It's hard to get different players to agree on this issue;

everyone wants to keep their piece of the pie. I think if there was a national boxing commission that would help. Someone like Teddy Atlas or Senator John McCain should run it.

McCain's a big supporter of boxing. Gerry Cooney's F.I.S.T. organization is a step in the right direction. They have provided guidance for several retired fighters. I would like to see Gerry's group expand to every state, almost like franchises.

He was at our most recent March meeting of the Baltimore chapter of the Veteran Boxers Association, of which I'm a lifetime member, to exchange ideas with us.

When you hang up your camera and tripod, how would you like to be remembered?
I hope never to hang them up until they hang me up, but I guess I would hope they say, "he did good quality work, and was respected by the magazines, the fighters and his peers" - that I treated everyone with respect.

Finally, what is the one saying you live your life by?
"Seize the day".

As always fight fans, keep reaching for the stars, and all your dreams can be fulfilled.

Interview conducted March 2002

Passion Runs Deep...

Up Close and Personal with World Renowned Boxing Tape Collector Lee Groves

Throughout my years of boxing writing, many readers have e-mailed after an interview to ask where they can get a tape of a fighter who was interviewed in my column. Also, many readers want to know how to get into trading, and where good sources are to ensure top quality tapes.

Well, Lee Groves, who has supplied me with wonderful quality tapes for my research, has amassed a collection of tapes that are some of the best quality out there, and which I totally vouch for. With that said, I thought since so many of you out there collect or wish to start, you would enjoy an interview with Lee, who not only has the largest collection I have ever seen, but truly knows his stuff when it comes to tape collecting and boxing.

How did you first become involved in collecting?

145

Ever since 1983 I had wanted to get a VCR to tape fights, but at that time the price of VCR's and tapes were cost prohibitive. On Christmas 1985, a BetaMax VCR was purchased but something was wrong with it and it had to be returned. The BetaMax was soon exchanged for a VHS compatible VCR, and I began taping in January 1986.

The first fight I ever recorded was Bobby Chacon vs. Arturo Frias, which was shown on the Spanish International Network (now known as Univision). At that time, still being cautious about the price of tapes, I was very selective about what fights to tape and keep, so I kept watching Chacon-Frias again and again until I practically had every punch memorized.

After a while I erased it, something I rarely do now. I have since re-acquired the fight in a trade. So the first fight on Tape 1 of my collection was Greg Haugen's one-round KO of Charlie "White Lightning" Brown on ESPN. After a while, I loosened my standards on what to keep and the tapes began to accumulate to where I am today: Approximately 12,000 fights on 1,620 tapes.

What fight is considered the most valuable, should someone have it in their collection?

Since I don't sell fight tapes, but only trade, I can't tell you which fight in my collection is the most valuable monetarily. However, in terms of fights that netted me the most trades, Joe Frazier-Oscar Bonavena I (complete) and Nino Benvenuti-Luis Rodriguez have each spawned four different trades.

So they were valuable in terms of my receiving much more footage than the fights themselves lasted. The fights no one else has are considered most valuable in the hobby. Some choose to keep those fights rare, while others use them as a way to further build their collections through trades.

How does one really get into collecting tapes and finding access to other collectors?
To my knowledge, the best place to find fellow collectors can be found in "Fight Game" magazine, where a column called "The Trading Post" runs. It lists names, addresses and e-mail addresses of those who have large collections of fight tapes. Ring Magazine had a similar column back in the 1980s, and that's how I was able to contact other collectors.

Also, attending the International Boxing Hall of Fame induction festivities every June is a great way to meet fellow hobbyists because you have the chance to network, exchange addresses and form long-term friendships face-to-face. Once you get established in the hobby, word of mouth helps a lot. If you have a good reputation in the hobby, people will seek you out.

How does one judge the quality of a tape?
The main quality collectors look for is picture sharpness. The original source of the fight has a lot to do with the quality of the fight. Some fights from the 1970s, before the era of satellite dishes, were taped by private collectors off local TV stations which can be fuzzy or have ghost images.

Sharper versions of these fights can be acquired from TV networks, but they are hesitant to give those out to the general public. With the advent of C-band satellite dishes and 18-inch DSS dishes, sharp images of all fights are easily obtained. Many hobbyists tape their fights in SP (two-hour) speed to ensure the sharpest picture and the least chance of disintegration over time.

Since I tape off satellite dishes as well, even my EP (six-hour) original can translate well onto a SP recording for someone else. I've found that LP (four-hour) speed is a pretty good compromise, offering a sharper picture than EP speed, but allowing a collector to tape twice as much footage on a tape than at SP speed. Other things collectors look for is whether there are "noise lines" on the top or bottom of the picture, whether the picture shakes, and whether a fight is complete or only has selected rounds.

What tape do you most cherish in your collection?

I cherish all my tapes like a shepherd cherishes all his sheep. If one tape comes up missing, I do all I can to find it and won't be satisfied until I do. However, the fight I watch most often is Betulio Gonzalez KO 12 Martin Vargas for the WBA Flyweight Title.

The picture quality is pretty poor, but the fight itself was amazing because they fought at a fast pace throughout, and that it was a tale of two halves. Vargas dominated the early rounds, pinning Gonzalez on the ropes and raining right hand bombs. Gonzalez dominated from Round 8 on, using guile and counterpunching to score the KO after Vargas got tired.

This fight was part of the "Cavalcade of Boxing" series that ran in the 1970s and early 1980s with Steve Bass doing blow-by-blow and Harold Lederman doing color. It showed many lighter-weight title fights, but this was the only fight of the series I have. If anyone out there has a tape of other fights in the series, I'd be very interested in talking with you.

To the best of your knowledge, what is the oldest fight on tape?

The first fight to be filmed was James Corbett and Peter Courtney in 1894, but the first World Heavyweight Title fight to be filmed was Bob Fitzsimmons vs. James Corbett in 1897. I have a 25-minute version that does not include the famous solar plexus punch, but I do have the KO sequence on another tape.

What are your best words of advice to the new collector?

Above all, be honest in everything you do. If a certain fight on your list has only partial rounds, say so. If there is a potential problem with a fight that someone has requested, bring it up with him before you mail the tape so he'll have a chance to make any changes if necessary. Be accurate when telling someone about the picture quality of a certain fight.

Let them know when you are mailing out their tapes so they won't be hanging by the mailbox day after day only to be disappointed. I always send my tapes in the U.S. via Priority Mail so the turnaround time would be short.

If someone asks you not to circulate a certain fight, don't do it because if you do, word WILL get back to the person who you promised and as a result, your name will become poison in the hobby. These are some of the little things that make a world of difference to those who receive your tapes. If you build a good reputation in the hobby, you will receive more tapes in the end because you have proven that you can be trusted.

Also, tape whatever you can because you never know when it can be of use. Managers are always looking for footage of preliminary fighters, and if you have that footage you will get your name out there. I have fights of Marco Antonio Barrera at age 15 when he fought on the undercards at the Arena Coliseo in Mexico City. Who would have ever guessed that he would become among the best fighters in the world?

Also, tape all the amateur boxing shows you can because future stars may be showcased and would make valuable trading material years down the road should they become successful as pros. Additionally, I was able to make a brief TV appearance on Classic Sports Network in 1998. The network was showing the first Archie Moore-Yvon Durelle Fight, but was missing Round 3.

I called the network immediately and informed them that I had the missing round in my private collection. They called me back a few weeks later and asked several questions about the picture quality, at what speed the tape was recorded, and so on. After I mailed the tape to them, the Classic Sports Network producers I met at the Boxing Hall of Fame induction festivities asked to tape a brief interview that was included on a show they called "Viewer Discovery Night." So you never know what may come your way.

As always fight fans, keep reaching for the stars, and all your dreams can be fulfilled.

Interview conducted December 2000

Going All the Way...

Up Close and Personal with Former IBF Light Heavyweight Champion William "Kid Chocolate" Guthrie

In my line of work you will always hear me talk about the good people I meet in boxing circles, while so many others will tell you the negative side of boxing. Well, as I sat in my home office with William Guthrie doing our interview, I realized just how much this man loves the sport of boxing. Most importantly, he cares about his fellow fighter's welfare and life's during their careers. Not to stop there, he also wants them to be taken care of long after they depart the ring ropes.

In life, I have always felt that when you click with someone who has your sincere feelings as their own, it is like two kindred spirits meeting. I felt this way with Will,

151

and look for us to be working together on local events in the Metropolitan area of Virginia, Washington, DC and Maryland.

First of all, tell the readers what you are doing today since we don't see you as much in the ring?

I have started a new company called Fair is Fair. Our goal at Fair is Fair is to move boxing forward all around the country. Our main focus right now is the World Team Boxing Association (WTBA) that I helped create. It will focus on professional team boxing and currently is up and down the East Coast. The main purpose of me doing this is to give professional boxers the opportunity, on a continuous basis, to sharpen their skills and stay busy. I want them to have the same opportunities that the NFL, NBA and MLB have.

What I mean is this Brad, in those sports you lose some and you win some. So many times in boxing a fighter loses and it's career death to them. I disagree with that and the reason I mention those other sports is, if any of those teams lose, they come back to play another day. It should be the same way in boxing and with my organization it will be.

What is the first event that we are going to see from you?

My first event will be November 18, 2000 at the Showplace Arena in Upper Marlboro, Maryland. It will pit Philadelphia fighters against the Virginia, Washington, DC and Maryland area fighters.

(*** To all of my readers in the Virginia, Washington, DC, Maryland, and points North and South. Let's get out there to support Will's venture into promoting his boxing show. He is putting together one heck of a card.)

How did you first get into boxing?

I was four years old when I first got into the sport. At that time, I was living in the projects in South St. Louis, Missouri. I always hung out with the big boys in the neighborhood and directly across the street was a community center where both Michael and Leon Spinks used to train as little boys. One day they put me in the ring and lied about my age making me five vs. four. I won the Diamond Gloves Diaper Weight Championship at the age of four.

You turned professional in May of 1989. It was right at the end of what has become a legendary era for Light Heavyweights. How do you think you would have faired against the greats in the early 80's such as Dwight Muhammad Qawi, Michael Spinks, Matthew Saad Muhammad and Eddie Mustafa Muhammad to name just a few?

I really don't know. Back in late 88, early 89, I had the opportunity to work out with Michael Spinks. We sparred and had lots of fun. To be honest, I would not put myself in that league and I have always felt that you cannot say what if, or what could have been unless you actually do it.

On July 19, 1997 you reached the highest level a professional fighter can reach by winning a World Title. In that fight, you stopped Darrin Allen for the IBF Light Heavyweight Title. How did it feel to hear, "And the new IBF Light Heavyweight Champion of the World, William Guthrie"?

Brad, that is a question that I have never been asked before. It's hard to put in words what I felt, but I will try. Thinking back on that night, I was one of the happiest people in the world. See, now that I held the title, I will go down in history as a Champion. When they look at the records they will see my name in the books and that Brad, is a great feeling to have.

Now that you had the IBF Light Heavyweight Title, how did it change your life?

It really didn't change my life. However, when I was in trouble and finally got myself out, I dedicated my life to doing the right things. People have not read about me doing this or doing that outside of boxing.

In the old days, there was one World Champion vs. three. Would you like to see it go back to that?

I think it's a hard thing to do because a lot of my fellow fighters would lose out because of the politics of boxing. They would never have a chance to fight for a title if there was just one belt. I know from the fans standpoint that one belt enables them to know the Champion, but from the fighter's standpoint, three is better.

You had a stellar amateur career in which you won several amateur titles. How do you feel about the current crop of amateur fighters coming out of the 1992, 1996 and 2000 Olympics?

I have a great deal of respect for these young kids coming out now. Unfortunately, I watched the scoring system and can't stand it. I wish more kids would come into boxing. We also need more professional boxers to get involved in amateur boxing. The fighters from before '88 were better prepared for the professional boxing. Back in my day I had over 600 amateur fights.

Today, you see less venues for amateur fighters to work on their skills. I think boxing teaches a young man respect for his fellow man.

Brad, let me give you an analogy. No matter how much I dislike you in your neighborhood, once we fight, we have a connection forever. You may live on the North side and me on the South, but no one ever comes in between us. We always will have a connection from that fight. These are things that only boxing can teach you.

What do you think the current state of boxing is?

I think boxing can improve and I want to boost it with my WTBA organization. I want this organization to help the fighters much more then it helps me. There will be rankings and belts. Ultimately, I would like to align myself with other organizations, but I will not shut a fighter down that is 4-12 because he still has a chance.

Who are your three favorite fighters of all-time and why?

First of all, Muhammad Ali. He was one of the classiest men in the history of boxing. His skill level was just amazing. He stood for his beliefs and never backed down. Second, Sugar Ray Leonard. Ray was a classy guy and believe it or not, they tried to put him in there with hand picked opponents. His management made mistakes, but Ray would overcome them with his amazing skills in the ring. Finally, Marvin Hagler. He was a determined man and did not care about a purse amount. He just wanted the Championship Belt. His passion was just incredible.

Who do you think won the Marvin Hagler vs. Sugar Ray Leonard fight?
I would have to say Ray did because he just stole the rounds with those flurries.

What is the greatest fight you have ever seen and why?
I would pick Marvin Hagler vs. Sugar Ray Leonard. I could watch that fight right now and it puts me in the mindset to go out and fight.

Do you favor a mandatory retirement fund for all boxers and if so, how would you like to see it accomplished?
Brad, I totally favor it. It must be well thought out and planned. Someone much smarter than I would have to be involved in it. I would get some outside Attorney Generals to be involved in it such as Elliot Spitzer, who is the Attorney General for NY. It just amazes me that we are professional athletes and unlike the other sports, have nothing set for a retirement.

Along with that, we need health insurance which you mentioned earlier. Currently, I am looking around to see how all fighters associated with my organization can have health insurance. I want all the fighters who are on my cards to be taken care of, and I will work very hard to ensure this becomes a reality.

What fight do you wish that you could have been in during your career that never materialized?

I wanted to really fight Roy Jones, JR.

If you could take a fighter from any era in the Light Heavyweight division, who would you like to fight in a dream match, and what would be the outcome in your opinion?

I would like to have fought Evander Holyfield at Light Heavyweight. He always had the same desire as I, or so I felt, to win a fight. With that said, I would have beaten him at that weight.

When you finally retire from boxing what do you want your fans to remember you for?

That I was a guy who cared about the profession of boxing.

Finally, what is the saying you live your life by?

"Do unto others as you want done unto you".

William wanted to add the following to our interview:

I would like for everyone who is a boxing fan and has a strong desire to see the sport of boxing move forward, to support the WTBA - not for me, but the boxers. You give these young men the opportunity to do what they have been blessed to do. They go in there and take a chance with their life each time out. I make a heartfelt promise that I will allow fighters to showcase their talents and make a way for them to get ahead. I want to be different from other promoters in the past.

William GUTHRIE
Nickname: "Kid Chocolate"

Weight class: Light Heavywieght/175 lbs

Amateur record: 1988: Olympic Trials Middleweight:
- Anthony Hembrick points
Professional: 28 fights; 26+ (21 KO), 2-
1995: United States Light Heavyweight
1997-1998: I.B.F. Light Heavyweight

- 1989 -
+ (May-1-1989, Saint-Louis) John Moore kot 2
+ (Jun-21-1989, Saint-Louis) Clarence Hutchinson kot 1
+ (Jul-27-1989, Saint-Louis) Roy Bedwell kot 1
+ (Nov-3-1989, Atlantic City) Chris Collins kot 3

- 1990 -
+ (Feb-16-1990, Saint-Louis) Randy Thomas kot 1
+ (Mar-24-1990, Mobile) Lee Smith ko 1
+ (Apr-27-1990, Mobile) David Gwynn ko 1
+ (Jul-28-1990, Atlantic City) Eric Cole kot 1

- 1991-1992: inactive -

- 1993 -
+ (May-6-1993, Saint-Louis) Anthony Campbell ko 2
+ (Aug-27-1993, Saint-Louis) Tim Knight 10

- 1994 -
+ (Apr-11-1994, Inglewood) Jimmy Bills ko 3

+ (May-5-1994, Las Vegas) Krishna Wainwright kot 6
+ (Jun-23-1994, Florissant) Darrell Kizer kot 2
+ (Nov-28-1994, Bridgeton) Don Penelton ko 2

- **1995** -
+ (Feb-6-1995, Bridgeton) Travis Meat ko 1
+ (Apr-25-1995, Cut Off) Ron Butler kot 3
+ (Oct-3-1995, Memphis) Jeff Bowman kot 3
+ (Nov-8-1995, New York) Richard Frazier ko 4 (United States, Light Heavyweight)

- **1996** -
+ (Jan-27-1996, Phoenix) Tim Hillie 10
+ (Feb-24-1996, Richmond) Jerome Hill kot 2
+ (May-18-1996, Las Vegas) John Kiser 10
+ (Jun-29-1996, Indio) Ramzi Hassan kot 6

- **1997** -
+ (Mar-28-1997, Boston) Jamie Stevenson ko 3
+ (Jul-19-1997, Indio) Darrin Allen kot 3 (I.B.F., Light Heavyweight)

- **1998** -
- (Feb-6-1998, Uncasville) Reggie Dwayne Johnson ko 5 (I.B.F., Light Heavyweight)

- **1999** -
- (May-9-1999, Minot) Michael Nunn kot 6

- **2000** -
+ (Mar-11-2000, Miami) Wesley Martin 8
+ (May-6-2000, Las Cruces) John Kiser 8

As always fight fans, keep reaching for the stars, and all your dreams can be fulfilled.

Interview conducted October 2000

60 Years in Boxing...

Up Close and Personal with Legendary Comedian Buddy Hackett

Recently, I had the great pleasure of interviewing someone who I feel is one of America's funniest comedians, and a truly a nice man. This man of course, is Buddy Hackett. To my younger readers, you will probably recognize Hackett from Herbie The Love Bug or more recently, the voice of the parrot in Paulie, but in fact, he has been around for some 50 years. We have had the honor to share in his wonderful humor during those years. Hackett is another gem from yesteryear who knows his boxing.

Tell me about the different fighters you have met over the years and how you were involved with them?
I met Joe Louis in Las Vegas when he was a casino host at Ceasar's and I used to play

160

golf with him, as well. I knew Rocky Graziano, who I met at the Nevele Country Club, when he was training to fight Tony Zale back in 1947 or '48. We stayed friends over the years, till I moved out West and whenever I came back to New York, we would see each other. I met Jake Lamotta, I think maybe through Rocky. Funny thing about Jake, he liked to be a comedian and tell jokes, which he did fairly well.

Jake was really a nice guy. His wife Vicki at the time, was so beautiful that you didn't want to pick your head up to look at her around him. Jake used to say, "go ahead you can look at her." In fact, I know where I met him at now, the Concord Hotel, where he stayed for the summer.

I met Muhammad Ali when he was still Cassius Clay and at that time only 21. I met him at Gold's Gym located in Miami Beach. At that time, I knew a guy named Joe Kalman, from Chicago, who also used to put fights on at the Marigold Arena there. He had a couple of kids who got in trouble when they held up a grocery store and shot somebody. They were going to get the electric chair, but could have spared their own lives if they would say they were sorry, or make a deal and they would not do it.

Joe and I, went to see Ali to ask if he would call those kids and have them change their minds to save their lives. I really didn't know that much about it, but went with Joe and talked to Ali. I believe Ali made the call. Ali went on to become a great man and to this day, if we are at a big function together, one of his guys comes over to me and will say "the Champ wants to talk with you." As soon as I walk over he starts to laugh and says, "I was going tell you a joke, but I can't tell you a joke." Ali is a great laugher, nice guy and just a very warm man.

How long have you followed boxing?
Since I listened to Jack Sharkey on the radio with my father back in 1930.

Who have you seen in your lifetime that you consider the greatest fighter of all-time?
Well I suppose it would be Harry Greb. I must say some great exciting ones were Kid Gavilian and Beau Jack. But pound for pound, I would say between Harry Greb and Sugar Ray Robinson.

What is the nicest venue you ever watched a fight at?
Well Brad, I see them mostly on Pay-Per-View at my home which is a pretty nice place. (I laughed hard when he said this.) I would have to say the old Madison Square Garden was a pretty nice place. It was a very exciting place and just hearing the announcer say, "Ladies and Gentlemen, Madison Square Garden Presents." This just gave you gooseflesh.

I also played Madison Square Garden many times for very big benefits. I remember working there in 1949 and followed Lena Horne. It was just quite a place to be. In fact, that reminds me, I was there one time for the opening of the circus for some publicity thing where I rode an elephant all around that place.

What era do you feel had the best fighters and why?
Well before TV came in, so the era would be the 1930's – early 40's before World War II. I feel this because we were coming out of the

depression. The depression started in the 30's and didn't end until the early 40's. The depression breeds boxers and other athletes because people have to make a living. If you have a talent such as in sports, then you have to pursue it and work very hard at it, which produced the very rough and tough fighters.

Later on, after the GI BILL, guys could go to college, learn a craft, trade, or just about business. So then, what would have been a great potential of flesh, didn't have to go into the ring. Later on when all the sports starting paying huge amounts of money, it became lucrative for people to go into sports after that. Nowadays what you're getting in boxing, is not quite as good as what it was back then.

Who are your top three favorite fighters of all-time?

Joe Louis, Rocky Graziano and Sugar Ray Leonard.

Since you have been in the entertainment business for many years, do you have any funny stories about any of the fighters you have met over the years?

Well first a funny story is the old one where the corner is saying to the fighter that the other guy is not laying a glove on you. The fighter then turns to the corner and says, "then you better watch the REF because someone is whacking the hell out of me!"

In today's boxing, are there any fighters that remind you of fighters from the old days?

Yes! Oscar Delahoya. I love to watch Oscar he is a throwback fighter to me who would have fit back in those days.

What is the greatest fight you have ever seen and why?

Joe Louis Vs Max Schmeling. The reason was, all of America back then was against the Germans. Of course Max was German, however, I want to say that later on, I found out that he was a very nice man. But back then all we heard in America was "Joe Louis", "Joe Louis", when I was a young man. Many years later, I met Joe Louis and I used to make him laugh so hard.

One time we were both sitting at Caesar's in the coffee shop and a woman came over and I said, "Joe, before we are through you are going to hit the canvas." Joe said, "If I fall don't count me." I used to make him laugh so hard he would fall down and I would start counting him out. It use to aggravate him that I would do this.

So anyway, the woman came over and said, could you gentlemen give me an autograph for a cripple? I said, "Oh yeah, show us the cripple!" You know, like she was lying. Joe went right on the floor and I started counting.

He kept saying "Buddy don't count (LAUGH) and say don't count Buddy again". HOLD ON! I have a great story for you Brad about Joe Louis. Joe showed up in a casino and of course everyone knew he was a gambler, who gambled all his money away. Joe was dressed in a black suit, black shirt, white tie and white cowboy hat.

While he is walking through the casino people are yelling "Hey Champ, let's shoot some craps. Here is five hundred play it and keep it." Joe replies, "no I am going to Sonny Liston's funeral today. I have to go to

Sonny's funeral." Another "Hey Champ here is five hundred." Joe says, "NO NO!" Then they say "Hey Champ, here's five thousand." Joe then says, "Sonny would understand."

Finally, in all your years as a boxing fan, what was the most brutal knockout you have ever seen in the ring?
When Emile Griffith fought Benny "The Kid" Paret. Paret went straight back, down to the canvas and laid there. I turned to a guy and said, "Paret is dead" and he was. Very sad thing.

As always fight fans, keep reaching for the stars, and all your dreams can be fulfilled.

Interview conducted April 2000

Moving Up...

Up Close and Personal with Boxing Trainer Asim Hanif

Over the course of the last three years, I have had the ultimate pleasure of meeting and becoming involved with some great talents in the Virginia, Washington, DC and Maryland areas. These talents are not just fighters, but trainers, writers, promoters, managers, fight doctors, judges, announcers, gym owners and matchmakers. Each one is adding something that I feel will have long-lasting, positive effects on the sport of boxing.

One such person is Asim Hanif, currently the trainer for several up and coming fighters in the Virginia area.

One thing that I admire about him is that he takes the time with each of his fighters, teaching them strategy, directing them on things to do. This is a great attribute for a trainer to have and will no doubt, take Hanif to the top of his craft in the years to come.

How did you first become involved in professional boxing?

I had a man in my life who was like my grandfather named Connie Bryant. He owned a gym located in Harlem called the Knights Gym. He trained Hector Camacho and Iran Barkley back in the day, to name just a few.

At that time, I had kickboxers training there. They thought I was just a karate guy and they were curious about me which led to questions on my background. Once they found out, they would ask me about conditioning tips and so on. This was around 1991 timeframe.

Who are some of the fighters that you have worked with who the readers would be familiar with?

Lou Del Valle and Saul Mamby. I didn't train these guys but advised them on conditioning. I took Derek Amos from small clubs to big arenas. He performed very well and only lost to fighters like Chris Byrd and Danny Williams, to name a few. It showed me what I could do when I had a fighter with talent to train.

What do you think of the current state of boxing?

I think it's healthy and getting really better right now. The networks are really starting to pick it up again which can only help it.

If you could play a key role in revamping the ranking systems, what changes would you make?

I think that you really have to look at the level of competition that a fighter faces when ranking them. You can't just go by how many wins, a gold medal, and media attention they have gotten. You must look at their level of competition and if they lost, who to?

So many organizations it seems place every thing on an undefeated record. I feel the IBF Trial and a subsequent action is going to clean this up.

Do you favor a mandatory retirement fund for all boxers and if so, how would you like to see it accomplished?

I do feel there should be a mandatory retirement fund and the commissions should have something similar to a 401K. I would also like to see a mandatory retirement age instituted as well. Bottom line: I think the promoters, as well as the fighters, should pay in and it should be a percentage match by both parties.

Who are your three favorite fighters of all-time and why?

First of all, Sugar Ray Robinson. He had so much finesse and power which he showed in several weight classes. Roberto Duran. He was so furious when he was a lightweight. He defined the word fighter. Finally, Marvin Hagler. He was the consummate professional who always came in there to fight.

What is the greatest fight you have ever seen and why?

Ron Lyle vs George Foreman. They both took a huge beating in there and both came back with Foreman finally pulling it out.

If you could have any fighter in the history of boxing to train, who would it be and why?

Alexis Arguello. He was a very smart boxer. He always sized up an opponent and made the necessary adjustments to win the fight.

Do you emulate any trainer that you have seen over the years and if so, what attributes do you take from him?

I would have to say two names. The late Victor Valle who worked with Gerry Cooney in his heyday. He taught me a lot about the theory in boxing. Secondly, Aldy Ochiai. He taught me you can never control another man but, you can control yourself. This is so true in boxing, which I feel is 90% mental. Also, this saying is true in life.

If you could choose an era in which you could train fighters, which would you pick and why?

I love the current era because I feel fighters are all around better athletes today.

When you finally retire from training, how would you like to be remembered in boxing circles?

I would like the people to remember that I did a good job with whatever I had to work with. Whether a fighter was high level or one who never became a big star, but gave the sport his all.

Finally, what is the saying you live your life by?

"You cannot control what another man does, but you can always control yourself".

Asim wanted to add the following to this interview:

I really feel that I am where I should be at this time in my life. My discipline comes from an early age of being trained in classical musical. It took a lot of hard work and that work ethic stuck with me over the years.

I love working with people, bringing the best out of them in the ring and in life.

As always fight fans, keep reaching for the stars, and all your dreams can be fulfilled.

Interview conducted May 2000

(R) Johnson sets up Stanciel for the big
knockout

Making Believers...

Up Close and Personal with NABF Welterweight Champion Golden "14 Karat" Johnson

At his best, an NABF Lightweight Title with
a win over James Crayton, with other big wins
over top rated Teddy Reid, Juan Lazcano and
Bobby Heath to regain an NABF Welterweight
Title. In addition, a gallant effort in his
first IBF Lightweight Title attempt against
quite possibly today's pound-for- pound
greatest fighter Sugar Shane Mosley.

At his worst, personal problems that
sidetracked his career for a short period of
time. This occurred right after his huge ESPN2
win over Teddy Reid. Now as many of my readers
know, I rarely if ever, will go into a

negative issue when I interview a fighter. Johnson isn't just any fighter. He is a close friend of mine and I wanted to get out the side of him that changed during that period of time; time that gave him one thing to think about and that was getting back to a world title shot.

During that period, I had no contact with him, but I knew we had forged a bond before then and that we would be in contact once he got his life straight. Well, that phone call came from Golden, as I knew it would. In that call, I heard a renewed love for life, boxing and most importantly family. With his constant companion wife Teddy at his side, Johnson is back and wants the boxing world to know it.

June 15th is yet another career defining fight for you against tough Vivian Harris. How is training going for this fight?

Brad, it's really going great for this fight. I have gone back to the basics and really worked on things I picked up when I was working with Oscar Délahoya.

Being friends, I already know you have truly dedicated your life to boxing since you had your personal problems. But for the many out there who follow Golden Johnson's career, let them know what is different this time around.

Well, I have overcome a lot of personal problems in my life and I have gotten through them. It's part of life and how you come back from them is what makes the difference. Even back to the Teddy Reid fight, I had those outside distractions, but fought outstanding in the ring. With my personal life at an all-time high, I should be a tremendous fighter this time around.

172

For the younger boxers out there, discuss some of the pitfalls they need to watch out for that you had to overcome in your boxing career.

First of all, the dedication is a must. When you first turn professional, start getting those wins under your belt. The media gets a hold of you and you can get full of yourself, losing that dedication that you truly need in this sport. The business side is very difficult in boxing. But don't let it get you down because we all go through it.

I know that a big factor in your huge win over Teddy Reid was the intense sparring you got with Oscar Delahoya when he was preparing for Sugar Shane Mosley. What things do you feel you improved on, being his sparring partner for a good period of time?

Being in camp with Oscar and being able to hold my own with one of the best fighters in the world, then to face some of my opponents, who are not on the same level, puts me in the mindset that I can beat them. Brad, the real thing I took away was a better mindset because it really did improve my confidence level.

If you win this fight and it puts you in the top 10, what champion would you like a crack at first?

It really doesn't matter who I face. The champions in my division are great champions and I know whoever I fight, I must be in great shape. In that fight, I must bring everything I have.

What inspired you to get into boxing?

My cousin former world champion Reggie Johnson and when he won his title, I really wanted to be in boxing.

What do you consider your best weapon in the ring at this point of your career?

I have always felt my mind is my best weapon. I am always thinking while I am in the ring.

What is the greatest fight you have ever seen and why?

Aaron Pryor vs. Alexis Arguello I. Aaron took punches especially the right-hand from Alexis that everyone else went to sleep from. Pryor shook it off like it was nothing. It appeared to me that Arguello lost his confidence from that and ultimately Pryor stopped him in the 14th round in what was a spectacular fight.

Do you favor a mandatory retirement fund for all boxers and if so, how would you like to see it accomplished?

Yes, I would like to see it done. It's going to be hard for a fighter just starting out. I feel that when a fighter makes around $15,000 to $20,000 for a fight there should be a percentage taken out. Also, the promoters should put some money in as well because they never take the punches.

I think if this can be done, you will see a lot less fighters walking around broke and coming back when they shouldn't, for the money.

When you finally retire from boxing, what do you want your fans to remember you for?

The great guy I was out of the ring. I always have time for my fans and I just want them to know that yes, I had pitfalls in my life, but I overcame them.

Finally, what is the saying you live your life by?
"You only have one life to live, so live it your way".

Golden wanted to add the following to our interview:
I have been to the doorstep in January 1999 against Sugar Shane Mosley and this time around, I am going through the door. Whoever they put in front of me, I will prevail. I am not going back down because I feel it's my time to come up.

Golden JOHNSON
Nickname: "14-KT"

Weight class: Welterweight/147 lbs

Amateur record: 95 fights; 85+, 10-
Professional record : 26 fights; 20+ (15 KO), 2=, 4-
1998: North America Lightweight
2001: North America Welterweight

- 1993 -
+ (Sep-3-1993, San Antonio) Chris George kot 1
- (Oct-9-1993, San Juan) Pedro Calderon kot 2

- 1994 -
+ (Feb-17-1994, San Antonio) Jaime Herrera kot 2

175

+ (Jun-7-1994, South Padre Island) Juan Zuniga 4

- 1995 -
= (May-27-1995, San Antonio) Gilbert Salinas 4
+ (Jun-20-1995, Fort Worth) Steve Trumble kot 2
= (Jul-19-1995, San Antonio) Danny Rios 6

- 1996: inactive -

- 1997 -
+ (Oct-5-1997, Killeen) Emmanuel Ford kot 2
+ (Nov-1-1997, Houston) Paul Ramirez kot 7
+ (Nov-19-1997, Baton Rouge) Emmett Davis ko 2
+ (Nov-25-1997, El Paso) Julian Romero injury 2

- 1998 -
+ (Jan-20-1998, San Antonio) Cesar Delgado 6
+ (Feb-8-1998, Lake Charles) Eugene Johnson 6
+ (Mar-26-1998, Houston) Raymond Flores kot 5
+ (May-1-1998, Austin) Benito Rodriguez injury 8
+ (Jun-6-1998, Las Vegas) Juan Lazcano kot 3
+ (Jul-26-1998, Ledyard) James Crayton 12 (North America, Lightweight)
+ (Aug-12-1998, Brownsville) Jesus Saldana ko 4
- (Oct-16-1998, Miami) Israel Cardona 12 (America, Lightweight)

- 1999 -
- (Jan-9-1999, Pensacola) Shane Mosley ko 7 (I.B.F., Lightweight)

+ (Apr-15-1999, Houston) Eduardo Martinez ko
3

+ (May-14-1999, Tunica) Miguel Arrozal kot 4

- 2000 -
+ (Jan-20-2000, Houston) Eldon Sneed kot 6
- (Mar-19-2000, Tunica) Wonder Tackie 10
+ (Jul-21-2000, Mount Pleasant) Teddy Reid
12

- 2001 -
+ (Mar-22-2001, San Antonio) Bob Heath kot 6
(North America, Welterweight)

As always fight fans, keep reaching for the
stars, and all your dreams can be fulfilled.

Interview conducted June 2001

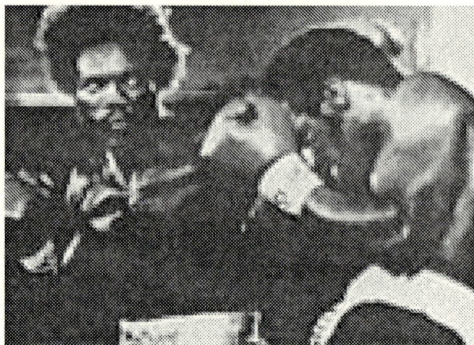

(L) Johnson brings it to WBA Light Heavyweight
Champion Michael Spinks

Almost There...

Up Close and Personal with Former Light Heavyweight Title Challenger Vonzell Johnson

In the late 1970's through the early 1980's, you had a Light Heavyweight division that was simply put, magical!

Up and down the rankings, there were noteworthy challengers and champions that gave a boxing fan a lesson each time out. I have recently watched old fight tapes from this era, and I am here to tell you, that if these guys fought in this era today, look out!

One such contender, who fought twice for the coveted belt in the Light Heavyweight division, was Vonzell Johnson. Vonzell was trained by the legendary Angelo Dundee and even trained at the gym I did, as an amateur. Who would have known some twenty years later, I would be interviewing him for my column.

I found Vonzell no different today than he was twenty years ago to a young amateur fighter, named Brad Berkwitt. Vonzell was very warm, expressed a true concern for both the amateur fighters he trains, and the professional's he watches on TV.

These are the elder statesmen of boxing who deserve all the respect in the world and should be turned to for advice on how to improve the state of boxing.

For the readers, what are you doing today since you have been retired from boxing for many years?

I am training amateur fighters at the Lulu Pearl Douglas Recreation Center (Named after Buster Douglas's Mother) in Columbus Ohio. I am an assistant manager of security for our Columbus Metropolitan library. I also worked Tom "Boom Boom" Johnson's corner for about five fights when he was the featherweight champion.

What inspired you to get into boxing?

When I was about 13, like most kids, you see or hear about Muhammad Ali (back then Cassius Clay). You think that could be you. What really got me into boxing was a fight I had in front of a recreation center, where the man who broke it up, made us go and put boxing gloves on to finish up the fight. Boxing stuck with me from that day on.

You come from what I consider to be, the Golden Era of light heavyweights, where you saw great champions and truly worthy challengers, such as yourself. What are your observations of the light heavyweights back then?

Brad, you are so right on your comments. You had world class fighters up and down the rankings with the possibility of the title changing hands each time out. It was all about maneuvering at that time. If you were matched right and came to fight, you were going to be a world champion.

Looking at your record, I notice you beat one of the Davis brothers, both of whom challenged for the light heavyweight title. Just how good was Johnny Davis?

Johnny was a pretty good puncher, but he really didn't have great boxing skills. If he couldn't get you out with that power, he would be outboxed.

Another observation looking at your record is, you turned professional in 1974 and it took you nearly 7 years to get a title shot. Why do you think that happened?

Very good observation Brad. What I know now and didn't know then was that my manager, Henry "Hank" Grooms out of Kalamazoo Michigan, was the problem. At that time, Hank had about five contenders. They included, Greg Coverson, Floyd Mayweather SR., Len Hutchins, Johnny Baldwin and myself. We all were ranked at that time.

I would have huge layoffs in between fights and always wondered, 'what happened'? Hank was telling me that nobody wanted to fight me. I found out later that no one could work with him to make fights because he thought he was the man, since he had all these contenders. We were basically blackballed because of his actions and his over-pricing of us.

When you finally did get a title shot, you faced WBC Lightheavyweight Champion Matthew Saad Muhammad. It was a tough fight, and I can remember it well. In the 11th you were stopped. But, in your very next fight, which was only a

little over 8 months later, you challenged WBA
Light heavyweight Champion Michael Spinks. How
were you able to get back-to-back title shots?

It was based on my performance against Saad
Muhammad, and of course, a lot of that was
having Angelo Dundee in my corner. If I would
have been with Angelo at the start of my
career, I feel I would have been a world
champion. Angelo had that kind of juice and
just could move his fighters like that.

**What made you retire after fighting Michael
Spinks for his WBA Light Heavyweight Title?**

I wanted a rematch with Spinks and went to
Angelo to tell him to get it. Angelo told me
that Butch Lewis said that I will never get a
rematch with Michael again. That kind of
discouraged me, and I lost the desire for
boxing.

**I remember you training at the same gym I
did, Allen Park located in North Miami Beach,
Florida. At that time, you had the legendary,
Angelo Dundee as your trainer. What was it
like working with Angelo?**

Angelo was a great cornerman. He has great
ring knowledge, and his ability to map out a
strategy is phenomenal. I have to give Del
Williams and Robert Mitchell out of Detroit
credit for training me. Angelo has an amazing
insight to boxing.

**What do you think of the current contenders
and champions in your weight class?**

With the exception of Roy Jones, JR., I feel
they couldn't be competitive in our days. With
that said, I feel Roy would have beaten a lot
of the contenders, but probably not the
champions.

Do you favor a mandatory retirement fund for all boxers and if so, how would you like to see it accomplished?

Yes I do. I love the sport of boxing and want to see all fighters taken care of. I think a certain percentage of a fighter's purse should be taken out each time. It then should be put into a fund. Finally, we need a regulated committee to oversee that the money is handled correctly.

What do you want your fans to remember you for?

I was a decent fighter who possessed above average skills and always was a gentleman in and out of the ring.

Finally, what is the saying you live your life by?

"If I can make a difference in one young man's life to get him away from drugs and crime, through boxing, then it was all worth it".

Vonzell would like to add the following to our interview:

I just want to say I think that the public should not judge boxing by the actions of a few fighters who don't do the right thing. In the history of boxing, there have been a few fighters who went left of the center. The remaining fighters should not get a black eye because of the few fighters who don't live up to the public's standards.

Vonzell Johnson

Weight class: Light Heavyweight/175 lbs

Professional record: 25 fights; 22+ (11 KO), 3-

- 1974 -
+ (12.11.1974, Indianapolis) Sylvester Wilder 4
+ (9.12.1974, Highland Park) Charlie Jordan ko 3

- 1975 -
+ (8.5.1975, Baltimore) Smokey Middleton 6

+ (22.5.1975, Baltimore) Wayne Mc Gee 6
+ (17.6.1975, Largo) Smokey Middleton 6
+ (25.6.1975, Toledo) George Mc Gee 8
+ (23.9.1975, Jacinto City) Aaron Solomon 6

- **1976** -
+ (22.4.1976, Seattle) Bruce Scott ko 3
+ (5.5.1976, Lake Tahoe) Terry Lee ko 6
+ (25.5.1976, Seattle) Eddie Owens ko 7
+ (6.10.1976, Las Vegas) Buddha Brooks ko 7
+ (27.10.1976, Las Vegas) Vern Mc Intosh ko 7
+ (24.11.1976, Las Vegas) Hildo Silva 10

- **1977** -
+ (27.3.1977, San Antonio) Tony Greene ko 4
+ (22.6.1977, Columbus) Gary Summerhayes 10
-   (23.8.1977, Nouvelle-Orleans) Jerry Celestine 10
+ (13.10.1977, Columbus) Ron Wilson ko 10
+ (26.11.1977, Columbus) Hank Gregory ko 2

- **1978** -
+ (22.6.1978, Kalamazoo) Chuck Warfield ko 7

- **1979** -
+ (26.9.1979, Windsor) Larry Sims 10

- **1980** -
+ (23.5.1980, Pontiac) Bill Hollis ko 3
+ (9.8.1980, Atlantic City) Johnny Davis 8
+ (13.12.1980, Miami) Ernie Barr 10

- **1981** -
-   (28.2.1981, Atlantic City) Matthew Franklin kot 11 (W.B.C.,Light-Heavyweight)
- (7.11.1981, Atlantic City) Michael Spinks kot 7 (W.B.A., Light-Heavyweight)

As always fight fans, keep reaching for the stars, and all your dreams can be fulfilled.

Interview conducted October 2000

(L) Howard Eastman and William Joppy trade jabs

Never Give Up...

Up Close and Personal with WBA Middleweight Champion William Joppy

Since I started writing about three years ago, I've had the absolute pleasure to interview and to be involved with some great fighters, managers, trainers and celebrities. Each one has given me some great moments.

Well, William Joppy is yet another example of why I love boxing and truly enjoy writing about it. Joppy was down to earth, more than willing to be candid, and loves being a champion who wants to take on the best in his division.

As you will read, we both share a lot of the same thoughts on boxing, which include wanting the best for the fighters and the fans.

What inspired you to get into boxing?
Boxing was something I always wanted to do as a youngster coming up. Unfortunately, I did not get into boxing until I was 20. I used to

go to the gyms and boxing events. At the time though, I was too immature, so I lacked the dedication to be a fighter. That's why I started late in the game because as you know, you have to eat, sleep and drink boxing.

If you could fight anyone out there right now, who would it be and why?

I would like to fight Felix Trinidad tomorrow, if I could. There is a question in everyone's mind about me being great or not. I need that caliber of a fighter right now in my career to elevate me. If I would fight say, Keith Holmes or Bernard Hopkins right now, it would establish me.

However, a SuperFight with Felix takes me to a whole different level. (I totally agree with William on this and in fact, said it on Glenn Harris's SportsTalk TV Show).

Who are your three favorite fighters of all-time and why?

Sugar Ray Leonard. He did it all in the ring. He could box, bang, and he was just naturally gifted. Even when he wasn't at his best, he looked good. Buddy Mcgirt. When he was young he was very slick in the ring. Finally, Mike Mccallum. He also had many tricks in the ring, too.

What is the greatest fight you have ever seen and why?

Sugar Ray Leonard vs Tommy Hearns I. You had two fighters both in their prime. They both had speed and great boxing ability. It just boiled down to who wanted it the most in there. Bottom line: It was one hell of a fight.

What are your words of wisdom to the young fighter just turning professional?

Number one, more than anything, TRAIN HARD. Number two, I have a boxing saying that goes, "Never duck no Rec". What I mean by that Brad is, you have a lot of guys in the gym who should be champions, but they are always worrying about who they are going to fight, or they don't want to spar certain guys in the gym. Guys like this Brad, don't make it. I have always been eager to fight everyone out there, and especially guys who are better than I, because it brings me to another level.

Bottom Line: You have to fight the best to be a true world champion, and you must have a killer instinct in there. I don't mean to sound vicious, but this is the hurt business and that's the way it must be.

Do you favor a mandatory retirement fund for all boxers and if so, how would you like to see it accomplished?

I totally agree with you Brad that we need a retirement fund for all boxers. However, it is partially part of the fighter's fault for winding up broke after a long career. A point that I think strongly backs up your hopes of a retirement fund is this, say you're in the Navy like you are or maybe if you're a lawyer, doctor or police officer. All of these professions you can do for many years. You can't box for that long and these guys get this money which is temporary.

Brad, people remember you from your last fight. So let's say that you make $500,000 for a fight. You have to pay taxes and your people. Lets just say that you lose so next time out, your going to make less. The point I am making Brad is this, these guys get this money and they go out and by the most expensive Mercedes Benz and all this fancy stuff and not realizing that when you lose, it's gone.

Bottom Line: I do favor a mandatory retirement fund from day one but as you can tell, I am stressing to fighters out there to be responsible with your money!

If you could personally fix the rankings systems, what changes would you make to them?

Brad, I really can't say. Sometimes the number one contenders are credible and others times they are not.

Who do you think you emulate in the ring?

Sugar Ray Leonard. I can do it all! I can fight backing up and coming forward. I can box and bang!

What do you consider your best weapon in the ring?

My right hand.

Who do you feel was your toughest opponent and why?

Peter Venancio. I had seen him fight many times, but not as good as the night he faced me. It was his first title shot and as so many fighters do, he rose up to the occasion. He really gave me a difficult time in that fight.

In your opinion what is the state of boxing today?

I think it's in trouble. It needs to go back to the days of Sugar Ray Robinson and Jake Lamotta. Back then we could tell who was the best in the world. Brad, I will tell you a thing that just happened to me the other day.

A young boy walked up to me and asked me who I am? I told him and he wanted an autograph, but he also said, "I thought Keith Holmes was the champion?"

I had to explain to him that we both had a piece of the pie. As you know Brad, back then you had only one real World Champion which left no confusion for the fans out there.

Is there any place to date, that you have not fought at, but would really like to?

I would love to fight in Jamaica outside, and over in Mexico in one of those bullrings, where Julio Cesar Chavez fought.

When you finally retire, what do you want your fans to remember you for?

I want to be remembered just like you remember Roberto Duran or Jake Lamotta. That's why I want a career defining fight. I need that to put me in that position. If I stop fighting today, I am not going to be mad at my career because I was a world champion. I wouldn't be totally satisfied, because I want to go down as one of the best.

That's why I said earlier, I need a Felix Trinidad to do this.

Finally, what is the saying you live your life by?

"Stay Focused"! Let me explain Brad, if I may. Whether it's boxing, or whatever you choose to do in life, you have to stay focused and not worry about what the next man is doing. By doing this, I feel there is no way you can't succeed.

If you do worry about what other people are doing or what they have, you are only taking a step back.

William Joppy
Weight class: Middleweight/160 lbs

Amateur record: 52 fights; 48+, 4-
1992: Olympic Trials Worcester Middleweight:
+ Eric Wright points
- Chris Byrd points
Professional record: 36 fights; 32+ (24 KO),
1=, 1-
1996-1997: W.B.A. Middleweight
1998-2001: W.B.A. Middleweight .

- 1993 -
+ (Feb-26-1993, Camp Hill) Dwayne Tennet 4
+ (Apr-30-1993, Woodbridge) Ken Ruffin kot 1
+ (May-12-1993, Baltimore) Shane Martin kot 3
+ (Jun-18-1993, Woodbridge) Tim Tisdale kot 1
+ (Aug-13-1993, Largo) George TAYLOR kot 3
+ (Sep-25-1993, Largo) Ivory Teague ko 2
+ (Oct-21-1993, Washington) Tyrone HAYWOOD ko 2

- 1994 -
+ (Jan-7-1994, Upper Marlboro) Willie TAYLOR kot 3
+ (Feb-17-1994, Upper Marlboro) Robert HARRIS kot 1
+ (Feb-27-1994, Atlantic City) Tony MC CRIMMION kot 2
+ (Apr-8-1994, Upper Marlboro) Ken Parker kot 2
+ (Apr-14-1994, Richmond) Muhammad SHABAZZ kot 5
+ (May-13-1994, Upper Marlboro) Carl Sullivan kot 4

+ (Jun-15-1994, Southwark) Carlos CHRISTIE 6
+ (Jul-30-1994, Las Vegas) Miguel Hernandez ko 3
+ (Aug-13-1994, Atlantic City) Richard EVANS 8
+ (Sep-20-1994, Washington) Tony Cartrell ko 2

- 1995 -
+ (Mar-1-1995, Fort Lauderdale) Tony MC CRIMMION ko 3
+ (Apr-29-1995, Landover) Joaquin VELASQUEZ 10
= (Sep-16-1995, Las Vegas) Rodney TONEY 12 (North America, Middleweight)
+ (Dec-7-1995, Upper Marlboro) Israel FIGUEROA ko 1

- 1996 -
+ (Feb-10-1996, Las Vegas) David BOONE kot 2
+ (Jun-24-1996, Yokohama) Shinji TAKEHARA kot 9 (W.B.A., Middleweight)
+ (Oct-19-1996, Upper Marlboro) Ray MC ELROY kot 6 (W.B.A., Middleweight)

- 1997 -
+ (May-10-1997, Miami) Peter VENANCIO 12 (W.B.A., Middleweight)
- (Aug-23-1997, New York) Julio Cesar GREEN 12 (W.B.A., Middleweight)

- 1998 -
+ (Jan-31-1998, Tampa) Julio Cesar GREEN 12 (W.B.A., Middleweight)
+ (Aug-28-1998, Las Vegas) Roberto DURAN kot 3 (W.B.A., Middleweight)

- 1999 -

+ (Jul-24-1999, Las Vegas) <u>Napoleon PITT</u> kot 1

+ (Sep-24-1999, Washington) <u>Julio Cesar GREEN</u> injury 7 (W.B.A., Middleweight)

- **2000** -
+ (Mar-3-2000, Las Vegas) <u>Fernando ZUNIGA</u> 10
+ (May-20-2000, Tunica) <u>Rito RUVALCABA</u> kot 1 (W.B.A., Middleweight)

As always fight fans, keep reaching for the stars, and all your dreams can be fulfilled.

Interview conducted May 2000

Boxing Champion

Musician

A Different Light...

Up Close and Personal with Undisputed World Light Heavyweight Champion Roy Jones, JR.

In any sport, throughout the years, there are many great athletes who come through the ranks; some great, and some larger than the sport because of their God-given talents. These talents go unexplained by some of the great minds of the world because these athletes transcend the norm. They will be discussed on porches, in barber shops and at summer picnics, for years to come.

Once such athlete in the sport of boxing, is Roy Jones, JR. His quickness, unorthodox style, amazing reflexes, and his complete, overall ability to just break down his opponent, cannot be explained by any panel on boxing, or taught in a classroom of hard knocks. It's a God-given talent at birth that is developed, and then when it matures, boxing fans are privileged to see it in the many rings throughout the world.

Since his professional debut on May 6, 1989, many things have been written about this man;

some positive, but as of late, too much that is negative. With that said, it's time for me to throw my hat in the ring and express my views which I have always stood by.

Jones, JR, has given many unbelievable performances against many top notch fighters throughout his career. Yet, the knock has always been, he doesn't fight the best. I disagree, I think he thoroughly dominates the best today and makes boxing's so-called critics, forget that the fighter in front of him, was a great fighter before the first bell rang.

Being around boxing for 27 years both in and out of the ring as a young amateur boxer, I can remember all the fighters we wish could have faced him such as, Marvin Hagler, Sugar Ray Leonard, Tommy Hearns, and Roberto Duran, to name just a few. If they were in their prime today, sure they could challenge him, and the boxing world would see how he'd perform.

Well, since that is not possible, its time to stop making dream fights and judging him on those. He needs to be judged on his ring accomplishments in the last 13 years.

In those 13 years, he dominated a fighter at one time who was pound for pound on everyone's list, by the name of James "Lights Out" Toney. He beat current undisputed Middleweight Champion, Bernard Hopkins and defended his title regularly, hardly losing a round in the fights that went the distance.

He willingly unified the titles, which is something boxing fans are screaming for with all the divisions, and he fought the best of his generation. As of late, everyone is screaming for him to fight Current WBO Light Heavyweight Champion Dariusz Michalczewski.

If the boxing world feels he should fight Michalczewski, and he's ranked number one through his ring efforts, and not placed at number one as so many are today, then sure he deserves a shot at him. But this shot should come on Jones, JR's terms - and in the United States. He is the World Champion and because he earned those belts through ring efforts, he dictates the terms.

Currently, he is showing that he is, in fact, diversified in many areas with the debut of his Rap Album, "Round One" which is climbing up the charts. And, at the time of this interview, he is currently shooting the Matrix II overseas in Australia. It's quite evident that Jones, JR is moving into other areas once he hangs up his boxing gloves.

Instead of the knocks, his career and recent business endeavors should be applauded and used as a blueprint for other fighters out there to follow. As Muhammad Ali stood up for what he has always believed in, so has Roy Jones, JR, and where Ali is praised for this, Jones, JR should be as well.

Now that the boxing side is addressed, let's discuss what this man has done far away from any spit buckets, cornermen and ring ropes. His charitable activities include touring with The Greatest, Muhammad Ali, on his cross-country goodwill campaign, delivering positive messages on life to school kids.

In addition, he spends countless hours speaking to today's youth on the importance of an education and staying off drugs. Though I have always felt that an athlete or any celebrity for that matter, is not required to be a role model, it is a welcome sight to see when someone as big as Jones, JR. welcomes the job of setting an example for today's children.

So with 2002 upon us, it's time to stop the negative press for a change and realize, that whether you like it or not, the name Roy Jones, JR. will go down in boxing history as one of the most talented fighters to ever step inside the coveted square circle, as well as a person who made a difference in this world we live in today.

In 1988, I was present at your going away party held at the Pensacola Civic Center to see you off to your moment in the sun, at the 1988 Seoul Olympics. Instead of rehashing what is already known about the horrible decision, talk about the wonderful memories that you had earning your place on the team, and being able to represent the USA.

Making the '88 Olympic team still has been the highlight of my life. Only one person represents the Country in each weight division. That is remarkable to be that one guy. This means that you are the best in the Country at that time.

On May 6, 1989, you turned professional in front of a sold out crowd at the Pensacola Civic center in Pensacola, Florida. I was at the fight with my wife. I can remember, we commented on the love in the arena that was felt towards you from the crowd of your hometown. What are your recollections of this very special night in your boxing career?

What a way to start a professional career. I felt as though they were repaying me for the way that I represented us all at the Olympic Games.

A little more than four years into your professional boxing career, you challenge Bernard Hopkins for the IBF Middleweight Championship of the world. What are your recollections of finally reaching one of your many dreams and to be standing in that ring on that night?

While he was coming to the ring, I was thinking, damn, this is what I was put on earth to do in my past time. I love this feeling. I only had one hand, but I had God with me. No way could he have beaten me.

When the decision was announced, and you heard, "And the New World Champion……" what did it feel like to have your hand raised and the belt put around your waist?

Once it was over, and the decision announced, I was like, Thank You God. I have wanted this for a long time and You finally blessed me with it. That took a lot of pressure off of my back.

You've fought and defeated Bernard Hopkins, James Toney, Mike McCallum, Virgil Hill, Thomas Tate, Eric Lucas, Montell Griffin, David Telesco and Eric Harding among others. Why do you feel you get knocked for not fighting anyone?

Because I don't have a promoter who fools people into thinking that a guy is going to kill me before I fight him, just to get people to watch it. They were great fighters, but one did not stand far over the next. But in my case, you have to look at someone like Jack Nicholas, Tiger Woods, Michael Jordan, or the greatest race horse of all time, Secreteriat. Nothing comes close to us in our fields, too often. Nothing can beat us when it comes time

for us to win. Roberto Duran beat Sugar Ray
Leonard at fighting on the inside. So, in the
second fight, Sugar got smart and realized
that he didn't have to prove anything to the
people. Everybody will watch a winner. Whether
they like the way he wins or not.

**Who do you feel was your toughest opponent
to date, in your career and why?**

A guy named Rollin Williams. Mainly, because
it was early in my career, and I had to show a
lot of patience, because he had an excellent
defense.

**Who are your three favorite fighters of all-
time and why?**

Muhammad Ali, Sugar Ray Leonard, and
Salvador Sanchez. Ali, because of his
willingness to die or go to jail for what he
believed. Sugar, because of his speed and
style of fighting, and his Olympic
performances. Sanchez, because he was simply
one of the best who ever did it. Skill for
skill, Salvador Sanchez and Sugar Ray
Robinson, would be a close tie with me.

**What is the greatest fight you have ever
seen and why?**

Thomas Hearns vs Sugar Ray Leonard I. The
hype and the fight turned out to be everything
that was promoted.

**Do you favor a mandatory retirement fund for
all boxers and if so, how would you personally
like to see it accomplished?**

I do, but I don't know how it would be
operated yet.

If you could have a hand in the ranking systems, how would you like to see them done?

Well, You have some type of box offs and the best fighters get the best rankings. Everyone wants to blame the alphabet organizations, but the networks are just as much to blame.

Many young male and female fighters look up to you and admire your ring skills. This month marks the 13th year of your successful boxing career. What words of wisdom can you offer to the many fighters out there just turning professional?

Learn the business before you sign anything.

Currently, you're shooting the Matrix II over in Australia. How is that going? And, are you finding any common threads between boxing and acting?

No common threads, but I like acting. The people treat you much better than the people of boxing do.

You have now successfully involved yourself in boxing, music, personal business endeavors, and we will see how the movie business turns out. What does the future hold for Roy Jones, JR?

Running a rap label called Body Head Entertainment. The album "Round One" is in stores now.

When you finally hang up the gloves, what do you want you're worldwide fans to remember you for?

I want my fans to remember me for standing up and doing things my way. Not bowing down to the systematic way of doing things. Never selling my soul for money. And also that the more people cheat me, the harder I go at them. Finally, I will not allow myself to be under anyone else's orders other than God's.

Finally, what is the saying you live your life by?
"God created us all. So if you think it's not right, or you are second guessing, just ask God. Or simply ask yourself, what would God want me to do"?

Roy has a very neat website where his fans can check his latest boxing events and many pictures he has, along with his CD should you want to order it online. Go to www.royjonesjr.com or www.bodyhead.com

****I would like to thank Chauntey Johnson of Body Head Entertainment for assisting me in this interview.

Roy JONES, JR.
Nickname: "RJJ"

Weight class: Light Heavyweight/175 lbs

Amateur record: 134 fights; 121+, 13-
1986: Golden Gloves Junior Welterweight:
1986: Goodwill Games: 3°
1987: Golden Gloves Junior Middleweights:
1988: Golden Gloves: 3°
- Gerald McClellan points
1988: Olympic Trials Junior Middleweights:
+ Frank Liles points
1988: Olympic Games Seoul Junior Middleweights:
+ Makalamba (Mal) ko 1
+ Michal Franek (Tch) points
+ Alexander Zaitsev (URSS) points
+ Richie Woodhall (G-B) points
- Si-Hun Park (South, Korea) points

Professional record: 47 fights; 46+ (37 KO), 1-

1993-1994: I.B.F. Middleweight
1994-1997: I.B.F. Super Middleweight
1996-1997: W.B.C. Light Heavyweight
1997: W.B.C. Light Heavyweight
1998-2002: World Light Heavyweight

- 1989 -
+ (May-6-1989, Pensacola) Ricky Randall kot 2
+ (Jun-11-1989, Atlantic City) Stephan JOHNSON kot 8
+ (Sep-3-1989, Pensacola) Ron Amundsen kot 7
+ (Nov-30-1989, Pensacola) David MC CLUSKEY kot 3

- 1990 -
+ (Jan-8-1990, Pensacola) Joe Edens ko 2
+ (Feb-28-1990, Pensacola) Billy Mitchum kot 2
+ (Mar-28-1990, Pensacola) Knox Brown kot 3
+ (May-11-1990, Pensacola) Ron Johnson ko 2
+ (Jul-14-1990, Pensacola) Tony Waddles ko 1
+ (Sep-25-1990, Pensacola) Rollin Williams ko 4
+ (Nov-8-1990, Pensacola) Reggie MILLER ko 5

- 1991 -
+ (Jan-31-1991, Pensacola) Ricky STACKHOUSE ko 1
+ (Apr-13-1991, Pensacola) Ed Evans kot 3
+ (Aug-3-1991, Pensacola) Kevin Daigle kot 2
+ (Aug-31-1991, Pensacola) Lester YARBROUGH ko 9

- 1992 -
+ (Jan-10-1992, New York) Jorge VACA kot 1
+ (Apr-3-1992, Reno) Art SERWANO ko 1

+ (Jun-30-1992, Pensacola) Jorge Locomotora CASTRO 10
+ (Aug-18-1992, Penascola) Glenn THOMAS ko 8
+ (Dec-5-1992, Atlantic City) Percy Harris ko 4

- 1993 -
+ (Feb-13-1993, Las Vegas) Glenn Wolfe kot 1
+ (May-22-1993, Washington) Bernard HOPKINS 12 (I.B.F., Middleweight)
+ (Aug-14-1993, Bay Saint-Louis) Thulane MALINGA ko 6
+ (Nov-30-1993, Pensacola) Fermin CHIRINOS 10

- 1994 -
+ (Mar-22-1994, Pensacola) Danny GARCIA ko 6
+ (May-27-1994, Las Vegas) Thomas TATE kot 2 (I.B.F., Middleweight)
+ (Nov-18-1994, Las Vegas) James TONEY 12 (I.B.F., Super Middleweight)

- 1995 -
+ (Mar-18-1995, Pensacola) Antoine BYRD kot 1 (I.B.F., Super Middleweight)
+ (Jun-24-1995, Atlantic City) Vinnie PAZIENZA kot 6 (I.B.F., Super Middleweight)
+ (Sep-30-1995, Pensacola) Tony THORNTON kot 3 (I.B.F., Super Middleweight)

- 1996 -
+ (Jan-12-1996, New York) Merqui SOSA kot 2
+ (Jun-15-1996, Jacksonville) Eric LUCAS injury 12 (I.B.F., Super Middleweight)
+ (Oct-4-1996, New York) Bryant BRANNON kot 2 (I.B.F., Super Middleweight)
+ (Nov-22-1996, Tampa) Mike MC CALLUM 12 (W.B.C., Light Heavyweight)

- 1997 -

- (Mar-21-1997, Atlantic City) Montell GRIFFIN disq.9 (W.B.C., Light Heavyweight)

+ (Aug-7-1997, Ledyard) Montell GRIFFIN ko 1 (W.B.C., Light Heavyweight)

- 1998 -

+ (Apr-25-1998, Biloxi) Virgil HILL ko 4

+ (Jul-18-1998, New York) Lou DEL VALLE 12 (World, Light Heavyweight)

+ (Nov-14-1998, Ledyard) Otis GRANT kot 10 (World, Light Heavyweight)

- 1999 -

+ (Jan-9-1999, Pensacola) Richard FRAZIER kot 2 (World, Light Heavyweight)

+ (Jun-5-1999, Biloxi) Reggie Dwayne JOHNSON 12 (World, Light Heavyweight)

- 2000 -

+ (Jan-15-2000, New York) David TELESCO 12 (World, Light Heavyweight)

+ (May-13-2000, Indianapolis) Richard HALL kot 11 (World, Light Heavyweight)

+ (Sep-9-2000, Nouvelle-Orleans) Eric HARDING retiring 11 (World, Light Heavyweight)

- 2001 -

+ (Feb-24-2001, Tampa) Derrick HARMON retiring 11 (World, Light Heavyweight)

+ (Jul-28-2001, Los Angeles) Julio Cesar GONZALEZ 12 (World, Light Heavyweight)

- 2002 -

+ (Feb-2-2002, Miami) Glenn KELLY ko 7 (World, Light Heavyweight)

As always fight fans, keep reaching for the stars, and all your dreams can be fulfilled.

Interview conducted May 2002

IFBA

INTERNATIONAL FEMALE BOXERS ASSOCIATION

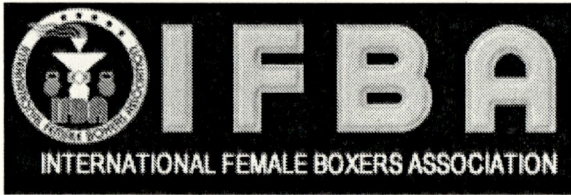

Moving In the Right Direction...

Up Close and Personal with International Female Boxers Association (IFBA) President Rick Kulis

When the name Rick Kulis is mentioned, it's associated with the pioneers of pay-per-view boxing events. He found his success in the early 1980's, when he developed the disposable trap technology that allowed cable systems across America, the opportunity to offer close circuit sporting events to their subscribers over pay-per-view television.

Kulis parlayed that early success into other business ventures and since February 1997, his passion has been the International Female Boxers Association (IFBA). As you will read, his goals are to move the sport of female boxing forward, giving the ladies a chance to shine, while earning the respect of becoming a champion. With these types of goals, we need more support for his organization, so the ladies of boxing have every chance to become a champion, which any fighter aspires to become.

How did you first get involved in the sport of boxing?

Boxing found me actually. During the early 80's, I was the Vice President of Sales, for SelecTV of America, which was an over the air pay-TV channel in Los Angeles and Milwaukee. While I was there, the company offered the infamous "No Mas" fight between Ray Leonard and Roberto Duran on pay-per-view and I was responsible for helping to sell the fight to our subscribers. Immediately following that fight, Sugar Ray Leonard vs. Tommy Hearns I was announced and I was approached by the President of our company to see if we could sell the pay-per-view rights to cable companies, as well as, to our over-the-air subscribers.

Prior to joining SelecTV, I worked in various positions in the cable television industry and I had worked on the technical side, as well as, in sales and marketing. Our Vice President of engineering at the time at Select TV was Mike Downs and I collaborated with him on how to make a live event available on cable Television.

We came up with the disposable trap. The device allowed cable company's to attach a filter to the back of a subscribers TV set to allow the signal to be seen on their TV without an addressable cable box. At that time only the Qube systems operated by the Warner Cable in two markets in the Midwest could show pay-per-view, so this device opened pay-per-view to the cable industry at large for the first time.

The Leonard-Hearns fight was a huge success on cable systems that used the trap, and immediately following that fight, Don King contacted me to use the device on the Larry Holmes vs Gerry Cooney heavyweight championship fight. For the next fifteen years we used the traps for almost every high profile pay-per-view boxing card and worked not only with Don King, but with Bob Arum,

Forum Boxing, ABC RSVP, Mirage Resorts and many others to present boxing on pay-per-view.

How did this lead to you creating the International Female Boxing Association (IFBA)?

I formed the IFBA in Feb of 1997, right after the George Foreman vs. Crawford Grimsley fight in Japan. During the Foreman fight, we distributed the event to hundreds of sports bars on closed circuit television and during the telecast there was a great women's bout that really stole the show. Our customers called us immediately asking about women's boxing and we felt we really had a new entertainment opportunity on our hands.

My publicist at the time was Matt Helreich and he encouraged me to form the IFBA and, through the Organization, we have sanctioned 41 women's world title bouts in the United States, Canada, South Korea and the United Kingdom.

For the readers, go into detail as to what separates yours from the rest, with so many female boxing organizations that have belts?

Our goal at the IFBA was to set the standard by which women's boxing was judged. When we started the organization, we worked with the Associated Boxing Commissions (ABC) to draw attention to the need for mandatory pregnancy testing. The universal acceptance of a two minute round. We worked with State Commissions to allow women to fight over 4 rounds, and we sought out, and found, a glove manufacturer to build a glove that would fit a woman's hand. This would add safety to the sport.

At the time we started the IFBA, only the Women's International Boxing Federation (WIBF) was active in women's boxing. While the International Women's Boxing Federation (IWBF) was already incorporated it was not active, and the International Boxing Association (IBA) was not even thinking about women's boxing.

Because we knew this sport needed television to survive, the IFBA worked with USA Tuesday Night Fights to form the first women's tournaments on TV. Later, our World Title bouts where seen on ESPN2, Fox Sports Regional Networks and pay-per-view, as well.

If you had two things that you would like our readers to take away from this interview about the IFBA, what would they be?

I think the first thing is that the IFBA is truly a champion in the sport of women's boxing. We know that it takes work to convince promoters to stage world class women's bouts and we work with promoters worldwide to convince them to give the women a chance.

Secondly, we are active with local commissions to alert them to mismatches and questionable managers that might be taking advantage of under skilled fighters in order to try make a buck. Also, we wanted to keep the commissions more knowledgeable about the women who fight in their states.

Why is it that female champions in any of the recognized organizations don't unify the titles as their male counterparts?

The problem with unifying the belts is the money. It is very difficult to get a promoter to sanction a women's championship bout in the first place and, when it comes to paying sanctioning fees, the promoters are looking for the cheapest fees they can find. Just recently we were approached to sanction a unified title, but when the promoter compared the sanctioning fees from our organization against another one, they opted for the cheaper organization.

With rating systems being knocked in the entire sport of boxing, what makes yours credible?

We do our best to make our ratings fair. We try hard to keep up with the fighters and how they perform. It is very difficult to keep up with the weight changes and records, but we try our hardest.

What do you think the current state of female boxing is in?

Currently women's boxing is a four and six round business. There is a lot of activity, but it is limited to one women's fight per card and usually only short fights. On the amateur level, the sport is booming and the amateur program is now active in many countries preparing the next generation of fighters to turn professional. We are slowly phasing in new faces in the professional ranks, with names like Martin, Collins, Webber, Guidi, Blackshear, etc. being replaced by Zaganas, Stone, Fettkether and Foster as fighters to watch.

Who do you feel are the top five ladies in boxing today?

Well that is tough question to answer without opening it up to spirited debate. But as a fan, I wouldn't miss seeing any of the Champions who represent the IFBA whenever I get a chance to see them in action.

Why do you think female boxing is not on more mainstream television on a regular basis?

The programming executives at ESPN, FOX, Showtime and HBO are in the male boxing business. Their shows are built around different levels of the sport and they do not see women's boxing as part of the male agenda. ESPN and Fox trend toward the everyday aspects of boxing featuring up and comers, current contenders and names of yesterday to fill out their shows.

HBO and Showtime are strictly in the Championship Boxing business with their telecasts being built around the fights, not an established time period. Bob Yalen at ESPN, and Brad Jacobs at USA Network, were the first television executives to give women's boxing a real chance.

Yalen put the first women's bout on national network television during an ABC Saturday telecast and Jacobs opened his doors to allow the first women's boxing tournament to air on USA Tuesday Night Fights. The ratings success of the tournaments gave the sport its own all-women's cards on ESPN2 and USA and the ratings really showed that the sport could be competitive with men's boxing in the same time period.

With the demise of USA Tuesday Night Fights and limited number of boxing dates ESPN2 could offer all-women's cards, the sport never really got a fair chance to show what it could do. Even though the ratings are tremendous, we haven't found a TV executive ready to give us our own time slot, so we will continue to beg for airtime and hope that the programming landscape changes to give us the shot we deserve.

Who are your three favorite fighters of all-time and why?

I really don't have three, for me it was the Fearsome Foursome — Sugar Ray Leonard, Roberto Duran, Marvin Hagler, and Tommy Hearns. Having the opportunity to work all their combined big pay-per-view fights, I could not wait for each one of them to climb in the ring. Each fight was filled with electricity and excitement and I was there to be a part of each one.

What is the greatest fight you have ever seen and why?

For me the greatest fight of my lifetime was Marvin Hagler vs Tommy Hearns for the undisputed Middleweight Championship of the World. It was Toe - toe nonstop action I can still see the fight in my mind today.

Do you favor a mandatory retirement fund for all boxers and if so, how would you like to see it accomplished?

The sport of women's boxing is not organized enough yet to talk about retirement funds. Certainly once the purses begin to escalate and the fighters see this sport as a place where they can earn their livelihood, the subject will have more merit.

When you finally pass on the reigns of the International Female Boxers Association, how you would you like to be remembered in female boxing circles?

Well, I am not in any hurry to pass the reigns on anytime soon. There is a lot of good work to be done on behalf of this sport and I hope the IFBA will be at the center of this. As for being remembered. I hope the IFBA will be remembered as the organization that helped establish the sport of women's boxing around the world, both as a live attraction and a solid TV product for generations to come.

Finally, what is the saying you live your life by?
"Life is what happens while others sit around making their plans".

Rick would like to add the following to our interview:
As of late, we have really made some great changes on our website with many exciting boxing pictures. Please take the time to check it out at: http://www.ifba.com

As always fight fans, keep reaching for the stars, and all your dreams can be fulfilled.

Interview conducted May 2002

Hercules, More Than Just A Greek Myth...

Up Close and Personal with Welterweight Contender Hercules Kyvelos

Many centuries ago, there was much talk about a mythical figure whose strength was more powerful than any mere mortal. Well, whether he existed can be debated, but the Hercules in this story, is leaving nothing up for debate in the ring.

From many accounts by boxing fans who have seen Hercules Kyvelos, there are no myths — just simple facts. These facts show his outstanding skills, huge heart and punishing power, which have the boxing world taking notice.

What are some of the differences you see between fighting in Canada and the United States?

Simply put, the United States is the world capital of professional boxing. For any fighter, whether you're from Canada, Russia or Australia, fighting in the United States is the zenith of professional boxing. You feel it in the venue on fight night and you feel it from the fans. Frankly, all roads in professional boxing ultimately lead to Las Vegas or Atlantic City.

This reality is reflected in the environment, the atmosphere. One of my joys is watching the old black and white tapes of fights from Madison Square Garden. I know twenty or thirty years from now, young fans will have the same thrill from some of today's classic bouts staged in the U.S.

And, for a fighter from Canada or elsewhere, fighting in the States is also a statement about being the very best in the sport.

In just 21 fights, you have proven that you are championship material. Why do you feel that when some fighters have the same amount of fights, they still do not look as you do in the ring?

I think some fighters choose only to learn from their defeats, but even in victory there's always something to learn, something to improve upon. There hasn't been a fight where I don't pour over the tapes later, picking up on the little things that might go unnoticed, the small techniques that can be improved. You have to keep a humble heart and an open mind, don't take things too seriously in the sport and from that you build your confidence as a fighter. Ultimately, it's the confidence that shows in the ring and inspires the fans.

In some of your big fights, you were down, but got back up to either stop your opponent, or win by decision. I attribute that to having heart, which cannot be taught. Explain your

definition of "heart" and why you have it for the younger fighters.

Having heart comes with the individual and how badly he wants things. Heart is not really something that someone can teach you, but rather it's something you have to teach yourself. You have to look deep inside, find the courage and strength and stay focused on the goal. As a fighter, you have to learn to channel bad things to your advantage. Flash knock downs can happen in the sport, but the fighter who has taught himself to overcome obstacles, to find success in his passion, gets up and finishes the job. The end goal is to win and occasionally there will be some obstacles and some adversity, but the champion rises above it.

If you could choose any champion in your weight class to challenge for your first world title, who would you like to face and why?

Right now with all the recent changes in the welterweight division, I'm not particularly focused on one fighter. I'm ready to take on any of the champions from the credible organizations and then start the process of unifying the titles. We'll see what the situation is after the Mosley - Forrest rematch in July.

Who are your three favorite fighters of all-time and why?

Ali - His mindset, aura and personality. He prevailed when he was the underdog - whether in or out of the ring. He revolutionized the sport and still, even today, is a positive role model for fans and boxers.

Roy Jones, JR. - Because he has the same ring instinct as Ali which makes him so dominant in his weight class.

And while he was not a professional boxer, I'd like to add Bruce Lee for his philosophy, spirituality, outlook and perspective of the fight game.

What is the greatest fight you have ever seen and why?

Definitely the Ali-Frazier I. It was a fight where both boxers stood toe-to-toe giving it everything they had - going to hell and back - showing the true heart that makes a champion. What it takes to be a great fighter, was on display that night.

Do you favor a mandatory retirement fund for all boxers and if so, how would you like to see it personally accomplished?

Yes. The yes is the easy part. Personally, I believe it's important to make a distinction between the part-time fighter and the full-time, the fighter who quits after a few bouts and the boxer who pursues his dream. Professional boxing is comprised of a large number of players: television networks, promoters, managers and, of course, boxers; whatever formula is used (for boxers who would be eligible for such a plan) must be fairly shared between all parties. I believe professional boxing can learn both from the successes and problems of the pension plan with the NHL Players Association.

To the young amateur and just-turned professional fighters in Canada who look up to you, what are your words of wisdom to them?

Be ready to bust your ass. Professional boxing requires a great deal of sacrifice, determination, sweat and commitment. It takes a lot out of a fighter to be the very best he can be. Talent alone is not enough, it's a tough business and you have to look out for yourself by putting a good, strong team together to help you achieve your goals.

Many readers may not know this, but you have a degree in Physical Education. How are you using your degree in your off-time from boxing?

Off-time? What off-time?

First, while I have a college degree, I'm actually half-way through a university degree in Physical Education. I've put university on hold while I pursue a world championship. With my available time, what I try to focus on is speaking to young people, encouraging them to stay in school, stay off drugs, the need for discipline in reaching your goals and the importance of faith in your life.

When you finally retire from boxing, how would you like your fans to remember you?

Naturally as a great fighter, but also as somebody who did something for the sport, helped improve its reputation. We need to bring fans back to the fights, to showcase boxers that parents want their children to see as role-models. All boxers have a responsibility to the sport, to raise it from some of the scandals of the past few years and return boxing to its past glory.

I'll try to do my end, and I hope that fans see this in me.

Finally, what is the saying you live your life by?

Luke 18:27

"The things that are impossible with men are possible with God".

***I would like to thank Dermod "D-Man" Travis of Pira Communications for helping make this interview possible.

Hercules KYVELOS

Weight class: Welterweight/147 lbs

Amateur record: Golden Gloves Canada:
1995: Tournoi Liverpool Welterweight:
+ Domenico Mura (Ita) points
- Michael Jones (Angl) points
1996: Tournoi Liverpool Welterweight:
+ Richard Murray (Angl) points
- Boris Kandez (Rus) points
1996: Olympic Games Atlanta Welterweight:
- Kamel Chater (Tun) points
Professional record: 21 fights; 21+ (11 KO)
2000: Canada Welterweight

- **1997** -
+ (May-14-1997, Montreal) Ryan JONES ko 1
+ (Jul-27-1997, Baton Rouge) John TRIGG ko 2
+ (Sep-30-1997, Bay Saint-Louis) Tim EDMONDS ko 2
+ (Dec-13-1997, Sheffield) Harry BUTLER 4

- **1998** -
+ (Feb-10-1998, Baton Rouge) Ray HARRIS kot 3
+ (Apr-3-1998, Montreal) David HORVATH ko 1
+ (May-12-1998, Kanata) Errol BROWN 6
+ (Sep-24-1998, Montreal) Ron PASEK ko 4
+ (Nov-27-1998, Montreal) Rodney TATUM 6

- 1999 -
+ (Feb-5-1999, Montreal) Rick STOCKTON kot 2
+ (May-28-1999, Montreal) Mathias BEDBURDICK kot 2
+ (Jun-29-1999, Montreal) Gilberto FLORES 8
+ (Oct-13-1999, Montreal) Greg JOHNSON 8
+ (Dec-10-1999, Montreal) Alex LUBO kot 3

- 2000 -
+ (Feb-15-2000, Montreal) Fitz VANDERPOOL 12 (Canada, Welterweight)
+ (May-9-2000, Montreal) Keith THOMAS kot 5
+ (Jun-16-2000, Montreal) Wayne BOUDREAUX 8
+ (Dec-15-2000, Montreal) Alex HILTON 10

-2001 -
+ (Mar-2-2001, Montreal) Charles WHITTAKER 10
+ (Dec-1-2001, Chester) Michael COVINGTON retiring

- 2002 -
+ (Feb-2-2002, Atlantic City) John MOLNAR 10

As always fight fans, keep reaching for the stars, and all your dreams can be fulfilled.

Interview conducted April 2002

Thanks for the Memories...

Up Close and Personal with Former Light Heavyweight Title Challenger Alvaro "Yaqui" Lopez

Before I get into this interview, I want to tell you how, an interview that has eluded me for quite some time, came to be. Back in November 2000, I did an interview for the boxing website www.fightnews.com with former IBF Super Middleweight Champion Murray Sutherland who campaigned as a Light Heavyweight before he dropped down to Super Middleweight. In that interview, I mentioned that Yaqui Lopez was also a boxer from Murray's era who always came to fight, and if anyone had contact with Lopez, it would be honor for me to do an interview with him.

Fast Forward——June 2001, I receive an email from a wonderful young lady who read the

Murray Sutherland interview when she found it by searching the internet when she typed in Yaqui's name, which pulled up my interview with Sutherland. She was doing this for a tenth grade project she was working on. Well, that project happened to be on her Uncle who turned out to be Alvaro "Yaqui" Lopez. The young lady turned out to be Ashley Lopez, Yaqui's very sweet niece.

I TRULY LOVE THE POWER OF THE INTERNET!!

The Alvaro "Yaqui" Lopez story is a fascinating one which starts with his birth under a bull ring in the Plaza de Toros San Pedro in Zacatecas, Mexico. He was raised for 14 years underneath the seats in an adobe garage of a famous Bullring in Zacatecas.

Young Lopez had dreams of becoming a Matador, but those dreams were shattered when in his teens, he got a shot at fighting a bull. After about four or five passes, the bull drove his horn into his ankle which shattered it. With that shattered ankle came shattered dreams of becoming a bullfighter.

Lopez always continued to dream about bigger and better things. Dreams turned to reality many years later when he met his soon to be father-in-law and manager, Jack Cruz. Cruz would take a young Lopez on a journey into boxing that few boxers ever will have a chance to experience.

It was a journey that saw Lopez challenge for the Light Heavyweight Title four times and the Crusierweight Title once. In three of those fights, many felt that Lopez should have won the belt against John Conteh and Victor Galindez (twice). All three of those bouts were lost by 15 round decisions and many as I said, felt the decisions should have gone to Lopez.

In his other attempt at a Light Heavyweight Title, he faced then Champion Matthew Saad Muhammad. The fight would go on to be the 1980 "Fight of the Year" by Ring Magazine. The first half of the fight was dominated by Lopez and in round eight (also named "Round of the Year"), Lopez pinned Saad Muhammad in a corner landing 20 consecutive blows. Muhammad somehow got out of that round, and stopped Lopez in the 14th round. If the fight would have been staged today, Lopez would have won by a TKO in the eighth round because they stop fights much sooner now, then back in his day.

One side note to the Muhammad fight. I was at the Boxing Hall of Fame this weekend and in fact, ran into Matthew Saad Muhammad. When I mentioned I just interviewed Yaqui, his face lit up with a big smile. He said, "Brad, in my two fights with Yaqui, he made me a better fighter because of his huge heart and the tough fights he gave me both times."

Shortly after his fight with Muhammad, Lopez moved up to crusierweight and challenged then Champion Carlos Deleon, who stopped him in four rounds. Lopez would go on to have one more fight as crusierweight, facing Bash Ali, dropping a 12 round decision. Both Lopez and Cruz felt it was time for Yaqui to retire and not go on as so many greats did before and after him, sometimes getting hurt.

From the very second Lopez and Cruz picked up the phone, I saw a closeness that you could hear when they spoke of their legendary run, which is still being written about today in boxing magazines.

When we finally got done with the interview, I chatted some more with Lopez and Cruz telling me some wonderful stories. Finally, as we hung up, Yaqui said, "Brad, I just want to thank you from the bottom of my heart for remembering me. I really appreciated the interview."

I was very moved by that and replied, "Yaqui, the honor was all mine. Thanks for giving {US} the fans, years of great excitement every time you stepped in the ring. Those memories will last a lifetime."

First of all, for the readers who talk about you as amongst the exciting Light Heavyweight's of the 70's and 80's, tell them what you are up to today?

I am retired now from a sanitation company where I drove big trucks. With my retirement, I get to spend lots of time taking care of my family, which I enjoy.

How did you first become involved in boxing?

I met my girlfriend, who would become my wife. She told me her father was a boxing promoter. I told her that I want to box. She was surprised when I said that, but took me to her father who got me started in the sport.

In your five title attempts, you faced John Conteh, Victor Galindez (twice), Matthew Saad Muhammad and finally, you moved up to Crusierweight. There you faced then champion Carlos Deleon. Briefly tell me your recollections of each bout?

John Conteh: When I went to Copenhagen to face him, we got over there three days before the fight. The first day, I can't sleep because of the time difference and very bad jet lag. My boxing equipment didn't arrive with me because they put it on another plane.

In the tenth round, I hit him with a big punch and they gave him an eight count. The referee also was messing with my trunks to give Conteh more time to get over the punch. There was not supposed to be an eight count. When the fight was finally over, I lost by a split decision. I feel that I won the fight.

Victor Galindez I: We traveled to Italy for that fight, and this time around we had a little more experience, since I had already fought once for the title. This time we went over there about 15 days prior to the fight. We took our own sparring partners. I felt I did very good in that fight and if you know about Galindez, he always threw lots of dirty punches and had other dirty tactics. The referee never took a point from him for any of this.

Victor Galindez II: When I was jogging over here in my hometown, I pulled my tendons in my left ankle which is the same one that got shattered in the bull ring many years before. This happened about 15 days before the fight. I told my father-in-law that I didn't want to back out of the fight. (This led to a great story told by Jack Cruz).

"When Yaqui messed up his ankle, we tried everything to get the swelling down. In fact, one old guy took us to an old Filipino healer. We had to take a fifth of whiskey to him, and he drank some combined with some other stuff he mixed, and spit it on Yaqui's leg while rubbing it with some type of powder." Funny thing, it really worked. I was very competitive in this fight and again, dropped a decision which I thought I should have gotten.

Matthew Saad Muhammad: In this fight, I was winning the first half of the fight and in the eighth round I had him almost out, and then Commissioner Jersey Joe Walcott was screaming for the referee to stop the fight. Only problem, the ref had his back to Walcott and didn't see him. Also, they told my corner we could not have smelling salts and after the fight, we went to his corner where they had about 15 broken capsules of smelling salts.

Carlos Deleon: I was in good shape and got caught by a good punch which stopped me.

These are all things that happen in boxing and not excuses, just recollections of those fights. I enjoyed each one and was honored to have had the chance to challenge as many times as I did.

In your days, you fought for the title and had 15 rounds vs. today's 12. Would you like to see the 15 brought back?

Yes! I think the 15 rounds show who is really in good shape and who is not.

Do you remember of any big fights you were approached with, but they didn't pan out?

We were supposed to fight John Conteh again in Africa in what would have been a rematch. The fight was all set and the Emperor of Uganda killed a bunch of people. He was the guy backing the fight and when he did that, it canceled out the fight.

If you had to take one of your fights to call a career best, which one would you pick?

When I fought Mike Rossman. We fought at Madison Square Garden and I was brought in to just be an opponent for him. Rossman at that time was number one. When I stopped him, I signed a contract that night to fight Galindez again. But what winds up happening is Rossman gets the shot instead, and beats Galindez.

What do you think of Roy Jones, JR. as the premier Light Heavyweight of today? How do you think he would have done with the fighters from your era?

I think Jones has good skills, but just doesn't have the same finesse that the boxers did in my era. We went 15 rounds in my day and I think Jones just couldn't hang, based on what I have seen him do today. I really think Michael Spinks could have beaten him.

I heard that you did a little acting in some movies (Fat City and Valentino Returns). How come you didn't pursue it more?

Yaqui said, with a chuckle, "I didn't do a good job acting. If I would have done a good job, they would have called me back."

If you could take any Light Heavyweight from any era and put him in the ring with you in your prime, who would that be, and what do you think the outcome would be?

Willie Pastrano. I think I would have out boxed him and took a decision.

Who are you top three favorite fighters of all-time and why?

Muhammad Ali. He was such a great Heavyweight Champion whose movement reminded me of welterweights I have seen fight. Also, he was very smart and can punch. Second, Jose Napoles. He was such a great defensive fighter. Finally, Carlos Monzon. He was not fast, but he would set you up with a right hand, and when he hit you, it was all over from that right.

What is the greatest fight you have ever seen and why?

I have seen lots of great fights in my lifetime. But I want to tell you that the recent fight with Prince Naseem Hamed and Marco Antonio Barrera was the greatest fight to me.

Out of 30 sports writers I think only two picked Marco to win. Both my father-in-law and I picked Marco to win, before the fight. Barrera showed me such heart in the Morales fight, which I felt he won. We thought if he had anything left, he would expose Hamed's weaknesses and he sure did. He put on a perfect fight, and it was so good to see him get the decision.

Do you favor a mandatory retirement fund for all boxers and if so, how would you like to see it accomplished?.

Brad, first of all, I think that is a very good question to ask. I think every fighter, after so many years, should have a pension coming in for all of his ring efforts. Lots of people don't realize what we have to go through to get in shape for a fight. We endure lots of pain, daily.

When I started boxing, there were no light heavyweights in Stockton, California. We would travel to Oakland Monday – Friday, and it was about a 75 mile trip. We did this four years straight. On top of this, I worked in a cannery.

I would wake up at 4:00 AM in the morning and go jogging. Then I would come home take a shower and then go to work at the cannery. I would get home around 2:00 PM and then we would jump in the car and go to Oakland to work out. I would spar with the number one contender at the time, middleweight, George Cooper.

There were other top fighters there that I had to spar with. They used to kick the crap out of me in the first four months. After about five months, nobody would show up because I reversed the beatings.

The reason I mention all this is because boxers endure these things, and this is why we need a retirement fund. I consider what a fighter does to become world class a full-time job. You could take out a certain percentage from each fighter's check and put it in the fund. I really hope this comes to be.

Now that you have been out of boxing for quite some time, how would you like your many fans to remember you?

I would like to be remembered by the way I retired. I knew when my legs were starting to go in my last fight, it was time to quit. I didn't go on as so many do.

Finally, what is the saying you live your life by?

"If you don't work hard, you will not go anyplace".

Jack Cruz wanted to add the following to our interview:

Yaqui has never been the type to brag, but I want the boxing people to know, that he goes to the schools and always talks to the kids about staying in school. He is always doing things to better our society and we are very proud of him.

Writers closing remarks:

As many of you know, when I conduct an interview which is really special to me, I have no problem saying it. It truly was an

honor to interview Yaqui, who indeed, is part
of my childhood memories. It was a time when
we had boxing on all the major networks, and
Lopez's image was forever forged in our boxing
memories.

I would like to thank Ashley Lopez again for
assisting me in making this interview
possible, and in addition, Jack Cruz, Yaqui's
father-in-law and manager.

Alvaro LOPEZ
Nickname: "Yaqui"

Weight class: Light Heavyweight/175 lbs

Professional record: 78 fights; 63+ (40 KO),
15-
  1978: North America Light Heavyweight
  1982: North America Cruiserweight

- 1972 -
+ (Apr-24-1972, Stockton) Herman Hampton 6
+ (Jun-2-1972, Carson City) Herman Hampton
ko 3
+ (Jun-16-1972, Stockton) Cisco Solorio ko 6
- (Jul-1-1972, Stockton) Jesse Burnett 8
+ (Oct-24-1972, San Carlos) Henry Tavako 6
+ (Nov-6-1972, Eugene) Mark Hearn ko 6
+ (Nov-29-1972, Stockton) Herman Hampton ko
7
+ (Dec-11-1972, Eugene) Van Sahib ko 2

- 1973 -
+ (Feb-8-1973, Stockton) Polo Ramirez ko 7
- (Mar-15-1973, Seattle) Al Bolden 10
+ (Apr-21-1973, Santa Rosa) Hildo Silva 10
+ (Jun-9-1973, Santa Rosa) Ron Wilson 10
+ (Jul-6-1973, Gardnerville) Dave Rogers ko
5

+ (Aug-3-1973, Reno) Ron Wilson ko 6
+ (Aug-22-1973, Tacoma) Herman Hampton ko 6
+ (Sep-20-1973, Stockton) Budda Brooks ko 5
+ (Nov-1-1973, Portland) Alfonso Gonzalez ko 2
+ (Dec-6-1973, Portland) Al Bolden 10

- **1974** -
+ (Feb-14-1974, Portland) Andy Kendall ko 5
+ (Mar-7-1974, Reno) Willie Warren 10
+ (May-10-1974, Stockton) Hildo Silva 12
+ (Jul-7-1974, Gardnerville) Joe Cokes 12
+ (Oct-11-1974, Portland) Bobby Rascon ko 6
+ (Nov-13-1974, Stockton) Hildo Silva 10

- **1975** -
+ (Mar-4-1975, Sacramento) Terry Lee ko 9
+ (Apr-8-1975, Sacramento) Lee Mitchell ko 6
+ (May-14-1975, Stockton) Mike Quarry 10
+ (Jul-3-1975, Gardnerville) Gary Summerhayes 10
- (Jul-31-1975, Stockton) Jesse Burnett 12
+ (Sep-24-1975, Stockton) Jesse Burnett 12

- **1976** -
+ (Feb-12-1976, Portland) Terry Lee 10
+ (May-3-1976, Stockton) David Smith 10
+ (Jun-30-1976, Stockton) Karl Zurheide ko 6
+ (Jul-17-1976, Stockton) Larry Castaneda ko 9
- (Oct-9-1976, Copenhagen) John Conteh 15 (W.B.C., Light Heavyweight)
+ (Nov-18-1976, Stateline) Clarence Geigger kot 5
+ (Dec-8-1976, Stockton) Pete Mc Intyre ko 6

- **1977** -
+ (Feb-18-1977, Stateline) Danny Brewer kot 6

+ (Mar-7-1977, Stockton) Larry Castaneda ko 8

+ (Apr-5-1977, Incline) Ron White ko 8

- (Apr-22-1977, Indianapolis) Lonnie Bennett kot 3

+ (Jun-17-1977, Miami Beach) Bobby Lloyd ko 5

+ (Jul-20-1977, Stockton) Manuel Fierro ko 3

+ (Jul-27-1977, Las Vegas) Benny Barra ko 5

- (Sep-17-1977, Rome) Victor Galindez 15 (W.B.A., Lightheavyweight)

+ (Oct-27-1977, Stockton) Chuck Warfield ko 4

+ (Dec-15-1977, Stockton) Clarence Geigger ko 4

- 1978 -
+ (Jan-12-1978, Los Angeles) Fabian Falconette ko 2

+ (Mar-2-1978, New York) Mike Rossmann retiring 7

+ (Mar-17-1978, Las Vegas) Ned Hallacy 10

- (May-6-1978, Camaiore) Victor Galindez 15 (W.B.A., Light Heavyweight)

+ (Jul-2-1978, Stockton) Jesse Burnett 15 (North America, Light Heavyweight)

- (Oct-24-1978, Philadelphia) Matthew Franklin ko 11 (North America, Light Heavyweight)

- 1979 -
+ (Jan-18-1979, Stockton) Wilfred Albers ko 3

+ (Feb-27-1979, Sacramento) Ivy Brown ko 3

+ (Sep-12-1979, Stockton) Ernie Barr ko 4

+ (Oct-4-1979, San Carlos) Bashiru Ali 10

- (Dec-1-1979, Rahway) James Scott 10

- 1980 -

+ (Apr-16-1980, Fresno) Pete Mc Intyre ko 8
+ (May-20-1980, Fresno) Bobby Lloyd ko 8
- (Jul-13-1980, Mc Afee) Matthew Saad Muhummad kot 14 (W.B.C., Light Heavyweight)
- (Oct-18-1980, Atlantic City) Michael Spinks ko 7
+ (Nov-29-1980, Lake Tahoe) Carl Ivy ko 3

- 1981 -
+ (Feb-14-1981, Lake Tahoe) Grover Robinson ko 4
+ (May-18-1981, San Carlos) George O'Mara kot 10
+ (May-27-1981, Stockton) Willie Taylor ko 7
- (Jul-24-1981, Reno) S.t. Gordon injury 7 (North America, Light Heavyweight)
+ (Nov-21-1981, Brisbane) Tony Mundine kot 3

- 1982 -
- (Jan-14-1982, Atlantic City) John Davis 10
+ (May-5-1982, Stockton) Alvin Dominey kot 6
+ (Jun-1-1982, Sacramento) David Smith 12 (North America, Cruiserweight)
+ (Jul-31-1982, Lake Tahoe) Ken Arlt 10
+ (Sep-9-1982, Stateline) Roger Braxton 10
+ (Nov-27-1982, Lake Tahoe) James Williams 10

- 1983 -
+ (Feb-19-1983, Incline) Mike Jameson 10
+ (May-7-1983, Stateline) Eddie Gonzalez 10
- (Sep-21-1983, San Juan) Carlos De Leon kot 4 (W.B.C., Cruiserweight)

- 1984 -
- (Sep-12-1984, Stockton) Bashiru Ali 12

As always fight fans, keep reaching for the stars, and all your dreams can be fulfilled.

Interview conducted May 2001

Lyle drops "Big" George Foreman

Class Personified...

Up Close and Personal with Former Heavyweight Title Challenger Ron Lyle

Ron Lyle is yet another heavyweight from the Golden Era of the 70's who I have had the privilege to interview, as of late. In his heyday, Lyle may have given boxing one of its most exciting fights when he faced two-time former Heavyweight Champion "Big" George Foreman on January 24th, 1976 in Las Vegas Nevada.

FAST—-Forward to June 2001 and the Boxing Hall of Fame weekend where I met Lyle, and found him to be yet another example of why I love boxing. He was bombarded by fans for his autograph, and we had to talk in between him signing. Anyone could tell he really enjoyed the love that was shown to him by so many boxing fans. He took the time to sign countless gloves, posters, pictures, and items put in front of him while he spoke to those same fans.

That same evening at the Banquet of Champions, Lyle got up in front of a packed room and gave a heartfelt speech that not only

235

evoked tears from himself, but there was not a dry eye in the house, including this writer and Burt Sugar, the MC of the evening. As Lyle spoke about his parents, along with his journey into boxing, you could feel his true passion for the sport that we both love.

Lyle, is a fighter who always gave 100% each time he stepped in the ring during that Golden Era of the 70's, in this writer's opinion. So to be able to recognize him here in my column, is an honor because I feel that so many of his era, not just in the heavyweight division, have gone far too long without the recognition they truly deserve.

First of all, for all the readers who bring up your name when the Golden Era of Heavyweights is mentioned, what are you doing today?

Currently, I am working with a young man named Farid Shahid who is from LA, and in the last five months, we have made some great strides in his boxing skills. This young man is very dedicated and listens well. He is only an amateur, but the skills are there, and he will be fighting towards the end of this month on an amateur card. Brad, I love boxing and really feel I can make a difference in some young man's life who has hopes, ambitions and dreams, by pointing him in the right direction to fulfill them. This is the first young man I have worked with, but in the past, I have worked with Michael Grant along with Lonnie Smith. I had Lonnie Smith when he knocked out Billy Costello at Madison Square Garden for the title. Bottom line: I really want to show the boxing world my capabilities with working with troubled youths to give them a chance to turn their lives around.

I had the pleasure to meet you for the first time this past June at the Boxing Hall of Fame in Canastota, New York. Was that your first trip and what were your observations of the Hall of Fame?

That was my first trip to the Hall of Fame. I have always dreamed of being judged by my peers who were all at the HOF this past June. In my life, I have always had this dream to be amongst my peers and respected. So when I made this trip and that happened, especially after I made my speech at the Banquet of Champions which aroused a standing ovation, my dream had come true.

My Mother, God rest her soul, told me, "If you hang in there and don't give up, in the end, you will be recognized for you what you have done." When I got up to make the speech, she was up in heaven looking down on me. In my life, I have never felt what I did on that night. (I was amongst that crowd which gave Ron a well deserved standing ovation. His tears of joy were sincere, and as I said earlier, there was so much love in the room for him which moved me to tears, as well.)

You were involved in many thrilling fights, but two in particular involved Earnie Shavers and former two-time Heavyweight Champion George Foreman. What are your recollections of those fights?

Earnie Shavers is the hardest puncher I have ever faced in my career. He is the first man to ever knock me off my feet. I didn't fall from losing my balance, slipping or being tired; he knocked me down with his sheer power, which caused the ground to come up to meet me. I really feel I came into my own in

this fight because I had always wondered, if I
got knocked down, would I get back up? My
question was answered in that fight. Brad,
Earnie is one of the nicest guys I have ever
known in boxing. (Knowing Earnie as well, I
totally second what Ron has said).

George Foreman is a tough fighter and a God-
fearing man. He was very strong and I truly
wish I could have fought him again, but was
never given the opportunity. He really is a
good man, and reminds me of my Dad.

**Who do you feel was your toughest opponent
in your boxing career and why?**

Muhammad Ali. The why is because he
represented so much in the world. When you
fought him, you were not just fighting the
man, you were fighting everybody. That was my
most gratifying fight because the respect I
had for this man along with the many things he
stood up for was amazing.

He stood up for black people as a whole,
putting up his life, swallowing that bitter
pill. I truly respected him for this. At that
same time, I knew I was a good athlete who
could match his athletic skills in the ring. I
feel that I did in that fight.

**In hindsight, what would you have done
differently in your attempt for the
Heavyweight Championship against Muhammad Ali?**

Nothing at all. I say that because when I
was in prison, God surrendered me that dream;
I never knew how it turned out. In it, I was
the champ and getting to that level to fight
for the title shot, was a very special thing
to me then.

You fought slick boxer, Jimmy Young, twice in your career and lost two decisions. What do you feel helped him beat you both times?

I feel I beat him both times. It's the nature of the business to have losses no matter what you think. Jimmy knows I won those fights, but I will not complain about it. Boxing has been very good to me and I totally respect it. It gave me a way out, to compete in society and for that, I am grateful to it.

What are your recollections of Jerry Quarry when you fought him?

Jerry was a very tough fighter. It was my first big fight in boxing. He was not given enough credit in boxing and really was a legit fighter in the ring. He had great combos with power; wasn't a big guy, but was in a big division. Bottom line: Quarry had a heart of a lion.

Who are your three favorite fighters of all-time and why?

Sugar Ray Robinson. I thought he was the greatest fighter I had ever seen, and that was at a time I didn't know that much about boxing, but knew how special he was. When I got into boxing, I really found out how great Robinson really was. Joe Louis was the Man! He could really punch and didn't need any room to do it in. All the rest of us needed room, but Joe didn't. He captured so many of our hearts. Finally, Muhammad Ali. He did so much for the sport of boxing, and it would not be to the point it is today, without him.

What is the greatest fight you have ever seen and why?

Aaron Pryor vs Alexis Arguello I. At that time, I thought Alexis had huge power, which he did show in that fight. It was an all out war with two great fighters. (As many readers already know, this is my favorite fight as well).

What big fights were you approached with, but never materialized?

Larry Holmes and Kenny Norton. One other was Joe Frazier and I didn't cry over that one, (Ron laughed when he said that) because Joe was a bad man.

Do you favor a mandatory retirement fund for all boxers and if so, how would you like to see it accomplished?

I absolutely do and it's way overdue! Every other sport has one, but boxing. There are so many pioneers who were involved in this sport and should have a pension fund. This is a great question, and I am glad you asked it. We need people such as yourself to keep bringing this out, so hopefully one day, it can become a reality.

How do you match the current heavyweights to your group?

I am going to give you my opinion from only a fighter's perspective. You always hear, the fighters of today couldn't compete with our group. If that's the case, then Ali, Foreman, Frazier, Bonavena, Chulvalo and myself to name a few, wasted our time, if these guys are not better than us. Every group has to be better than the group before them, because they are learning from the one behind them. Now, I think the fighters of today, are bigger and stronger. However, do they fight for the same

240

reasons that we fought for? That is where the breakdown comes in. They are better, but are they sacrificing more to gain, or to get less?

I don't think you can say these guys could or couldn't match up with us. That's like saying, Joe Louis will knock Ali out. I don't think so. Ali could use the ring against Louis, but if he got in Joe's range, he had the opportunity to win. This it not taking anything away from Louis because without him, there would be no Ali.

Without Ali, there would have been none of us. Each fighter contributes something to the next generation of fighters to carry on and it's what they do with that knowledge which is totally in their hands.

I have a copy of your fight against Muhammad Ali for the Heavyweight Championship of the World. On that tape, you're being interviewed by the legendary Howard Cosell and holding your own. What are your memories of Cosell?

Howard Cosell was a tribute to the sport of boxing. He really helped promote boxing, and in the case of Muhammad Ali, he made him bigger than life. In his way, he meant well and elevated the sport. We all have faults and Howard was no different from you or me.

What made you return to boxing after 14 years of being gone?

I really wanted to see if I could do it. The desire for boxing has never faded away in my heart. Here is an old quote, "Old fighters never die, they just fade away."

Now that you are retired from boxing, how do you want your many fans to remember you?

That I was a standup guy and every time I went to the post, I gave my best.

Finally, what is the saying you live your life by?

"Respect yourself, so you can respect others".

Ron wanted to add the following to our interview:

I would really like to thank the people in charge of the Boxing Hall of Fame in Canastota, New York for their warm hospitality to me. I have always wanted to be respected by my peers, and when they gave me a standing ovation at the Banquet of Champions put on by the HOF, it answered my question, if I was respected. For this, I will always be indebted to them at the Boxing Hall of Fame.

Writers closing comments:

As everyone knows, I will always share my joy of an interview when I feel it was special. Not only was this interview special, Ron gave me one of the greatest compliments I have ever received as a boxing writer when he said, "Brad, I appreciate this. You don't know, that I bit my tongue for years after I retired the first time from boxing. You are the first person who has ever asked me these type of questions and as you can see, I have been waiting to answer them." These are the things that make this journey so wonderful for me.

Ron Lyle

Weight class: Heavyweight/Unlimited

Amateur record: 29 fights; 22+ (17 KO), 3=, 4-

Professional record: 52 fights; 44+ (32 KO), 1=, 7-

- 1971 -
+ (Apr-23-1971, Denver) A.J. Staples ko 2
+ (May-22-1971, Boston) Art Miller ko 5
+ (Jun-22-1971, Stateline) Gary Bates ko 4
+ (Jul-16-1971, New York) Edmundo Stewart ko 5
+ (Jul-24-1971, Lake Geneud) Leroy Caldwell ko 9
+ (Aug-11-1971, Las Vegas) Frank Niblett ko 7
+ (Sep-11-1971, Las Vegas) Eddie Land ko 2
+ (Oct-10-1971, Denver) Manuel Ramos 10
+ (Nov-10-1971, Las Vegas) Joe Lewis ko 3
+ (Nov-26-1971, Denver) Jack O'Halloran ko 4
+ (Dec-18-1971, Denver) Billy Drover ko 2

- 1972 -
+ (Jan-22-1972, Denver) Chuck Leslie ko 3
+ (Mar-25-1972, Denver) George Johnson ko 3
+ (May-10-1972, Las Vegas) Mel Turnbow ko 7
+ (May-25-1972, Omaha) Mike Boswell kot 9
+ (Jul-11-1972, Denver) Vicente Rondon ko 2
+ (Sep-29-1972, Denver) Buster Mathis ko 2
+ (Oct-28-1972, Denver) Luis Faustino Pires kot 3
+ (Dec-9-1972, Denver) Larry Middleton ko 3

- 1973 -
- (Feb-9-1973, New York) Jerry Quarry 12
+ (Apr-14-1973, Missoula) Bob Stallings 10
+ (May-12-1973, Denver) Gregorio Peralta 10
+ (Jun-11-1973, Philadelphia) Wendell Newton 10
+ (Jul-3-1973, Oklahoma City) Lou Bailey 10

+ (Aug-15-1973, Denver) Jose Luis Garcia ko 3
+ (Oct-4-1973, Denver) Juergen Blin ko 2
+ (Oct-31-1973, Baltimore) Larry Middleton 10
= (Nov-17-1973, Francfort) Gregorio Peralta 10

- **1974** -
+ (Mar-19-1974, Denver) Oscar Bonavena 10
+ (May-21-1974) Larry Middleton 12
+ (Jul-16-1974, Denver) Jimmy Ellis 10
+ (Sep-17-1974, Seattle) Boone Kirkman kot 8
+ (Dec-13-1974, Nouvelle-Orleans) Al Jones ko 5

- **1975** -
- (Feb-11-1975, Honolulu) Jimmy Young 10
- (May-16-1975, Las Vegas) Muhammad Ali kot 11 (World, Heavyweight)
+ (Sep-8-1975, Denver) Earnie Shavers ko 6

- **1976** -
- (Jan-24-1976, Las Vegas) George Foreman ko 5 (United States, Heavyweight)
+ (Sep-12-1976, Utica) Kevin Isaac kot 7
- (Nov-6-1976, San Francisco) Jimmy Young 12

- **1977** -
+ (Mar-20-1977, Las Vegas) Joe Bugner 12
+ (Sep-14-1977, Las Vegas) Stan Ward 10

- **1978** -
+ (Jun-3-1978, Denver) Horace Robinson retiring 8

- **1979** -
+ (Apr-6-1979, San Diego) Fili Moala ko 8
+ (May-12-1979, Las Vegas) Scott Ledoux 10

- (Dec-12-1979, Phoenix) Lynn Ball kot 2

- **1980** -
+ (Jun-19-1980, Tacoma) Al Newman kot 10
+ (Aug-23-1980, Inglewood) George O'Mara ko 10
- (Oct-24-1980, Uniondale) Gerry Cooney ko 1

- **1981-1994: inactive** -

- **1995** -
+ (Apr-7-1995, Erlanger) Bruce Johnson ko 4
+ (May-12-1995, Erlanger) Tim Pollard ko 2
+ (Jun-9-1995) Ed Strickland ko 2
+ (Aug-18-1995, Denver) Dave Slaughter kot 2

As always fight fans, keep reaching for the stars, and all your dreams can be fulfilled.

Interview conducted October 2001

A Trip Down Memory Lane...

Up Close and Personal with Legendary Singer Al Martino

When my wife Gwen called me to the phone and told me Al Martino wanted to speak with me, I had no clue what it could be about. Well, I was delighted when he said, "Brad, Jerry Vale gave me your phone number after you did the interview with him on boxing. I am a big boxing fan and wondered if you would be interested in doing an interview with me?" I told Al it would be an honor, and this turned out to be a very special interview.

While conducting our interview, I discovered that in addition to music, Al had a totally different love, and that was his love of the sport of boxing. This love materialized from his following the sport over many years, some of those during "The Golden Era" of boxing.

Martino, being in show business for more than fifty years, has met and been involved with some great fighters, which has given him tremendous insight into the sport.

As a result of having numerous hits throughout his legendary career, such as Here In My Heart, Spanish Eyes, and Daddy's Little Girl, to name just a few, Al was afforded the opportunity to travel the world and see many great fights. For the younger generation, you may remember Martino as singer Johnny Fontane, in this writer's personal favorite movie of all-time, The Godfather.

Tell me about the fighters you knew over the years and how you were involved with them?

I go back a long ways with boxing. I can remember when I was a young boy I used to listen to all of Joe Louis's fights on the radio and especially remember the one with Max Schmeling.

Later when TV came out and was just in its infancy, I was glued to it, watching the fights as well. My family would look forward to all the boxing matches and boy did we watch them. I distinctly remember watching the Rocky Graziano Vs Tony Zale fight. Rocky was a close friend of mine for many years. Rocky and I used to see each other in New York and in fact, we did a couple of shows together.

Brad, let me tell you, to be friends with these fighters was to me, one of the most gratifying and exciting ventures in my life. I was friendly with Joe Louis and of course, Rocky Marciano. Rocky and I were very close and used to room in the same hotel together in

Boston called the Logan Motel. Rocky and I used to get together in Boston and talk boxing over dinner on many a night at Mother Anna's where I used to see the Kennedy's as well. As you grow in this business you have the opportunity to meet so many of the wonderful fighters.

I have to tell you a story about Muhammad Ali who is a fan of mine. Muhammad almost bought my house in Cherry Hill, New Jersey back in about 1964 - 65. I had just built the house because as you may know, construction is my hobby which started when I was a young boy. My father, brother, and I, used to build houses. I built this wonderful house in Cherry Hill which was not a big home, but was completely surrounded by a big seven foot high wall and iron gates.

Well, one day I looked out the window and there was Muhammad Ali sitting in a car right in front of my house. He had someone knock on my door. He said "We would like to buy your house". Seconds later the big man walked in. He then said to me "I like your house a lot and I have been watching you build it. Is it for sale"? I told him that I would love to sell it to you, but it took me almost a year to build it with my own hands and sweat so I really can't sell it.

Muhammad said, "If I offer you twice as much as you paid for it will you sell it?" I said "no I just can't." What finally happened is they pulled away and I only got one more call from them. I told them I was still thinking about it. Ali eventually moved to another area close by in New Jersey where he bought a house. The funny thing now .is I should have sold it to him because when I did sell it, I didn't get very much for it.

Who, in your lifetime, do you feel is the greatest fighter of all-time?

Well, that's like asking me what's my favorite finger? When these guys become champions it's because they are the best out there. If they are the best then they have to be your favorite, in my opinion. Fighters such as Joe Louis, Muhammad Ali, and Rocky Marciano. I just can't say one is better than the other unless you put them all in the ring and the best man wins.

Brad, thinking about these guys makes me think of another funny story I would like to tell you. When I first starting singing in New York City, I wanted a job at the Copacabana nightclub. I didn't know how to go about getting it and back then, I had no one representing me.

I met this guy who really looked like a wiseguy. He told me that he could get me a job at the Copa. At that time, Jack Entratter owned the Copa and later on became famous with the Sands Hotel in Las Vegas. This is around the late 40's say 1948 or 49. He took me over to the Copa. Jack said, "Let him get up and sing a song". I did and the wiseguy asked Jack, "what did you think about my singer?"

Jack replied, "I didn't like him." So the wiseguy said, "you don't like him as a singer we will make him a fighter." Of course I couldn't fight and that never happened. That's a true story.

What is the nicest venue you have ever seen a fight at?

I would have to say Madison Square Garden. You know it hasn't been that long since big fights went on at other places like they used to have at the Garden. You always can look back and say I saw those fights at Madison Square Garden.

What era do you feel had the best fighters and why?

Well, first of all, I will answer the why. The why is television. Television was so important to boxing because it brought it forward the same way it has brought golf forward. If Tiger Woods played back in the days when Ben Hogan played, he would not have been as known. Now, the era would be the late 40's, 50's, and 60's when I really went out of my way to see the fights.

Who are you top three favorite fighters of all-time and why?

Well Ali is on top. He was the most exciting, charismatic, articulate, and funny. He could come up with some of the funniest lines. Next, Rocky Marciano. Rocky was just so tough. Finally, Sugar Ray Robinson who was a good friend of mine. He got into show business and we worked the room together at the Latin Quarter up in Boston. He really was a great fighter and had a good act.

Are there any fighters today who remind you of the old days?

I would say Oscar Delahoya a little bit. You see what it is Brad, television is so different today than when it came out of its infancy. When I watched Rocky Graziano fight Tony Zale, that was the first time I saw a live fight. It left an impression that you never forget. Now, TV is different today, because you don't see many fights on it like in the old days.

Everything is Pay Per View. This really makes a difference. I wish they would show the old fights here like they do in Germany. Once a week, they show the old fights and it's exciting to see them. They need to show them in the states and I am sure they can, because the networks own fight films.

What is the greatest fight you have ever seen and why?

Well, the greatest fight I saw, and it's not because of the fight, but because it involved two great champions, one ex-champion and one soon-to-be champion, was Rocky Marciano Vs Joe Louis. I was glued to the TV set. In my heart and believe it, I wanted Joe to win. I didn't want Joe to lose, even though I liked Rocky and we were friends. In my mind Brad, I said "Hey Rocky pass this one up or let Joe win." It broke my heart to see Joe lose.

If I was Rocky, I would not have taken the fight. Here, I will give you an idea. I made a record called Here in My Heart back in the early 50's. I recorded the song, produced it, and paid for it myself. It went on the air in Philadelphia and started to become a big hit.

Well, RCA Records heard about it and called Mario Lanza. At that time, Mario was the biggest star in the world and they told him to cover my record. They told him I was going to have a big hit with it, but if he did it, it would knock me right out of the box.

When I heard about that, I called Mario and told him this was my big opportunity to break into show business with a hit record. I asked him would he consider passing on covering Here in My Heart? You know what he said? He said, "Well why not? You're from Philadelphia and I am too. I will tell RCA that I will not do it." That was real CLASS! That's what I wish happened in the Louis fight.

Finally, in all your years as a boxing fan, what is the most brutal knockout you have ever seen?

I would say Rocky Marciano vs. Jersey Joe Walcott I. That was some punch Rocky landed and those close ups were something else. I remember pictures of Walcott's face being distorted.

For more information about Al Martino you can visit his website at www.almartino.com

As always fight fans, keep reaching for the stars, and all your dreams can be fulfilled.

Interview conducted May 2000

Big Heart...

Up Close and Personal with Junior Welterweight Del "The Hatchet" Matchett

One of the wonderful things about being able to cover boxing matches is the chance to meet so many wonderful young men and women. These men and women have dedicated their hearts and souls to boxing. One such young man is, Del "The Hatchet" Matchett.

This young man has touched my life with his big heart, and I consider him a younger brother - not by blood, but by choice. I recently sat down with Matchett in my home office and conducted a special interview. We had so much in common, including being big movie buffs and most importantly, huge fans of my favorite fighter of all-time, Aaron "The Hawk" Pryor.

When Del and I finished our interview, we sat and watched old tapes of Aaron that Del had never seen before. Matchett, being the great technician in the ring that he is, really appreciated my buddy Aaron's unbelievable talent.

In fact, I gave Del a thrill of a life-time when I called Aaron and let him talk to him. Aaron, as always, was kind to Del and offered him any assistance that he could to further his career.

What inspired you to get into boxing?

I first got into boxing because it was a neighborhood thing. My cousin took me to the boxing gym. Since I really didn't play any sports in High School, such as basketball or football, it gave me plenty of time for boxing.

What are your observations of the fight game such as contract negotiations, pay and getting fights?

I am easygoing and don't complain about the negotiations, so it makes it easier to complete them. As far as getting fights, it's hard to find opponents who will push me to the next level, but at the same time, be on my level. The pay cuts, I have no problems with because there are things that I just can't do, that the good people around me take care of. They deserve to get paid what they do.

What are your words of wisdom to the young fighter just lacing up the gloves?

When you get into the pro ranks you must be serious about it. In the amateurs I played around when it came to training. Right now, I am always in the gym and love to train. By taking this seriously, it has built my confidence and taken my boxing skills to another level.

How was your transition from the amateurs to the pros?

It was fairly easy because a lot of people in the Maryland and Washington, DC area knew me from my amateur days and in fact, many were approaching me to go with them when I turned pro.

If you could emulate any fighter who would it be and why?

To be honest Brad, I take different things from many fighters, such as Oscar Delahoya, where he studies an opponent. I like how Trinidad stays focused throughout a fight. Then of course, there is Roy Jones, JR. who is so awkward, you can't tell where he is coming from with his style. Roy is so relaxed and confident in the ring and that is also how Muhammad Ali was. So, there is a group of fighters with qualities I would like to emulate.

How long have you followed boxing?

Brad, to be honest, I never really have followed boxing except for the really big fights.

Who are your top three favorite fighters of all-time and why?

Sugar Ray Robinson because of the great technician he was in the ring. Roy Jones, JR. because I have never seen a fighter be in control of a fight the way he is. Finally, Sugar Shane Mosley because of speed, power and aggressiveness.

Who do you pick in the upcoming Oscar Delahoya vs "Sugar" Shane Mosley match?

I have to go with Mosley. I feel someone is going to get knocked out in this fight and I think Shane is the one who is going to knock out Oscar.

What is the greatest fight you have ever seen and why?

Well I don't follow much boxing, but out of the fights that I have seen, I would say Erik Morales vs Marco Antonio Barrera. There was so much action in that one and Marco should have gotten the decision.

Do you favor a mandatory retirement fund for all boxers and if so, how would you like to see it accomplished?

I think there should definitely be one Brad. It's like the full-time job I work. I put money away in a 401K. We should have insurance, as well. I know the risk is high for an insurance company, but we need to do something about insurance, too. I feel the same as you do Brad, with paying in at day one of your pro career.

What went through your mind the very first time you stepped into the ring as a professional?

I felt very comfortable in there as I did when I was an amateur. One funny thing I do recall Brad, is my first opponent had a beard and our faces rubbed up against each other and it felt so funny. It dawned on me, that we were not wearing any headgear as we did in the amateurs.

Even though you don't have the opportunity to fight in 15- round matches today, would you like to see them re-instated?

Yes I would. If they could fight that long in the old days then why not today? I was really into 15-round fights back in the day. I know they dropped the rounds because of safety reasons, but the 13th - 15th were the true championship rounds to me.

What do you think females in boxing?
They are getting paid way too much. I wish I could get paid as much as them. The talent is not there in the female fighters. From what I see, it's more entertainment than boxing.

Do you have a particular location you want to fight at one day and why?
I want to fight in Las Vegas because I have never been on the West Coast to fight and everyone always goes to Las Vegas to see the big fights.

How many fights do you feel a fighter should have before he challenges for a world title?
I feel he should have 20 fights. I can only answer this in regards to me and feel the way my career is going, I will be ready to challenge for a world title after 20 fights.

How do you feel about boxing going back to the old days when there was only one title and one real world champion?
I think it should be one title because you're the King of the Hill. That is one heck of an accomplishment to be the one world champion out there in your respective weight class.

After you have achieved, or attempted to achieve all of your goals in boxing, how would

you like your fans from the start to remember you?

Remember me as a person who got the glory from Jesus! In addition, a fighter who came in the ring always ready to fight.

Finally, what is the saying that you try to live by?

"I can show you better then I can tell you".

Del MATCHETT
Nickname: "The Hatchet"

Weight class: Junior Welterweight/140 lbs

Professional record: 20 fights; 16+ (8 KO), 1=, 3-

- **1998 -**
+ (Sep-16-1998, Glenarden) John LOCKETT kot 4
+ (Nov-3-1998, Woodlawn) Donnie PARKER kot 1
+ (Nov-24-1998, Washington) Terrell DAVIS kot 2
+ (Dec-16-1998, Glenarden) Ben WAGABA 4

- **1999 -**
+ (Feb-5-1999, Pikesville) George BEST kot 4
+ (Apr-9-1999, Waldorf) Kelvin DALY kot 5
= (May-13-1999, Glen Burnie) Kenito DRAKE 8
- (Jun-25-1999, Ledyard) Anthony CHASE 4
+ (Sep-27-1999, East Saint-Louis) Germaine SANDERS 8
+ (Nov-19-1999, Washington) Quentin WILLIAMS 6

- **2000 -**
+ (Jan-27-2000, Glen Burnie) Awel ABDULAI 8

+ (Mar-1-2000, Woodlawn) <u>Cornell SHINHOLSTER</u>
ko 2
+ (Mar-23-2000, Glen Burnie) <u>Tyrone JACKSON</u>
<u>II</u> kot 3
+ (May-11-2000, Glen Burnie) <u>Damone WRIGHT</u> 8

As always fight fans, keep reaching for the
stars, and all your dreams can be fulfilled.

Interview conducted June 2000

Leaving a Legacy...

Up Close and Personal with WBC Welterweight Champion Sugar Shane Mosley

On June 17, 2000, a new gunslinger came to town by the name of Shane. He was unlike the legendary gunslinger Shane played by Alan Ladd in my all-time favorite Western, "Shane". He didn't have Brandon De Wilde to run behind him yelling, "Come Back Shane"! This Shane did not ride out into the sunset, and boxing couldn't be happier about his stay. Of course, by now you know the Shane in this piece is none other than, Sugar Shane Mosley.

About four months prior to his bout with Oscar Delahoya, I wrote a piece, and talked about him on subsequent TV shows I did where I said he would beat Oscar by a decision. Well, my prediction rang true, and if they fight again, I will go with Shane once again.

Now with that said, Shane Mosley and Oscar Delahoya are both to be commended on giving diehard boxing fans such as myself, a great fight where you saw two warriors give you their all.

I recently caught up with Shane at his training camp in Big Bear Mountains, CA where he was training for his upcoming title defense against Antonio Diaz.

What inspired you to get into boxing?
At a young age, I used to go to the gym with my Father and really started liking the sport. My fondness for it grew and still goes till this day.

Being very close to my late father, I really appreciate the relationship I see between you and your father especially in the boxing arena. When so many other Father & Son relationships in boxing fail, what keeps yours so strong?
Its foundation is based on mutual respect and trust between two people. Being that he is my father, I trust all his decisions. We really have a great communication between us.

First of all I want to commend you on your huge win over Oscar Delahoya. It was a victory I wrote about 4 months before it ever happened, picking you to win a decision. What went through your mind when they started announcing the decision and you heard Oscar was up on one score card?
I knew that I beat him fair and square. With this in my mind, when I heard the one judge gave him the UPS on me, I said to myself, "They are going to try and give it to him". I knew in my heart, along with all the fans around the world, I won that fight. That alone was a victory.

What is your motivation to continue to endure all the hard things a boxer must go

through to achieve all the well deserved things you have?

I strive for excellence and want to be the best in the boxing ring everytime out. I want the fans to know that everytime out, they are going to get a great fight and their monies worth. Bottom line: I want to be the King of the Hill.

For the young amateur boxers out there, what are your words of wisdom to them?

Again, as I said earlier, strive for excellence. Never second guess yourself and always have confidence in yourself.

If you had a chance on one special night to be in the ring with any fighter from any era, who would it be, and what do you think the outcome would be?

I would pick Sugar Ray Leonard. I feel that my speed and ability to outwit him would make me the winner in that match by taking a great decision.

Who are your three favorite fighters of all-time and why?

First, Sugar Ray Robinson. He had great thinking ability, power, and was just a masterful boxer. Second, Muhammad Ali. I loved how he boasted about himself. He would make predictions and then fulfill them.

Finally, Sugar Ray Leonard. He was like the Golden Boy, Oscar Delahoya. He won the Gold in the Olympics and just had the same type of glamour. Also he had just incredible charisma to go along with his outstanding skills in the ring.

What is the greatest fight you have ever seen and why?

Marvin Hagler vs Tommy Hearns. They just gave everything that they had. Marvin just had more willpower and better legs to survive the onslaught that Tommy brought to him. Tommy should have boxed him and I think there might have been a different outcome.

Do you favor a mandatory retirement fund for all boxers and if so, how would you like to see it accomplished?

I really do favor a fund, Brad. I would like to see it done, but it is difficult because of the large differences, such as what I make, and say, a club fighter. Lots of fighters at my level would not want to put money into a pot to help those other guys. However, I do feel that we at the top should put a percentage in to help out other fighters, and I would be willing to put money into it.

They in turn would have to put money in, as well. Promoters should put a percentage into the fund, too. Finally, the sanctioning bodies should have a retirement fund set up for the fighters and along with this fund, they need to have health insurance.

What super fights, such as when Hearns fought Hagler, do you feel are out there for you?

I think Oscar, the second time around, will be a super fight when I clean out the welterweight division, possibly the winner of Vargas - Trinidad if I move up. If the price and the hype are right, I am there. Brad, I want to fight the best out there!

When you finally do hang up the gloves, what do you want you're legion of fans to remember you for?

That I was a good guy who gave back to the sport of boxing. It would be nice to also be remembered that I was a great fighter of this era. Brad, I love this sport with all my heart and always give it 100%.

Finally, what is the saying you live your life by?

"You live by the gun, you die by the gun".

Shane would like to add the following to our interview.

I just want to say to all the fans out there to watch my upcoming fight on November 4, 2000 with Antonio Diaz. I am going to put on a spectualar show. Currently, I am really working out hard, here at Big Bear to get in shape.

Finally, I really want to thank all my wonderful fans out there. I look forward to seeing all of you in New York next month.

Shane MOSLEY
Nickname: "Sugar"

Weight Class: Welterweight/147 Lbs

Top of Form 1
Amateur record: 242 fights; 230+ 12-
1988: United States Featherweight:
- Kelcie Banks
1988: Golden Gloves Lightweight:
- Tonga Mc Clain
1988: Olympic Trials Lightweight:
- Richard Armstrong
1989: United States Junior Lightweight:

+ Steve Johnston
+ Rodney Garnett
1989: W.C. Juniors San Juan Lightweight:
- Anibal Acevedo (P-R) points
1990: United States Junior Lightweight:
+ Patrice Brooks
1990: Goodwill Games Lightweight:
- Artur Grigorjan (URSS)
1991: World Cup Junior Welterweight:
- Candelario Duvergel (Cub)
1992: United States Junior Welterweight
+ Stevie Johnston points
1992: Olympic Trials Worcester Junior Welterweight
+ Orlando Hollis points
- Vernon Forrest points
Professional record: 35 fights; 35+ (32 KO)
1997-1999: I.B.F. Lightweight
2000: W.B.C. Welterweight

- **1993** -
+ (Feb-11-1993, Hollywood) Greg Puente ko 5
+ (Apr-24-1993, Inglewood) Arnulfo Villa ko 1
+ (Jul-21-1993, Reseda) Pey Castillo ko 1
+ (Aug-25-1993, Hollywood) Roberto Urias ko 5
+ (Sep-27-1993, Inglewood) Miguel Pena ko 1
+ (Oct-25-1993, Inglewood) Juan Aranda ko 2
+ (Dec-6-1993, Inglewood) Paulino Gonzalez ko 2

- **1994** -
+ (Jan-20-1994, Irvine) Francisco Rodriguez ko 2
+ (Feb-4-1994, Oxnard) Lorenzo Garcia ko 5
+ (Mar-26-1994, Pomona) Oscar Lopez 10
+ (Apr-29-1994, Santa Cruz) Lorenzo Garcia kot 3

265

+ (Jun-30-1994, Irvine) John Bryant ko 8
+ (Jul-24-1994, Los Angeles) Narciso Valenzuela ko 5
+ (Aug-6-1994, Pomona) Mauro Gutierrez kot 9
+ (Sep-9-1994, Los Angeles) Louis Ramirez kot 10
+ (Nov-12-1994, Santa Cruz) Jose Luis Madrid ko 4

- **1995** -
+ (Apr-12-1995, Woodland Hills) Raul Hernandez ko 2
+ (Jul-21-1995, Anaheim) Mauricio Aceves ko 1

- **1996** -
+ (Jan-23-1996, Biloxi) Mike Bryan kot 1
+ (Nov-1-1996, Indio) Ramon Felix kot 1
+ (Dec-21-1996, Uncasville) Joseph Murray retiring 3

- **1997** -
+ (Feb-6-1997, Beverly Hills) Elias Quiroz ko 2
+ (Apr-9-1997, Westmont) Mike Smith ko 4
+ (Aug-2-1997, Uncasville) Philip Holiday 12 (I.B.F., Lightweight)
+ (Nov-25-1997, El Paso) Manuel Gomez ko 11 (I.B.F., Lightweight)

- **1998** -
+ (Feb-6-1998, Uncasville) Demetrio Ceballos ko 8 (I.B.F., Lightweight)
+ (May-9-1998, Atlantic City) John-John Molina kot 8 (I.B.F., Lightweight)
+ (Jun-27-1998, Philadelphia) Wilfredo Ruiz ko 5 (I.B.F., Lightweight)
+ (Sep-22-1998, New York) Eduardo Morales kot 5 (I.B.F., Lightweight)

+ (Nov-14-1998, Ledyard) Jesse Leija kot 9 (I.B.F., Lightweight)

- 1999 -
+ (Jan-9-1999, Pensacola) Golden Johnson ko 7 (I.B.F., Lightweight)
+ (Apr-17-1999, Indio) John Brown kot 9 (I.B.F., Lightweight)
+ (Sep-25-1999, Temecula) Wilfredo Rivera ko 10

- 2000 -
+ (Jan-22-2000, Las Vegas) Willy Wise kot 3
+ (Jun-17-2000, Los Angeles) Oscar De La Hoya 12 (W.B.C., Welterweight)

As always fight fans, keep reaching for the stars, and all your dreams can be fulfilled.

Interview conducted October 2000

Road Warrior...

Up Close and Personal with Lightweight Contender Sue Mullett

On April 26, 2002, at the Palace Indian Gaming Center located in Lemoore, California, current WIBF number #7 ranked Jenifer Alcorn (12-0, 8 KO's) takes on WIBF #9 ranked, Susan Mullett (7-6, 4 KO's), for the vacant WIBF Lightweight Championship of the World.

This will be Mullett's second shot at a world title in her last two fights. In her first attempt at a world title, she faced current champion The "Raging Beauty" Isra Girgrah for the vacant UBA Lightweight Championship. Mullett put up a game effort, but was stopped within four rounds.

At that fight, I had the opportunity to interview both Mullett and Girgrah at an exclusive Fightnews press conference. Mullett showed true class and, it's finally a pleasure to bring her solo to my column.

How is training going for your upcoming fight?

Training is going very well. I'm doing a lot of conditioning drills that my trainer, Sam Jones, wants and I have some great sparring partners.

What adjustments have you made that fans will see since your last attempt at a world title?

Going into my last fight, which was over a year ago, I had some physical problems that I was having trouble adjusting to, or compensating for. My conditioning was good, but it affected my mental conditioning some.

I never stopped training in the past year, but Sam has had me change some of my routines and the results have been great.

Any predictions for your fight?

I don't like to make predictions, but I am going to California and bring back the title. That is why I train and that is where my career has been aimed. I feel very fortunate to be given not just one, but two chances at a world title.

How long have you followed boxing?

For about as long as I can remember. I started in martial arts when I was 8 and into self defense with full contact training when I was 12. My instructor was a former AAU North

American and National Champion and I've been hooked ever since.

Do you feel that, since you first turned professional in women's boxing, the sport has moved forward? .

I think it has moved forward in some ways. There are many more skilled female boxers out there and they are finally getting some respect and recognition as boxers, not just 'female boxers'. Unfortunately, the same promoters that hurt 'boxing' also hurt 'women's boxing'. The sport has taken a step backward in that regard.

The early fighters fought any and everybody. Isra Girgrah fought one of the better fighters, Deirdre Gogarty, in her pro debut and went on to fight Christy Martin in a fight I thought she won. Jane Couch, Marischa Sjauw, Kathy Collins and many others, have fought just about all comers. I don't mean to leave out any names, but there are too many to list. The computer rankings on the women's boxing page shows an opponent rating that will tell who has been in with the best. Now, just like the men, there are many 'fighters' with 'unblemished' records, but no shine to them. Some promoter backs them and brings in 'professional opponents' to build their records. I don't have anything against building a fighter - not a record, but you have to step up the competition at some point, not just feed them punching bags.

Also, there is still not enough money in women's boxing. It is very tough when a champion has to have a full time job and train on top of that. It has come a long way, but there is a long way to go.

What inspired you to get into boxing?

Many factors entered into the decision, but the driving force was to find out how good, or bad I was. It is very hard to tell when you work out with guys 40-100 pounds heavier all the time.

What are your words of wisdom to the young ladies out there who want to pursue a professional boxing career?

You can do whatever you want. It is up to you. But you need the right people to guide and help you. Find the best people you can with which to surround yourself. You need a team that can take you as far as you can go and you have to be able to trust them to make decisions in your best interest. Then, go for it.

If you could emulate any fighter who would it be and why?

I have two. They are the two people who have trained me, in life and in the ring. Pat Malone, an AAU National and North American Champion and undefeated as a professional boxer - as good a friend and instructor a person can wish for, since long ago.

Sam Jones, my professional boxing coach, great friend, and an undefeated professional boxer. They both have tremendous fighting skills and a never-quit attitude, in the ring and in life.

Who are your three favorite fighters of all-time and why?

Danny "Little Red" Lopez - I never thought he had the best skills, but his heart took him to the top and made him beat 'better' fighters. He had a 'never say die' attitude.

Roberto Duran - great skill and never stopped throwing punches. Third place is up for grabs, Arguello, Hagler, Hearns, Pryor, Palamino. I love them all.

What is the greatest fight you have ever seen and why?

That is another hard one to answer. Fights are great in different ways. I think the Thrilla in Manilla was probably the most exciting, and the ultimate test of courage by both Muhammad Ali and Joe Frazier.

What do you consider your best weapon in the ring?

Combinations, I don't like to rely on one weapon, there is always room for follow-up.

What went through your mind the very first time you stepped in the ring as a professional fighter?

I still remember the little details. I was nervous, anxious, ready to go, but Sam kept me settled. He wouldn't let my nerves take away my fight game. The last thing Sam said before the bell rang for the 1st round was "don't throw your right until you hit her with your jab." She was taller with a longer reach, which I followed to a tee. I never heard the crowd, but I heard Sam say "3", which called for a hook to follow my right. The fight ended shortly after.

Do you favor a mandatory retirement fund for all boxers and if so, how would you like to see it accomplished?

I would like to see boxers taken care of much better. A retirement fund would be hard to set up. As for "all boxers", some fight a few times and get out, some without backing, become professional opponents with terrible records, but make more than a lot of others. Maybe a percentage of a fund paid, based on fights/rounds boxed.

One idea I think has merit, would be a minimum per-round pay and then a percentage of the gate/profit set aside for the boxers, with a percentage set aside for boxers who suffer career-ending or disabling injuries in the ring. The way it is now, the promoters make a killing (I know, not always and not on small club fights). Also, many factors would have to be, considered but not enough time or room, here.

When you finally hang up the gloves, how do you want your fans to remember you?
I hope they remember me as someone who always gave her best in and out of the ring.

Finally, what is the saying you live your life by?
"Any journey starts with the first step".

Susan Mullett
Weight class: Lightweight/135 lbs

Professional record: 13 fights; 7+ (4 KO), 6-

- 1997 -
+ (Nov-26-1997, Youngstown) Teara SANDERS kot 1

- 1998 -
- (Mar-3-1998) Vicki WOODS 4
+ (Mar-27-1998) Teara SANDERS ko 2

- (Jun-30-1998, Atlantic City) Ulia VOSKOBOINIK tko5

- 1999 -
- (Jan-22-1999, Cleveland) Sabrina HALL 4
- (Jul-10-1999, Allentown) Maureen HENRY 4
+ (Sep-17-1999, Parma) Debbie WADE 4
+ (Nov-5-1999, Parma) Brenda RODRIGUEZ 4

- 2000 -
+ (Jan-29-2000) Heather SHOFFNER KO3
+ (Mar-24-2000, Parma) Kristin ALLEN kot 1
+ (Apr-17-2000) Theresa GAULDEN 4
- (Sep-15-2000, Atlantic City) Isra GIRGRAH 6

- 2001 -
- (Jan-12-2001, Atlantic City) Isra GIRGRAH kot 4

As always fight fans, keep reaching for the stars, and all your dreams can be fulfilled.

Interview conducted April 2002

Old School...

Up Close and Personal with Former WBA Light Heavyweight Champion of the World Eddie Mustafa Muhammad

In what clearly was a magical time in boxing there were fighters such as Eddie Mustafa Muhammad who ruled among many of the top 10 light heavyweights in the world. If you doubt this statement, I can back it up by fact.

Fact— Every top notch light heavyweight contender who I have interviewed or spoke with from Yaqui Lopez, Murray Sutherland, Vonzell Johnson, and Matthew Saad Muhammad to name just a few, always throws Eddie's name into the mix of their respected division that ruled in the mid 70's to early 80's.

Fact—With all that great talent, Muhammad rose to the top by winning the WBA Light Heavyweight Title from another warrior who doesn't get enough credit, Marvin Johnson. This great win secures his place in boxing history.

In a division today, that has Roy Jones, JR. at the top, and no one really in sight to beat him who currently is ranked as a light heavyweight, it makes a true boxing fan like me wish Roy were around in Muhammad's era, to show how great he really is. Many will say Roy could beat them as well. That may be so, but what dream matches could have been made!

First of all, for all the readers who bring up your name when the light heavyweight division was full of so many outstanding fighters who, on any night, could have been champion, what are you doing today?

I am a teacher of the art of self defense. First though, I am trying to spread the word of Islam because people have to know what Islam means. Islam, as you know means peace. The people who did those attacks on the Pentagon, New York City and finally, the plane that fell in Pennsylvania, is not what is taught in Islam. It's up to guys like myself, Muhammad Ali and other prominent Muslims to take a stand and let them know that is not true Islam to take innocent lives.

To this day, I feel a strong need to go out and continue to spread the correct word which I do. This is what I am currently doing. (**** (Writer's note: In a world that has greatly changed since September 11, 2001, one needs to listen to this heartfelt answer and take solace in knowing that we all must live together in this world, peacefully).

In 1971, you faced former undisputed Middleweight Champion Vito Antuofermo in the amateurs. What are your recollections of him and could you see that he had the talent to go on to be a champion?

No question in my mind Brad. Vito defines the saying, "What you see is what you get." He was a great, great competitor who was not an exceptional boxer, but his thing was stamina and constant pressure. He always threw punches in abundance. The only downfall for him, was he cut so easy. Bottom Line: I had no doubt, based on his fierce competitiveness, that he would be a champion.

On March 11, 1977, you won a big fight against Matthew Franklin who would go on to become Matthew Saad Muhammad and the Light Heavyweight Champion of the World. What do you recall about this fight?

I can recall that Saad hit me the hardest I have ever been hit in my life. In fact, he hit me so hard that in the first round, when he knocked me down, I split my trunks. We were on TV on channel five at that time. I think it was called Metro Media back then. It's ironic you asked about Vito earlier because he fought Eugene "Cyclone" Hart on the same card. They ran into the back and put Vito's trunks on over my trunks in the corner. That really was a funny experience, Brad.

On October 19, 1977, you reached the crowning moment of any fighters career when you earned the chance to challenge for the title. In that fight, you faced tough Champion, Victor Galindez. One thing you have in common with another warrior from your era who I interviewed, Yaqui Lopez, is that you both dropped highly disputed decisions to him. I feel both of you beat him and should have had your hands raised as the new champions. Why do you think decisions always seemed to go his way when he was clearly beaten?

I fought him in Turin Italy and that really was a hometown advantage for him since he was promoted from that area. Going into that fight, I knew I could beat him. My training and confidence in myself was very high at that time. I can remember, Victor and I were at a press conference where he would always try and get the best of his opponent. When we were done, we both had to go to the men's room, which he went in first. I went in behind and closed the door. I then told him, "I am going to kick your ASS come Saturday and you may not understand what I am saying, but you understand my facial expressions". Just some of my recollections of the whole fight.

On October 13, 1978, you traveled to Rahway State Prison to face former light heavyweight contender James Scott who you dropped a decision to. What are your recollections of Scott and fighting in a prison?

He was a great, conditioned fighter and I had no problems going into the prison to fight him because I was the number one contender. I didn't have to fight him, but I did because he felt he was the best in the world. I wanted to prove who really was. I had seen him fight some other times at the prison and I really knew I could beat him. Brad, I took this guy too lightly and he beat me fair and square.

On March 31, 1980, shot number two comes for your chance at the Light Heavyweight Title, and this time you faced very tough Marvin Johnson. In a great match, you knocked out Johnson to secure your place in boxing history as a world champion. What do you recollect about that fight?

I remember it well because it was a four fight title card. It was the most watched boxing card on TV up until that time. The card had "Big" John Tate vs. Mike Weaver for the WBA Heavyweight Title, Larry Holmes vs. Leroy Jones for the WBC Heavyweight Title, Sugar Ray Leonard vs. Davey "Boy" Green for Ray's title and of course Marvin Johnson and me for his title. 9:00 PM, the fight was on and I always thought, how ironic that Marvin and I shared the same room on the Olympic team and now we are fighting each other for his belt.

I knew I had to bring my lunch because I was going to be there for a little while with Marvin. I take my hat off to him because he is a great competitor and comes to fight, which really made it easier for me. I showed them all what I was made of, especially in my body punching and just everything, I did on that night.

What was it like to hear, "And the new Light Heavyweight Champion of the World"?

It was a blessing and a relief to me. I knew when I first starting boxing, and this is not being braggadocios, that it was destined for me to become a champion.

After making two successful defenses of your belt, you faced Michael Spinks and lost your title on a 15 round decision. What do you recollect about this fight and just how good was Spinks as a fighter?

First of all, people didn't know I was in the hospital for a lot of my preparation for that fight because I threw my back out. When I fought Renaldo Snipes, I left the hospital, fought him, and went back into the hospital to only come out again to fight Spinks.

I am not taking anything away from Michael because I really think he is a real decent person and a great, great fighter. But if I was a hundred percent, there would be no way he could have beat me.

On December 11, 1981, you fought on a boxing card that took place in Nassau, Bahamas. Many may not even know about that card, but it involved the legendary Muhammad Ali, in what would be his last fight. He dropped a 10 round decision to Trevor Berbick. What was that whole atmosphere like?

Brad, Ali and I are real close, like family. I would never tell him to retire because it is basically up to him or anybody to decide on their own. It was not a sad occasion, but we knew that you cannot do this forever because this is a young man's sport. All we can do while we are there, is leave an impression for the younger guys coming up the ranks. That is what Ali did for me by just being with him and hanging out.

I give a lot of credit and thanks to Muhammad Ali during my run for the title. He let me stay in his camp for free and we sparred a tremendous amount of rounds together. By being around him for about three years, it took me to another level, boosting my confidence and skills to the highest plateau.

Brad, on that night it really was magical because we saw the end of a great era because Ali transcended boxing, which is something he happened to do. God put him on earth to be a great ambassador, to not just black people, but ALL PEOPLE. Finally, I must say, I learned my humbleness from him, what to do and how to handle life by being with this great man.

I always get a kick when a fighter has a walk-on or an acting role in a movie. Many may not know this, but you played yourself in Body and Soul, the 1981 remake of the 1947 great boxing flick that starred the late, John Garfield. The remake also had Muhammad Ali in it playing himself. What was that set like?

It was so much fun. You had Leon Issac Kennedy and Jayne Kennedy with us hanging out on the set. We did our work and it was a ball.

On December 21, 1985, you again challenged for the IBF Light Heavyweight Title held by then champion, Slobodan Kacar. You dropped a 15 round decision. Kacar is a fighter who you never hear about today. What do you recollect about this fight and Kacar as a fighter?

I have to be realistic with you, like I have always been. I almost killed him with my body shots. After the fight, all of the participants went to a dinner from the event. Kacar went to the event for a very short time and they had to rush him to the hospital because he had internal bleeding. If you look at his record, he didn't fight for about a year because he was healing from our fight.

Brad, I feel the decision should have gone to me easily, but both times I fought overseas in championship bouts, I got robbed on decisions. As a fighter, he was a good amateur and won a gold medal for Yugoslavia. As a professional he was OK. He was never the same after our fight.

Who are your three favorite fighters of all-time and why?

First, Sugar Ray Robinson. He did it all in the ring and was the blueprint for all of us

to become, with things like hooking off the
jab, backup punching and so much more. Number
two, but really tied at number one, is
Muhammad Ali. He transcended boxing and really
was a Man of All Seasons. Finally, a tie
between Joe Louis and Jack Johnson.

Johnson was so controversial in his day, but
he walked the walk and talked the talk. All
guys should do this. Louis, for the simple
reason he was a credit not just to his race,
but the human race by the way he represented
himself in his athletic accomplishments.

**What is the greatest fight you have ever
seen and why?**

I have a tie. Ron Lyle vs. George Foreman.
That fight was action packed and each man got
knocked down to get back up and knock the
other down. That is what fans come to see. My
other one, which is a tie, was Bruce Curry vs.
Monroe Brooks. Brooks was winning the entire
fight and I think it was the last minute in
the ninth round, Curry knocked him out with a
left hook, out of nowhere. You could have
counted to 500 and he was still out.

**Do you favor a mandatory retirement fund for
all boxers and if so, how would you like to
see it accomplished?**

That's happening now. I am involved with
doing this with my good friend Linda Hawkins
who contacted me, along with Akbar Salaam and
Mike Tyson, who are the catalysts for doing
this retirement fund. We started about six
months ago on this. It will be one, across the
board, for everybody.

**Since you have found great success as a
trainer, what are your words of wisdom to the**

many ex- fighters who would like to follow in your footsteps?

The reason I have had success with some of the fighters I am involved with is because I don't try to make them fight like I used to fight. I take what they bring me and add on to it. You always have to keep adding till they find themselves.

Now that you are retired, at least as a former world champion from boxing, how do you want your fans to remember you?

When the going got tough, I handled my business. At times, I came up on the losing end even though there were a couple of times I should have won. If I would have killed the guy overseas, I still couldn't have gotten the decision. I always gave everything I had in the ring.

Finally, what is the saying you live your life by?

"Do unto others as you would have done unto you".

**Eddie Mustafa Muhammad
(AKA Eddie GREGORY)
Nickname: "The Flame"**

Weight Class: Light Heavyweight/175 lbs

Amateur record: 1971: Golden Gloves New York Welterweight:
+ Vito Antuofermo
Professional record: 59 fights; 50+ (39 KO), 1=, 8-
1980-1981: W.B.A. Light Heavyweight

- **1972** -

+ (Sep-15-1972, New York) Dave Wyatt ko 4
+ (Sep-16-1972, Boston) Jose Pagon ko 1
+ (Sep-29-1972, New York) Pete Pagon ko 3

- **1973** -
+ (Feb-1-1973, North Bergen) Percy Hayles ko 1
+ (May-17-1973, North Bergen) Billy Wilson 6
+ (Jul-9-1973, New York) Jose Anglada 8
+ (Sep-24-1973, Philadelphia) Elwood Townsend ko 1
- (Dec-3-1973, New York) Radames Cabrera 10

- **1974** -
+ (Apr-8-1974, New York) William Classen 8
= (May-10-1974, Marseille) Max Cohen 10
+ (Aug-26-1974, New York) Eugene Hart ko 4
+ (Nov-25-1974, New York) Mario Rosa ko 8

- **1975** -
+ (Jan-14-1975, Philadelphia) Steve Smith ko 4
+ (Apr-28-1975, Philadelphia) Don Cobbs ko 2
+ (Jun-16-1975, Philadelphia) Len Harden ko 10
- (Aug-18-1975, Philadelphia) Benny Briscoe 10

- **1976** -
+ (Mar-8-1976, New York) Hildo Silva ko 7
+ (Apr-29-1976, Kingston) Dino Walker ko 6
+ (Jun-28-1976, New York) Otis Gordon ko 4
+ (Jul-14-1976, Philadelphia) Lee Barber ko 4
+ (Oct-1-1976, New York) Jimmy Owens kot 10
+ (Oct-29-1976, New York) Frank Davila ko 2

- **1977** -
+ (Jan-18-1977, New York) John Wilburn ko 3

+ (Mar-11-1977, Philadelphia) Matthew Franklin 10

+ (Sep-16-1977, Wilmington) Eddie Phillips ko 4

- (Oct-19-1977, Turin) Victor Galindez 15 (W.B.A., Lightheavyweight)

- 1978 -

+ (Feb-15-1978, Las Vegas) Jesse Burnett kot 10

+ (Mar-12-1978, Bamako) Ba Sounkalo 10

+ (Apr-14-1978, Fort Lauderdale) Nat Gates ko 6

+ (Jun-2-1978, Jersey City) Ray Elson ko 2

+ (Jun-14-1978, White Plains) Ed Turner ko 4

+ (Aug-18-1978, Newark) Chuck Warfield ko 1

+ (Sep-6-1978, White Plains) James Dixon ko 1

- (Oct-13-1978, Rahway) James Scott 12

- 1979 -

+ (Jan-26-1979, New York) David Conteh kot 8

+ (Feb-26-1979, New York) Pat Cuillo 10

+ (Jul-10-1979, Atlantic City) Lee Royster ko 5

+ (Jul-16-1979, New York) Fred Brown kot 3

+ (Aug-31-1979, Long Island) Johnny Wilburn ko 1

+ (Nov-28-1979, Hauppauge) Kid Samson kot 4

- 1980 -

+ (Mar-31-1980, Knoxville) Marvin Johnson kot 11 (W.B.A., Light Heavyweight)

+ (Jul-20-1980, Mc Afee) Jerry Martin kot 5 (W.B.A, Light Heavyweight)

+ (Nov-28-1980, Los Angeles) Rudy Koopmans injury 4 (W.B.A., Light Heavyweight)

- 1981 -

- (May-17-1981, Atlantic City) Renaldo Snipes 10
- (Jul-18-1981, Atlantic City) Michael Spinks 15 (W.B.A., Light Heavyweight)
+ (Dec-11-1981, Nassau) Michael Hardin kot 8

- 1982 -
+ (Aug-7-1982, Philadelphia) Pablo Ramos 10
+ (Oct-2-1982, Las Vegas) Lottie Mwale ko 4

- 1983 -
+ (Jan-22-1983, Stateline) Jerry Celestine 10

- 1984 -
+ (Jun-29-1984, Iles Caimans) Andy Russell ko 1

- 1985 -
+ (Feb-9-1985, New York) Tyrone Booze 10
+ (Mar-21-1985, Detroit) Oscar Holman disq.7
+ (Apr-3-1985, Galveston) Ricky Myers kot 4
+ (Jun-18-1985, Atlantic City) Ricky Parkey 10
+ (Aug-22-1985, Detroit) Elvis Parks ko 1
- (Dec-21-1985, Pesaro) Slobodan Kacar 15 (I.B.F., Light Heavyweight)

- 1986-1987: inactive -

- 1988 -
+ (Feb-4-1988, Newark) Prince Ray Davidson kot 7
+ (Mar-24-1988, Newark) Melvin Epps 10
- (Oct-21-1988, Newark) Arthel Lawhorne kot 3

As always fight fans, keep reaching for the stars, and all your dreams can be fulfilled.

Interview conducted November 2001

Norton admires his work

The Spoiler...

Up Close and Personal with Former WBC Heavyweight Champion Ken Norton

Kenny Norton, as the legendary Howard Cosell used to call him with affection, grew up in the small rural town of Jacksonville, Illinois. He went from small town hero to world level star on March 21, 1973, when he not only defeated the great Muhammad Ali, but broke his jaw in the process.

Recently I caught up with Ken and found him to be very open, extremely funny, and more than willing to talk about his boxing career, along with his incredible life. Our interview was to last only thirty minutes, but next thing I knew, it was an hour later, and we still were talking.

That's how much we enjoyed each other's conversation. Ken, I always felt, came from the Golden Era of heavyweights, and let me explain why I say this. I take nothing away from the current crop of heavyweight contenders, and especially hold Lennox Lewis in high regard. I think, that what he has done in his last four fights, is good for boxing. Now with that said, in Ken's Golden Era you had so many great fighters such as, Muhummad Ali, Joe Frazier, Earnie Shavers, George Foreman, Larry Holmes, Ron Lyle and even Jerry Quarry, who has to be given credit for being very tough. On any given night, any of these fighters could beat one another. Today, we just don't see that type of competition out there. This is why I will always have fond memories of his era.

First of all, for the readers what are you doing today?

I'm still in recuperation from my accident and working on my voice a lot. I finally feel I have gained back quite a bit. Currently, as well, I am getting involved in a project that centers around NASCAR racing. I will be behind the scenes. We are putting together the Ken Norton Racing Team.

I can remember watching you as a young kid on "The A Team" and of course, in "Mandingo". Why did you not pursue a more active movie career?

"You watched me as a young kid?" Ken said with a chuckle. He then said, "You're calling me old"? This he said with even a bigger chuckle. Well, Brad at that time, I was in the heart of my boxing career. I did it so it would open doors after I quit boxing. I was a single parent at the time, and I had my son Kenneth to raise. I wanted him to have the best things in life.

289

I can always remember Howard Cosell affectionately calling you Kenny. What was it like to be interviewed by him?

After the first Ali fight, we became friends. When he interviewed me, we already were very close and being his friend, made it so much easier to do the interview. I am very appreciative of our friendship and what he did for my career as a boxer.

I have always felt you were a very exciting fighter who always came in the ring and seemed to be in great shape. One thing I always noticed and wondered about, was the crab-like defense you used to block punches. Where did you learn that style from?

I started that style in the Henry Clark fight. It really worked for me to block punches, and it just developed.

Of all the fights you ever had, who do feel was your toughest opponent and why?

I would have to say, George Foreman. His power was unbelievable.

You fought two murderous punchers in your career when you faced Earnie Shavers and George Foreman. Who do you consider the harder puncher?

That's a hard question, Brad. "I did not have a meter in my body when I got hit," Ken said with a chuckle. I would have to say George Foreman.

Being in the military currently, and knowing that you were in the Marine Corps., working in the same field as I, please tell the young readers what you feel they could gain from being in the military?

First of all, I grew up quickly in the Marines, learning to lead people, and to follow, and it enabled me to really be able to help others.

I have always felt that you should have retained your WBC Heavyweight Championship Belt when you defended against Larry Holmes. Why is it that in a fight that was so close, you were not given an immediate rematch?

Brad, I have always wondered the same thing. The way I looked at it at the time, Don King was Larry's promoter and they did not want to fight me again. I have always felt to take a champion's belt, you have to beat him decisively. Larry Holmes did not do that to me.

When fighting Muhammad Ali and beating him the first time, did you ever imagine that the fight would go down in history as much as it did?

I really didn't. When Muhammad fought Bob Foster, I was on his undercard and faced Henry Clark. That was the first time I had ever met Ali. After our fight, I went over to him and told him I hope that the result of this fight does not hurt our friendship. Brad, funny thing, I was not even friends with him, but I just felt so close to him.

In fact, one of my daughters and his daughter live together. One day my daughter called me about six or seven months ago, and told me someone wants to speak to you. My mind was not thinking it was Ali. He told me, "Norton, LET'S DO IT AGAIN!" We really get along well today and I am also close with Joe Frazier.

You were always built like a body builder. Did that come from weight training or, what other methods did you use to get that build?

I never used weights in my life. I did start to use them during my recovery from my auto accident. I grew up in a rural town and I used to throw bales of hay which will build up anyone.

What big fights were you approached with that never materialized?

There was supposed to be a fourth fight with Ali. That's about it.

Do you favor a mandatory retirement fund for all boxers and if so, how would you like to see it accomplished?

I really do. There is no system set up for the fighters. In addition to the fund, there should be a health package to go with it. After a fighter gets to a certain point in his career where he is making decent money, he automatically should have an amount deducted to go into a retirement fund. The more he makes the more he would pay in and it would go into a pot for all fighters to be able to draw from it. Promoters should pay into it as well. They make a lot of money off the fighters and they never take one punch.

How do you compare the heavyweight division of today to the days when you were in it?

Number one, I would say that our era which included, Joe Frazier, Muhammad Ali, George Foreman, Earnie Shavers, Ron Lyle and myself, were like in the top 7 at that time. Nowadays, you don't see that type of competition in the top seven heavyweights in the world. Also, they fight 12 rounds vs. the 15 round distance in my day.

I feel we were more dedicated, in my opinion. I really liked the 15 round distance and you really had to be in shape to do this. Today they are tired by the 8th round.

What is greatest fight you have ever seen and why?

George Foreman vs. Ron Lyle. That was the first time I really saw two big men really go at each other and not duck. Each would get knocked down and get back up. Neither fighter wanted to give up. I think Ron could have beaten anyone on that night.

Finally, what is the saying you live your life by?

"Sooner or later, the man who wins, is the one who thinks he can".

Ken would like to add the following to our interview:

I would like to say that my foundation for hard work basically came from the direction of my father. When he passed away a couple of years ago, it was like taking half of my heart away from me.

Also, I raised my son basically by myself which formed a good bond between us with a strong mutual respect for one another. Even though we had our problems once, the respect and the friendship is what got us back together, where we could overcome what happened in the past. We promised each other, should that ever happen again, we would always get together and talk it out.

Writers closing comments:

You have read a very candid interview that Ken Norton was more than willing to grant me.

I hold the utmost respect for him as a man first, then, for being a great fighter.

Ken Norton

Weight class: Heavyweight/Unlimited

Professional record: 50 fights; 42+ (33 KO), 1=, 7-
1978: W.B.C. Heavyweight

- 1967 -
+ (Nov-14-1967, San Diego) Grady Brazell ko 5

- 1968 -
+ (Jan-16-1968, San Diego) Sam Wyatt 6
+ (Feb-6-1968, Sacramento) Harold Dutra ko 3
+ (Mar-26-1968, San Diego) Jimmy Gilmore ko 7
+ (Jul-23-1968, San Diego) Wayne Kindred ko 6
+ (Dec-5-1968, Los Angeles) Cornell Nolan ko 6

- 1969 -
+ (Feb-11-1969, Woodlands Hills) Joe Hemphill kot 3
+ (Feb-20-1969, Los Angeles) Wayne Kindred ko 9
+ (Mar-31-1969, San Diego) Pedro Sanchez ko 1
+ (May-29-1969, Los Angeles) Bill Mc Murray kot 7
+ (Jul-25-1969, San Diego) Gary Bates ko 8
+ (Oct-21-1969, San Diego) Jose Luis Garcia ko 3

- 1970 -

+ (Feb-4-1970, Las Vegas) Aaron Eastling ko 2
+ (Mar-13-1970, San Diego) Stanford Harris ko 3
+ (Apr-7-1970, Cleveland) Bob Mashburn ko 4
+ (May-8-1970, San Diego) Ray Ellis ko 2
- (Jul-2-1970, Los Angeles) Jose Luis Garcia ko 8
+ (Aug-28-1970, San Diego) Ray Wallace ko 4
+ (Sep-26-1970, Woodlands Hills) Chuck Leslie 10
+ (Oct-16-1970, San Diego) Roy Harris ko 2

- 1971 -
+ (Apr-24-1971, Woodlands Hills) Steve Carter ko 3
+ (Jun-12-1971, Santa Monica) Vic Brown ko 5
+ (Aug-7-1971, Santa Monica) Chuck Haynes ko 7
+ (Sep-29-1971, San Diego) James Woody 10

- 1972 -
+ (Feb-17-1972, San Diego) Charlie Harris kot 3
+ (Mar-16-1972, San Diego) Jack O'Halloran 10
+ (Jun-5-1972, San Diego) Herschel Jacobs 10
+ (Jun-28-1972, San Diego) James Woody kot 7
+ (Nov-21-1972, Stateline) Henry Clark kot 9
+ (Dec-13-1972, San Diego) Charlie Reno 10

- 1973 -
+ (Mar-30-1973, San Diego) Muhammad Ali 12
- (Sep-10-1973, Los Angeles) Muhammad Ali 12 (North America, Heavyweight)

- 1974 -
- (Mar-25-1974, Caracas) George Foreman kot 2 (World, Heavyweight)

+ (Jun-24-1974, Seattle) Boone Kirkmann retiring 8

- 1975 -
+ (Feb-13-1975, Oklahoma City) Reco Brooks ko 1
+ (Mar-24-1975, New York) Jerry Quarry kot 5
+ (Aug-14-1975, Saint-Paul) Jose Luis Garcia ko 5

- 1976 -
+ (Jan-10-1976, Las Vegas) Pedro Lovell kot 5
+ (Apr-30-1976, Landover) Ron Stander kot 5
+ (Jul-10-1976, San Diego) Larry Middleton kot 10
- (Sep-29-1976, New York) Muhammad Ali 15 (World, Heavyweight)

- 1977 -
+ (May-11-1977, New York) Duane Bobick ko 1
+ (Sep-14-1977, Las Vegas) Lorenzo Zanon ko 5
+ (Nov-5-1977, Las Vegas) Jimmy Young 15 (Wins WBC Heavyweight Title)

- 1978 -
- (Jun-9-1978, Las Vegas) Larry Holmes 15 (W.B.C., Heavyweight)
+ (Nov-10-1978, Las Vegas) Randy Stephens kot 3

- 1979 -
- (Mar-23-1979, Las Vegas) Earnie Shavers kot 1
= (Aug-19-1979, Bloomington) Scott Ledoux 10

- 1980 -
+ (Oct-31-1980, San Antonio) Randy Cobb 10

- **1981** -
- (May-10-1981, New York) Gerry Cooney ko 1

As always fight fans, keep reaching for the stars, and all your dreams can be fulfilled.

Interview conducted September 2000

Former WBA Lightweight Champion Sean O'Grady serves as interview analyst for [...] Networks's premier Boxing Series, "USA TUESDAY Night Fights."

Throwback...

Up Close and Personal with Former WBA Lightweight Champion Sean O' Grady

"Bubblegum" was his nickname and he had plenty of pop in his bubble. Sean O'Grady in his heyday, masked an impressive record of 81 wins against 5 losses and a whopping 70 knockouts. By the way, his career lasted only eight years 1975 – 1983. His total fight record can be divided by three, and that would equal the number of fights a modern day fighter has in his career, on the average.

During our interview I found his personality to match the one you see on television, which I have always thought was funny and down to earth. Growing up I closely watched tough fighters such as O'Grady, and having the wonderful job of now interviewing them all of these years later, is a true joy, to say the least.

How did you first get into boxing?
Both my parents were promoters so I grew up around the sport. Pat O'Grady, my father, always owned a gym and had a promotion company. My dad had been in the boxing business since he returned from World War II, so as you see, I totally grew up in the boxing world.

Looking at your impressive record (81-5, 70 ko's) it jumped out at me that in only an 8 year career, you had all those fights. Also, in one year alone, you had 26 fights which is more than some fighters have in an entire career. I really consider you a throwback fighter, which is compliment. Did your management want you to have all those fights, or was it your idea?
First of all Brad, I turned pro when I was 15 years old. It was my management's idea, but I was able to fight that often because you could have a four round fight on Tuesday and then have one on say, Thursday. It was easy back then to have many four round fights. Look at the amateur fighters, who I have the utmost respect for, and if you look in these tournaments, they fight everyday.

Looking at boxing today, it's different with the media and now, the internet. I had to do something different to become known, which I think was done through my father's direction. By fighting so much, was the way I think my father envisioned me getting really noticed.

My dad grew up in the golden era of boxing in the early 40's and 50's, when it was easy for a fighter to have over 300 fights in a career. Bottom Line: My dad wanted me to emulate that as closely as I could.

In your fight against Jim Watt, I can remember you being way ahead on points. Watt knowing that, intentionally head butted you opening a terrible cut. I also remember all the bad things surrounding that fight such as death threats and just total madness. Discuss that fight, and do you feel that your impressive showing earned you the shot so quickly against then, WBA Lightweight Champion, Hilmer Kenty?

To be honest Brad, when he butted me, what was going through my mind, was his head! (We both really laughed at that answer). As you know the fight was staged in Glasgow, Scotland which was in his backyard. A lot of the war had bled over to Scotland, so downtown Glasgow was hostile towards me, because of my Irish background.

As a result, we constantly got death threats and it was really scary every time I left the hotel to run into people who were just adamantly against me. When he butted me in the head, it really was appalling, and started me thinking what do I do back to him? I started thinking I had my mother, grandmother, sisters and the rest of my family sitting ringside.

It occurred to me that I was in some real trouble because of the bad cut and if I did something back to him, would they go after my family for my actions? Brad, it was totally a scary experience to even get out of town after the fight. We needed a police escort which took us right from the arena to the airport. I do think the performance I gave against Watt did earn me the title shot against Hilmer Kenty.

In your fight with Hilmer Kenty you struck gold by winning the WBA Lightweight Title. What happened to you being the champion and defending the belt?

The title was stripped from me by a judge. To be honest, I don't really know all the circumstances around it, and really have hesitated to find out, because I really don't want to know. From what I understand, Kenty had some kind of contract made between the number one contender to challenge for his title. Subsequently, five months later, I was stripped of the Lightweight Title.

How were you involved in the WAA, and if I remember correctly Monte Masters was it's first Heavyweight Champion?

Wow Brad, you really did your homework. My father was in charge and it started around 1981. I fought for the WAA Lightweight Title against Andrew Ganigan. He was from Hawaii, and really did hit me with a Hawaiian Punch.

Since you turned professional in 1975, what changes have you seen to date, that have made the sport of boxing better?

There have been changes to the sport that have made it better such as shorting the rounds to help in the safety of the fighters. There are lots of things that need to be changed, and because of so much politics in boxing, it's hard to get them instituted. I don't think it has improved as rapidly as the other mainstream sports.

I would like to see profound changes made, and there are just so many to go into. I would love to be asked what changes I feel need to be made, and to date, never have. I feel the ideas for the changes need to come from the fighters because they are the ones in there taking all the blows.

I would like to see a David Stern or say Marc Ratner have control of the panel to better the sport of boxing. (I totally agree with this answer and fighters such as Sean, should be on a panel that makes these changes).

You retired in 1983. Has the urge to come back even today, crossed your mind? If so, why have you not done it like so many others have?

I have thought about it, but I really didn't want to come back and possibly risk injury, or not looking good at all in the ring. Most fighters, and I'm no exception, love to hear the roar of the crowd. When you're in there and they are rooting you on, it's a hard thing to give up. Even in my TV career, I may get someone to come up and say, "great job", which I appreciate. However, it will never equal the fans cheering you on when you're in the ring.

What big fights were you approached for, but never materialized?

We were approached with Ray Mancini, Alexis Arguello and Aaron Pryor, to name just a few. The lightweight division at the time was very hot.

What is the real reason Tuesday Night Fights went off the air?

It was a direction change for the network, and they wanted to cut back on their sports. They had a change in the ownership, and they wanted to take it in another direction.

What were some of the things on Tuesday Night Fights that you implemented?

"In the Gym" and "In this Corner", to name just a few. The great thing about our show is we had the freedom to do what we wanted. Working with Al Albert was so great. Al was so giving and very knowledgeable. I learned so much over the 13 years I was there.

To me you have made the transition quite easily to commentating. For all those out there yearning to get behind the mic, what are your words of wisdom to them?

I talk to these kids on all the shows that I have done over the years and get asked this question. I have to say, number one thing is getting your education so you can be articulate when you do get behind a mic. EDUCATION IS THE KEY!

Do you favor a mandatory retirement fund for all boxers and if so, how would you like to see it accomplished?

I sure do Brad. The big question is how do you pay for it? I think the answer is television. All the other big sports have their retirement fund subsidized by these big television contracts. That is why I mentioned Daniel Stern or Marc Ratner types earlier who could oversee this retirement fund. It would take a very strong person to make sure it is done correctly. In addition, fighters, promoters, a percentage of the ticket sales could go into it. Football, Baseball and Basketball all have it. Why are we so far behind? The ones suffering are the fighters, and it really is time to get this enacted! (Once again, I totally agree, and that is why I always ask this particular question. I know

so many people read it, and I am hoping that
one day soon, something will be done about it
throughout the United States and Overseas to
help out the fighters!)

**What is the greatest fight you have ever
seen and why?**

Sugar Ray Leonard vs. Tommy Hearns I. It
beat me out for Fight of the Year. It deserved
to be number one. Leonard hit Hearns with a
left hook in the fourth round that wobbled
Hearns, but could not land that hook again
until the 13th round. It was a spectacular
finish. It defines what being a man is all
about. That fight had everything a fan could
ever ask for in a fight.

**Finally, what is the saying you live your
life by?**

"One day it will all be worth it".

Sean would like to add the following to our
interview:

I would just like to say that I have been
very lucky and met a lot of wonderful people
throughout my career. Being a fighter is
something I am very proud of.

Sean O'GRADY
Nickname: "Bubblegum"

Weight Class: Lightweight/135 LBS

Professional record: 86 fights; 81+ (70 KO),
5-

1979-1980: United States Lightweight
1981: W.B.A. Lightweight

- **1975** -

+ (Jan-21-1975, Oklahoma City) David Tyhes ko 1

+ (Feb-4-1975, Oklahoma City) Willie Johnson ko 1

+ (Feb-18-1975, Oklahoma City) Joe Matthews ko 1

+ (Mar-4-1975, Oklahoma City) James Word ko 1

+ (Mar-18-1975, Oklahoma City) Muhammad Muffleh ko 1

+ (Apr-1-1975, Oklahoma City) Rocky Matthews ko 2

+ (Apr-15-1975, Oklahoma City) Tyrone Taylor ko 1

+ (May-6-1975, Oklahoma City) Earl Booth ko 1

+ (May-17-1975, Little Rock) David Williams ko 1

+ (May-20-1975, Oklahoma City) Ramon Campos 6

+ (Jun-3-1975, Oklahoma City) Ramon Perez ko 3

+ (Jun-9-1975, Dallas) Earl Booth ko 1

+ (Jun-17-1975, Oklahoma City) Ezequiel Campos ko 1

+ (Jul-1-1975, Oklahoma City) Simmie Black ko 4

+ (Jul-9-1975, Memphis) Ramon Reyes ko 3

+ (Jul-15-1975, Oklahoma City) Ramon Campos 10

+ (Aug-5-1975, Oklahoma City) Victor Luna ko 1

+ (Aug-19-1975, Oklahoma City) Harvey Wilson 10

+ (Sep-2-1975, Oklahoma City) Billy Miller ko 3

+ (Sep-4-1975, Omaha) Harvey Wilson 8

+ (Oct-21-1975, Oklahoma City) Raul Carrez ko 1

+ (Nov-4-1975, Oklahoma City) Ramon Reyna ko 2

+ (Nov-18-1975, Oklahoma City) Tony Ramirez ko 3

+ (Nov-20-1975, Omaha) Roberto Rodriguez ko 3

+ (Dec-2-1975, Oklahoma City) Luciano Medina ko 4

+ (Dec-16-1975, Oklahoma City) Bubba Thompson ko 3

- 1976 -

+ (Jan-6-1976, Oklahoma City) Shannon Williams ko 2

+ (Jan-20-1976, Oklahoma City) Ken Connors ko 1

+ (Feb-3-1976, Oklahoma City) Luis Martinez ko 1

- (Feb-25-1976, Los Angeles) Danny Lopez ko 3 (United States, Featherweight)

+ (Apr-6-1976, Oklahoma City) Domingo Luna ko 3

+ (Apr-20-1976, Oklahoma City) Manuel Tarazon ko 3

+ (May-4-1976, Oklahoma City) Frank Amano ko 1

+ (May-18-1976, Oklahoma City) Eliseo Estrada ko 3

+ (Jun-1-1976, Oklahoma City) Blackie Sandoval ko 1

+ (Sep-7-1976, Oklahoma City) Joe Medrano ko 3

+ (Sep-21-1976, Oklahoma City) Richie Puentes ko 2

+ (Oct-5-1976, Oklahoma City) Danny Young ko 1

+ (Oct-19-1976, Oklahoma City) William Curtis ko 2

+ (Nov-2-1976, Oklahoma City) Esteban Olvera ko 6
+ (Nov-16-1976, Oklahoma City) Jose Cazares ko 2
+ (Dec-7-1976, Oklahoma City) Raul Carreon ko 5
+ (Dec-21-1976, Oklahoma City) Francisco Robles ko 2

- 1977 -
+ (Mar-1-1977, Oklahoma City) Earl Large ko 9
+ (Mar-15-1977, Oklahoma City) Melvin Jameson ko 1
+ (Apr-5-1977, Oklahoma City) Chango Guillen ko 1
+ (May-17-1977, Oklahoma City) Davey Sanchez ko 2
+ (Jun-6-1977, Oklahoma City) Jerome Smith ko 1
+ (Jun-22-1977, New York) David Vasquez 10
+ (Jul-19-1977, Oklahoma City) Ricardo Flores ko 2
+ (Sep-6-1977, Oklahoma City) Gilberto Lara ko 1
+ (Oct-25-1977, Anaheim) Jose Olivares ko 5
+ (Dec-6-1977, Oklahoma City) Bill Pearish ko 2

- 1978 -
+ (Mar-17-1978, Las Vegas) Eddie Freeman kot 1
+ (Mar-23-1978, Omaha) Ramon Campos ko 1
+ (Apr-16-1978, Los Angeles) Romeo Anaya kot 3
+ (May-1-1978, Omaha) Harvey Wilson ko 2
+ (Jun-10-1978, Oklahoma City) Shig Fukuyama kot 5
+ (Oct-11-1978, Denver) Al Franklin ko 6

+ (Nov-16-1978, Oklahoma City) Freddie Harris ko 7

+ (Nov-29-1978, Oklahoma City) Paul Garcia ko 5

+ (Dec-7-1978, Oklahoma City) Beau Jaynes ko 2

- 1979 -

+ (Jan-25-1979, Oklahoma City) Marion Thomas ko 2

+ (Feb-16-1979, Little Rock) Juan Garcia ko 2

+ (Mar-17-1979, Oklahoma City) Jose Hernandez 10

+ (Apr-28-1979, Oklahoma City) Roberto Perez ko 5

+ (Jul-19-1979, Oklahoma City) Dieter Schantz kot 2

+ (Sep-21-1979, Tulsa) Jose Martinez ko 4

+ (Oct-23-1979, Oklahoma City) Arturo Leon 15 (United States, Lightweight)

+ (Dec-15-1979, Oklahoma City) Ramiro Hernandez kot 4

- 1980 -

+ (Jun-10-1980, Oklahoma City) Scotty Freeman ko 2

+ (Jul-27-1980, Omaha) Gonzalo Montellano 12 (United States, Lightweight)

+ (Sep-9-1980, Oklahoma City) Carlos Villacana kot 5

+ (Sep-25-1980, Oklahoma City) Jose Gonzalez ko 3

- (Oct-31-1980, Glasgow) Jim Watt injury 12 (W.B.C., Lightweight)

- 1981 -

+ (Mar-17-1981, Oklahoma City) Jose Cabrera 10

+ (Apr-12-1981, Atlantic City) Hilmer Kenty 15 (W.B.A., Lightweight)
  7.1981: WBA strips title.
+ (Sep-25-1981, Oklahoma City) Jeff Morgan 10
- (Oct-31-1981, Little Rock) Andrew Ganigan ko 2

- **1982** -
+ (Feb-9-1982, Oklahoma City) Sultan Saladin kot 4
+ (Mar-18-1982, Oklahoma City) Lupe Sanchez ko 3
+ (Apr-3-1982, Denver) Jose Hernandez kot 4
+ (Jun-8-1982, Denver) Oran Butler ko 1
- (Oct-27-1982, Atlantic City) Pete Ranzany 10

- **1983** -
+ (Feb-10-1983, Northbridge) Jose Luis Gonzalez kot 5
- (Mar-20-1983, Chicago) Johnny Verderosa kot 4

As always fight fans, keep reaching for the stars, and all your dreams can be fulfilled.

Interview conducted September 2000

Champion Forever...

Up Close and Personal with Former WBA Heavyweight Champion Greg Page

Remember these words, "MANDATORY RETIREMENT FUND"? I have been calling for one for the last four years that would include medical coverage for all fighters. If boxing had one, would I be doing an article to help draw attention to the plight of former WBA Heavyweight Champion, Greg Page?

Yes, I would be interviewing him, but it would it have to start out on a sad note. Reality is, there is sadness in this story, but much cheer as well. On December 1, 1984 in Sun City, South Africa, Page cemented his place in boxing history by dethroning then WBA Heavyweight Champion Gerrie Coetzee, via an eighth round knockout.

Page would lose his title in his first defense against Tony Tubbs via a 15 round decision. He would go on to fight for several years, but he would not find the same successes as he did earlier in his career.

310

However, his dream of becoming a top contender and challenging for another world title would not go away. This dream would lead to tragedy when, on March 9, 2001, Page would face journeyman, Dale Crowe in a fight that was staged in Erlanger, Kentucky.

In this fight, which would be Page's last, he was knocked out in the tenth round. Page was carried from the ring and slipped into a coma, shortly after. There was much speculation on that night whether Page should have even been cleared to fight.

We may never know the answer to him being cleared to fight, but I feel that if a mandatory retirement fund were in place, it may have deterred Page from coming back, like so many other fighters before him have done. As I said earlier, there is sadness in this story, but rather than leave you on a sad note, just remember, Page was a champion in the ring, and currently, he is fighting like a champion out of the ring to gain as much normalcy in his life as he can.

First of all, how are things going with your rehabilitation since you were injured in the ring?

My recovery has been one day at a time. I don't remember a whole lot about it. I have seen video footage of me in therapy almost 2 months after I was injured. I could hardly sit up by myself. They had to sit me in a reclining wheelchair with special made straps to keep me from falling over.

Has the Kentucky boxing commission done anything to assist you in offsetting your medical bills?

I have not heard a word from anyone of the Kentucky Athletic Commission. That is disappointing, because I trusted Jack Kerns. I took him to be a man of his word. Yet, not one of them has called and asked about me, sent a card or anything. I have read and heard that they supposedly have an active investigation going on regarding the events that night. I don't know. What I do know is this, and can say it freely, is that no one has contacted me, any of my corner people, my wife or anybody else as far as I know who was at the fight, or part of the fight. How can they "actively investigate" yet never talk to anyone who was there?

Is there any truth to the rumor that you should have not been cleared to fight, yet you still were allowed to get in the ring?

I felt like I was very capable of fighting, obviously, or I would not have been in there, in the ring. I have heard that people have been accused of talking me into fighting. To them, I can only say, at that point in my life, no one was making decisions about Greg Page's career, but Greg Page. I want to make that clear - no one, not Patty, not my trainer nobody, but me. The fight details were given to me, and based on my conversations and promises from Jack Kerns, I took the fight.

Should I have been fighting? I felt like I was ready. Yes, I truly believed that fighting Dale Crowe was an opportunity. I thought it would be a stepping-stone to bigger and better things; a shot at a heavyweight title again. I also know that the commissioner talked to me and one of my friends who helped negotiate the fight and about making Louisville a big name in boxing once again. We talked about having televised fights in Louisville again.

I have been a vocal supporter of a mandatory retirement fund for all boxers and along with it, medical insurance. First of all, do you support one and, if there was one in place that you had money coming in from, that you paid into during the 22 years you fought up to the Crowe fight, would you have still stepped into the ring at the age of 42?

First of all, I do not believe in a mandatory retirement age. They don't have it in basketball, baseball or football to name a few sports. People are different. Their bodies age differently. I do however, believe in boxing reform. Boxing needs to be safer. That is what I want to see. Not mandatory retirement based on age. What I mean is if a fighter is 40 and is still physically fit, can pass strict, unbiased physicals, then I feel like he should still be able to fight. I do support setting up a pension fund system and also mandatory medical insurance for boxers. The promoters, the managers and sometimes the trainers make all the money and the fighter has to get what's left.

Some system should be included in boxing reform if it is going to be a true reform that will make boxing safer and protect the fighters, and that has to include pension plans, insurance, as well as, tougher nationwide regulations!

As far as, would I have still fought? Yes, I had been training hard and was ready to fight. I wanted a shot at the championship. I was raised in Kentucky; what would be more appropriate than for me to be the Heavyweight Champion of Kentucky?

For other boxing families that don't have the marquee name of Greg Page, but tragically have to deal with a ring injury of their loved one, what are your words of wisdom to them in dealing with everything you have, to this point?

I have to tell them to trust in the Lord. God alone has brought me this far. You never know what you have in store for you, what is in God's plan for you. Early on in my career, I didn't care about the business end of things. I just went out and boxed. I had people around me that I thought had my back, but they were making bad choices that ended up as bad choices for me. I let my family run things for me and I ended up bankrupt.

Then I moved out to Vegas and let other people take care of things for me, who may or may not have had my best interest at heart. When you are down as far as you can go, God will lift you up. HE knows what you need and will put you with the people that you need to be with, when you need to be with them. A year before I was hurt, God reunited me with an old high school friend. We both had gone through painful divorces and we started seeing each other. After I got hurt, people tried to make choices for me that I would never have made for myself, if I had not been comatose. Patty carried all of my troubles on her shoulders and stood up for me. God put her with me because HE knew what I would be going through and knew I would need someone strong to stand up for me.

As a young man, I remember a very exciting fight you had on the undercard of the WBC Heavyweight Championship between Champion

Larry Holmes and top contender Randall "Tex" Cobb. You faced then top contender James "Quick" Tillis. If I remember correctly, you came off the canvas early to stop him in the eighth round for the United States Boxing Association (USBA) Heavyweight Title. What are your recollections of that fight?

Man you are good. You know your boxing. You dug way back to get that one! I went into that fight knowing I could beat him and I just couldn't believe that he knocked me down. He was a fast fighter, living up to his nickname "Quick". A hard puncher, not the hardest puncher I had faced. In case you are wondering that probably was "Razor" Ruddock.

Early in your career, there were constant comparisons to you being the next Muhammad Ali. Did that put a lot of stress on you to attempt to fight at his level?

It put a lot of pressure on me. First, I was too young to have that kind of pressure put on me. You know that being from the same town, the same high school, you know. Nobody could fight like Muhammad, but Muhammad. I told people to let me fight and be me. Each fighter should have his own style, maybe they are similar to each other, like Ali's rope-a-dope or the Ali shuffle, you know a little of this or a little of that and it becomes your own style. I had my own style, especially early on. Kind of like my shaking of my shoulders.

Early in your career you fought many top contenders, beating most of them. Do you feel the level of competition in your earlier career, by far exceeds today's heavyweight contenders?

When I was coming up, fighters had skill and style. Today, it seems like they are all about brute force, knocking you out as fast as they can with no style or finesse. Some of them go on intimidation factors.

On December 1, 1984, you reached the pinnacle of your career when you dethroned then WBA Heavyweight Champion, Gerrie Coetzee knocking him out in the eighth round. What are your recollections of that magical evening?

Like that R. Kelly song, "I Believe I Can Fly". It was the most tremendous feeling in the world. Man it was great! To go to another man's country, his homeland, being the underdog, like I was. People told me that I'd never win, and amount to anything. Even Don King thought that I would lose, but I knew I would win. It was a tough fight, but I went up in that man's backyard and took his belt from him. I fought a good fight and it felt great to watch him fall. I didn't care much about South Africa. I caught a lot of stuff for going over there. Nobody else would, so I did. Besides those dagole' baboons used to run after me when I was doing my running over there. I was glad to get back home.

Who do you feel was your toughest opponent in your career and why?

Believe it or not it was George Chaplin. His head was so small it was hard to hit. He head butted me a lot. He did a lot of crazy jumping around. The most fun I had at a fight other than beating Coetzee was when I fought Scott LeDoux in the Bahamas. I danced around and made fun of him before I finished him off. I trained hard for that fight and he took me lightly. Then I got in trouble with my mom for the way I acted at that fight. She said "I acted like a fool."

Were there any big fights in your career that were close to being signed or signed that fell out?

I signed a contract (while we were in Canada,) to fight Tyson but, because of Don King, that fell through. Larry Holmes refused to fight me. They stripped him of the belt and then they created the IBF so Larry could have a belt. I called him a "chicken livered coward". I still think he was.

Who are your three favorite fighters of all-time and why?

Muhammad Ali- He has a fantastic jab and very fast hands. Muhammad is poetry in motion. He was just great to watch. I have to admit, I patterned myself after his style, somewhat. He was just real graceful.

Joe Louis- He had a good jab too. He was also very talented and fun to watch.

Sugar Ray Robinson- He was fast, flurrying his punches. I wanted to copy that fast punching jabbing he always would do.

Jersey Joe Walcott- His great footwork and his great moves. Okay, so that was four. Sorry!!

What is the greatest fight you have ever seen and why?

That would have to be when my friend, Aaron Pryor fought Alexis Arguello the first time in 1982. Pryor had great stamina and Arguello had graceful style. Pryor was straight up tricky in that fight - he was there, then he wasn't, and he popped up somewhere else. It was an awesome fight to see. I can still picture it in my mind.

Now that you are retired from boxing, how would you like your fans to remember you?

As a fast punching heavyweight who had a great heart. I fought hard, and I hope I am remembered as a nice guy! I would like to think that I gave my fans some exciting fights during my career and that they enjoyed watching me fight! I also helped a lot of people along the way.

Finally, what is the saying, if you have one that you live your life by?

"Believe in the knockout power of the Lord".

This was designed for me and it was on the back of my robe as I entered the ring for the last time as a fighter. The Lord has been with me every step of the way!!

Greg would like to add the following to our interview:

This past year has been very tough on me mentally and physically. I will never be the same Greg Page again. My daily memory is not great, but old stuff is still all there. I say things and then I forget and repeat myself. Sometimes I say things that I wish I hadn't, but Patty reminds me that I had a very severe brain injury and that I can't help it sometimes.

In the past year, besides being critically injured, I went through a terrible divorce and lost absolutely everything. I had a house that was almost paid for and everything, and they gave it to my ex-wife. Yet, I can't be bitter. At least I know my girls have a home. And besides, God let me live. I am poor, but I am alive!

I am still learning to be faithful to God's word, but I'm just a man and I fall sometimes. Sometimes I worry about what the future will bring. I'm broke and I just found out that the house that we have rented for the past 2 years will have to be sold because the partners are splitting up the assets. I don't have credit to buy it and I get scared sometimes cause I don't want to be homeless, but then I remember that God will provide for me. I get cards and letters from fans all around every now and then, and I do enjoy that and I hope that they keep on sending them.

My address is:

Greg Page

208 W. Kenwood Way

Louisville, KY 40214

When you are down and out, you find out who really cares for you. I got married in October of last year to a woman, who is tough, but she loves me for me and we started out as very good friends. She is, has, and always will be there for me. She loves me as I am broke, and crazy as a roach! I don't guess that it can get much better than that.

****A special thanks has to go to Patricia Love-Page and Brad Cooney for assisting me in this interview.

Greg PAGE

Weight class: Heavyweight/Unlimited

Amateur record: 101 fights; 90+, 11-

Professional record: 76 fights; 58+ (48 KO), 1=, 17-

1981-1984: United States Heavyweight

1984-1985: W.B.A. Heavyweight

- 1979 -
+ (Feb-16-1979, Louisville) Don Martin kot 2
+ (Jun-1-1979, Louisville) Jerry Mc Intyre ko 1
+ (Aug-19-1979, Bloomington) James Knox ko 2
+ (Sep-22-1979, Los Angeles) Oliver Philipps ko 4
+ (Oct-18-1979, Philadelphia) Frankie Brown ko 3
+ (Nov-24-1979, Bloomington) James Reid ko 1
+ (Dec-14-1979, Atlantic City) Ira Martin kot 1

- 1980 -
+ (Feb-1-1980, Louisville) Victor Rodriguez ko 1
+ (Mar-8-1980, Las Vegas) Claman Parker ko 1
+ (Apr-5-1980, Louisville) George Chaplin10
+ (May-16-1980, Lexington) Larry Alexander ko 6
+ (Sep-12-1980, Louisville) Leroy Boone kot 6
+ (Oct-2-1980, New York) Dave Johnson ko 6

- 1981 -
+ (Feb-7-1981, Atlantic City) Stan Ward kot 7 (United States, Heavyweight)
+ (Apr-11-1981, Kiamesha Lake) Marty Monroe kot 6 (United States, Heavyweight)
+ (Jun-12-1981, Detroit) Alfredo Evangelista ko 2
+ (Aug-22-1981, Atlantic City) George Chaplin 12 (United States, Heavyweight)
+ (Dec-11-1981, Nassau) Scott Ledoux ko 4 (United States, Heavyweight)

- 1982 -

+ (May-2-1982, Atlantic City) Jimmy Young 12 (United States, Heavyweight)
- (Jun-11-1982, Atlantic City) Trevor Berbick 10
+ (Nov-26-1982, Houston) James Tillis kot 8 (United States, Heavyweight)

- 1983 -
+ (Feb-12-1983, Cleveland) Larry Frazier 10
+ (May-20-1983, Las Vegas) Renaldo Snipes 12 (United States, Heavyweight)
+ (Oct-15-1983, Miami Beach) Rick Kellar kot 2

- 1984 -
- (Mar-9-1984, Las Vegas)Tim Witherspoon 12 (W.B.C., Heavyweight)
- (Aug-31-1984, Las Vegas) David Bey 12 (United States, Heavyweight)
+ (Dec-1-1984, Sun City) Gerrie Coetzee ko 8 (W.B.A., Heavyweight)

- 1985 -
- (Apr-29-1985, Buffalo) Tony Tubbs 15 (W.B.A., Heavyweight)

- 1986 -
- (Jan-17-1986, Atlanta) James Douglas 10
+ (Mar-30-1986, Edmonton) Funso Banjo disq.8
- (Jun-12-1986, Los Angeles) Mark Wills kot 9
+ (Nov-22-1986, Las Vegas) Jerry Halstead ko 8

- 1987 -
+ (May-30-1987, Las Vegas) James Broad 10
- (Jul-24-1987, Sydney) Joe Bugner 10

- 1988: inactive -

- **1989** -
+ (Mar-24-1989, Louisville) David Mauney ko 1
- (Apr-25-1989, Las Vegas) Orlin Norris 12 (North America, Heavyweight)
+ (May-12-1989, Struthers) Harry Terrell kot 2
+ (Jul-21-1989, Atlantic City) Charles Woolard ko 2

- **1990** -
+ (Mar-17-1990, Las Vegas) Mathias Fleming kot 1
- (May-19-1990, Las Vegas) Mark Wills kot 6

- **1991** -
+ (Mar-19-1991, Las Vegas) Mark Young kot 3
+ (Jun-8-1991, Saint-Louis) Fred Whittaker ko 2
+ (Nov-29-1991, Las Vegas) Joey Christjohn kot 1

- **1992** -
- (Feb-15-1992, Las Vegas) Donovan Razor Ruddock kot 8
+ (Jun-26-1992, Cleveland) James Smith 10
- (Sep-12-1992, Las Vegas) Francisco Damiani 10
+ (Dec-13-1992, Las Vegas) Kevin P. Porter kot 8

- **1993** -
+ (Jan-30-1993, Memphis) Dan Murphy kot 3
+ (May-7-1993, Las Vegas) Mike Faulkner kot 8
- (Aug-6-1993, Bayamon) Bruce Seldon kot 9

- **1994-1995: inactive** -

- 1996 -
+ (May-16-1996, Virginia Beach) Robert Jackson kot 1
+ (Jun-12-1996, Raleigh) James Birch Smith kot 1
+ (Jun-15-1996, Wentworth) Tyrone Miles ko 1
+ (Jul-23-1996, Chesapeake) Frankie Hines kot 1

- 1997 -
+ (May-20-1997, Nashville) Armando Furrubiartes ko 1
+ (Jun-10-1997, Nashville) Joe Barnes kot 1
+ (Jun-17-1997, Nashville) Frankie Hines ko 1
+ (Jun-24-1997, Nashville) Wes Black kot 1
+ (Aug-24-1997, Nashville) Robert Boykin ko 1
+ (Sep-9-1997, Nashville) Moses Harris kot 3
+ (Sep-23-1997, Nashville) Nate Jones ko 1
+ (Dec-2-1997, Nashville) James Holly kot 1
+ (Dec-9-1997, Nashville) Harry Daniels 4
+ (Dec-16-1997, Nashville) Kenneth Bentley kot 1

- 1998 -
= (Jan-31-1998, Tampa) Jerry Ballard 10
+ (Mar-27-1998, Atlantic City) Marion Wilson 8
+ (May-19-1998, Nashville) George Harris kot 1
- (Oct-23-1998, Atlantic City) Monte Barrett 10

- 1999 -
+ (Mar-27-1999, Gary) Harry Daniels ko 2
- (Apr-1-1999, Worley) Artis Pendergrass 10

+   (Jun-18-1999,   Fayetteville)   Tim Witherspoon retiring 8

-      (Nov-14-1999,   Portland)   Jorge   Louis Gonzalez 10

- 2000 -
+ (Feb-9-2000, Rosemont) Terrance Lewis ko 7
- (Jun-29-2000, New York) Robert Davis kot 8
+ (Oct-9-2000, Louisville) Mark Bradley kot 1

- 2001 -
(Mar-9-2001, Erlanger) Dale Crowe ko 10

As always fight fans, keep reaching for the stars and all your dreams can be fulfilled.

Interview conducted June 2002

Leaving Footprints for Life...

Up Close and Personal with Five Time World Champion Vinny Paz

Vinny Paz formally known as Vinny Pazienza is an Italian American who is very proud of his heritage. On many occasions, we have spoken, shared laughs and discussed life's up and downs. So, to conduct this interview was a true delight for me.

Vinny's story is truly an inspirational one that became legendary in boxing history when he made a comeback from a car accident that broke his neck.

To come back in the ring like he did, and to fight with the same tenacity, is something that should guarantee him induction into the International Boxing Hall of Fame. If they don't feel his career merits it, then I say, start a new category called Warriors which he qualifies for the moment they put the new category into effect.

Paz won his first World Title in the lightweight division beating Greg Haugen for the IBF Lightweight Championship on June 7, 1987. In his first defense on February 6, 1988, he faced Haugen again and came up on the short end of the stick, losing a 15 round decision.

Paz would move up in weight class and face then tough champion, Gilbert Dele, for his WBA Junior Middleweight Title on October 1, 1991. This fight saw him, in my opinion, at the best he ever looked in the ring, and for his efforts he knocked out the champion in the 12th round, earning him his second World Title. Shortly after his fight, he was involved in a car accident that broke his neck. He was out for a little over a year. He somehow, to the amazement of every boxing fan in the world, came back and to date, has given the fans some great wars.

If you ever have the chance to meet my dear friend, and I say this from the heart, take the time to talk with him. You will thoroughly enjoy a man who is a very special human being in this world.

What inspired you to get into boxing?

I would like to say the movie Rocky, but actually, I started boxing when I was 6 with this youth organization in Rhode Island, until I was 12 years old. The league only went to 12, so I took off then. When I was 14, I went to see Rocky and that's all it took. I wanted to box from then on.

When you step into the ring, you not only bring your boxing skills, but a showmanship

that is seldom seen in today's boxing? Why do you think that is?

I don't really know why they don't. I like to do it because I like getting the crowd into the fight.

Would you like to see 15 rounds reinstated in boxing?

Yes, because it shows the heart of a real champion. I feel that the 13th - 15th rounds are true championship rounds. (I totally agree with this answer.)

If Vinny Paz could personally change the ranking systems what changes would he make?

I would lessen the weight divisions which are now at 17, to 8. Then, only have two governing bodies.

How do you feel about the claim that rankings are bought?

That's the way of the world. It's not right, but as they say, "That's Life".

Do you favor a mandatory retirement fund for all boxers and if so, how would you like to see it accomplished?

Brad, that's a very hard subject to talk about. I would like to see it regulated for guys who are real fighters, not ones coming in and out of the game. A guy like me has been fighting for most of his life, and then you have someone else who only comes in and has 12 fights. He then disappears from boxing. He should not get the same benefit as someone like myself who has been doing this for almost 20 years. If they can get this thing regulated, it would be a beautiful thing for all fighters.

I do agree with you they should pay in from day one according to their purse, but the promoter should pay in as well because they don't take any punches, train and do all the things that we have to do to become a successful fighter. I love my promoter and he works his tail off for me, but still he doesn't have to get in there and take the punches.

Who are your three favorite fighters of all-time and why?

Number one is Muhammad Ali. I really started boxing because of him and he truly was my inspiration.

Second, Roberto Duran because I loved him in there, and he was just so tough. Finally, Aaron "The Hawk" Pryor. He was one of the most exciting non-stop fighters in the sport of boxing.

What is the greatest fight you have ever seen and why?

Marvin Hagler vs. Tommy Hearns. The big build up to the fight, and then it was an absolute raw battle in there. It was all or nothing and I love that.

What are your words of wisdom to the young fighter who is just lacing up the gloves?

If you're going to do this, have your whole heart and soul in it. Stay strong and keep the faith. If you feel it's getting too thick for you, then you should get out.

Would you like to see boxing go back to the old days when you only had one belt and one real world champion?

No! There are lots of good young kids out there who are trying to make something with their lives. You will eliminate them from making money and doing great things. I know it's great for the fans, but it minimizes the money for the fighters. The fans don't see what these fighters have to go through behind the scenes.

Say that you have a guy in a particular weight class such as Roy Jones, JR. who is so dominant and can not be beaten. It allows for that kid who has lots of skills and works his heart out, but will never beat a Roy Jones, JR. Well, before Roy won all the titles, he may have had the chance to challenge and possibly win one of those belts, allowing him to make some money for all his hard efforts.

Who do you feel was your toughest opponent and why?

Gilbert Dele, when I won the WBA Junior Middleweight Title. It was the hardest fight I was ever in because it was just physically exhausting. I never once felt this way in a fight like I did between the 7th and 8th rounds. In fact, really in the 8th round he was pressing me and I was just moving, punching in combinations, and landing while he kept pressing me. He was a very hard puncher and I remember saying to myself in the 8th round, I don't know if I can keep this guy off of me. This is ridiculous. I just can't keep this guy off me! Right after I said that, in my mind I then said, 'Hell no, don't even think like that! DIE if you have to!' Brad, I never felt like that in a fight until that night.

In your opinion, what do you feel the state of boxing is?

It's not very good because of the bad judging and all these investigations where the bad stuff gets the media attention. There really aren't a lot of flamboyant boxers out there to take the sport up, and it's lacking truth. It's sad because there is not a lot of publicity that goes with boxing.

It should be a mainstream sport like Major League baseball, NFL, and the NBA. Boxing right now just does not seem to be able to get it together like that. Brad, I want to tell you something. If boxing was regulated like those other sports, and I broke my neck, came back a year later, I would have been on a box of Wheaties.

When you finally retire from boxing, what do you want your legions of fans to remember you for?

That I was a good entertaining fighter with a lot of skill who just made a lot of people happy.

Finally, what is the saying that you live your life by?

"Let it fly"!

Vinny PAZ

Nickname: "The Pazmanian Devil"

Weight class: Super Middleweight/168 LBS

Amateur record: 112 fights; 100+, 12-
1982: C. North America Las Vegas Lightweight:
- Ramon Goire (Cub) points
Professional record: 55 fights; 46+ (29 KO), 9-
1987-1988: I.B.F. Lightweight

1991: United States Junior Middleweight
1991: W.B.A. Junior Middleweight

- 1983 -
+ (May-26-1983, Atlantic City) Alfredo Chino Rivera kot 4
+ (Jun-30-1983, Atlantic City) Keith Mc Coy ko 3
+ (Jul-10-1983, Atlantic City) Pat Dangerfield ko 2
+ (Aug-16-1983, Atlantic City) Ed Carberry ko 2
+ (Aug-31-1983, Atlantic City) Rafael Alicia ko 2
+ (Sep-9-1983, Las Vegas) Ricardo Moreno kot 3
+ (Sep-24-1983, Totowa) Jim Zelinski ko 2
+ (Oct-27-1983, Atlantic City) Rob Stevenson ko 1
+ (Dec-2-1983, Warwick) Emilio Diaz injury 2
+ (Dec-14-1983, Totowa) Jose Cheo Ortiz kot 6

- 1984 -
+ (Feb-26-1984, Beaumont) Dave Bell kot 4
+ (Apr-15-1984, Atlantic City) Mike Golden 8
+ (Aug-29-1984, Atlantic City) Richie Mc Cain 8
+ (Nov-17-1984, Riva del Garda) Bruno Simili kot 3
- (Dec-1-1984, Milan) Abdel Marbi injury 5

- 1985 -
+ (Mar-27-1985, Atlantic City) Antoine Lark kot 6
+ (Sep-18-1985, Atlantic City) Jeff Bumpus 10
+ (Nov-26-1985, Atlantic City) Melvin Paul kot 2

- 1986 -
+ (Feb-5-1986, Providence) Joe Frazier kot 7
+ (May-18-1986, Providence) Harry Arroyo 10
+ (Sep-18-1986, Providence) Nelson Bolanos kot 6
+ (Nov-8-1986, San Juan) Roger Brown kot 4

- 1987 -
+ (Feb-8-1987, Providence) Roberto Elizondo kot 10
+ (Jun-7-1987, Providence) Greg Haugen 15 (I.B.F., Lightweight)

- 1988 -
- (Feb-6-1988, Atlantic City) Greg Haugen 12 (I.B.F., Lightweight)
+ (Jun-27-1988, Providence) Felix Dubray kot 4
+ (Oct-4-1988, Chicago) Ricky Kaiser kot 3
- (Nov-7-1988, Las Vegas) Roger Mayweather 12 (W.B.C., Junior Welterweight)

- 1989 -
+ (Apr-14-1989, Atlantic City) Jake Carollo kot 2
+ (Jun-11-1989, Atlantic City) Vinnie Burgese kot 10
+ (Nov-27-1989, Providence) Eddie Van Kirk kot 5

1990 -
- (Feb-3-1990, Atlantic City) Hector Camacho 12 (W.B.O., Junior Welterweight)
+ (Aug-5-1990, Atlantic City) Greg Haugen 10
- (Dec-1-1990, Sacramento) Loreto Garza disq.11 (W.B.A., Junior Welterweight)

- 1991 -

+ (Jul-2-1991, Providence) Ron Amundsen 12 (United States, Junior Middleweight)
+ (Oct-1-1991, Providence) Gilbert Dele kot 12 (W.B.A., Junior Middleweight)

- 1992 -
+ (Dec-15-1992, Ledyard) Luis Santana 10

- 1993 -
+ (Mar-6-1993, Ledyard) Brett Lally kot 6
+ (Jun-26-1993, Atlantic City) Lloyd Honeyghan kot 10
+ (Oct-26-1993, Ledyard) Robbie Sims 10
+ (Dec-28-1993, Aspen) Dan Sherry ko 11

- 1994 -
+ (Apr-5-1994, Ledyard) Jacques Leblanc 10
+ (Jun-25-1994, Las Vegas) Roberto Duran 12
+ (Nov-8-1994, Ledyard) Rafael Williams 10

- 1995 -
+ (Jan-14-1995, Atlantic City) Roberto Duran 12
- (Jun-24-1995, Atlantic City) Roy Jones kot 6 (I.B.F., Super Middleweight)

- 1996 -
+ (Aug-23-1996, Atlantic City) Dana Rosenblatt kot 4

- 1997 -
- (Dec-6-1997, Wembley) Herol Graham 12

- 1998 -
+ (Jul-26-1998, Ledyard) Glenwood Brown 10
+ (Nov-6-1998, Ledyard) Arthur Allen 10

- 1999 -
+ (Jan-8-1999, Ledyard) Undra White kot 9

+ (Apr-9-1999, Ledyard) Joseph Kiwanuka 10
+ (Jun-25-1999, Ledyard) Esteban Cervantes 10
- (Nov-5-1999, Ledyard) Dana Rosenblatt 12

- 2000 inactive -

As always fight fans, keep reaching for the stars, and all your dreams can be fulfilled.

Interview conducted May 2000

Pearl calls off Leonard vs Hearns I

Little Big Man...

Up Close and Personal with Legendary Referee Davey Pearl

Webster's Dictionary defines the word referee as follows:
"A sports official usually having final authority while administering a game." Well, I want to add another couple of words to Webster's definition. They are, dedicated, caring, and professional, which is how Davey Pearl is defined, in my opinion. The pleasure derived from interviewing a man I have always felt, added something positive to the sport of boxing, is a life-long memory to cherish. Standing only at 5'4, he was a giant way before they even gave that title to referee, Mills Lane.

Pearl has been the referee in so many great bouts which include; the first, Sugar Ray Leonard vs. Tommy Hearns fight for the undisputed Welterweight Title of the World and

Larry Holmes vs. Earnie Shavers for the Heavyweight Title.

As you will read, boxing is this very sweet man's life, as I found out while talking to him for almost an hour, enjoying every minute of it.

First of all, it's a pleasure to interview someone I have always felt was a positive force in boxing. For the readers who always bring up your name when we talk about great fights, what are you doing today?

I'm waiting to get a fight! Brad, it's my whole life and I have been refereeing for about 35 years now. The fights don't come too often anymore and I miss them. I really don't do many fights anymore, and it looks like they are retiring me, I am guessing.

What was the first fight you ever refereed and what was the outcome?

Well, the first one was a Cruiserweight fight in Las Vegas. The promoter came over to me and wanted to know if I wanted to do it? I said yes and then he asked me if I had any boxing shoes in my car? I went and got a pair of bowling shoes to wear. Now, the funny thing Brad, in the first round one of the fighters hit me right on the chin, and you know what? I didn't feel a thing because my adrenaline was so pumped up. Now, of course, the fans are hollering because they always like to see an official get hit or go down. So, in the middle of the second round, I stopped and faced the crowd. I snapped my fingers over my shoulders, than proceeded to holler to them, mosquito bite. That was the first and last time I ever got hit in the ring Brad.

What do you think of the state of boxing today?

I have got to go with evidence such as in Las Vegas for example, where all the hotels are putting on fights. They wouldn't go back to boxing unless it would help them. We are getting lots of fights around here. The simple fact that hotels and lots of smaller venues are putting on fights, is a good sign to me.

Since you had the opportunity to referee in 15-round fights, would you like to see them come back?

I loved the 15-round fights and I never had a problem going the distance with the fighters.

Do you think there should be only two judges and the referee judging the fight, like in the old days?

I think the greatest thing that ever happened for guys who want to be referees, is that they changed this rule. They should thank their lucky stars.

Who are your three favorite fighters of all-time and why?

Well, Larry Holmes is one. I did about 5 or 6 fights of Larry's. All but one, were title fights. I was very happy to get them, and that he had that much confidence in me to do his fights. I have total respect for Larry. Davey then said, "Brad sometimes I tell people my favorite fighter and they want to boo me off." I replied, 'I would never do that to you.' Davey then said, "Sonny Liston." Liston, as you know Brad, was not liked by too many guys in Las Vegas. In fact, as far as they were concerned, he was a bum. They would always jump on my back and ask how could you run with a guy like that?" The way I use to get them off my back, is by telling them that I used to run with him every morning for five years on the golf course. Well, you do that, and you get to really know someone. Brad, nobody knew Sonny Liston like I did. I still get calls once or twice a month, asking me questions about him. I will tell you an interesting story Brad, concerning Sonny.

I was in his corner when he fought Chuck Wepner and I was really not supposed to be there. I got the word that the fight was fixed against him. I did not know what to do or how strong to come on. It's very tough to accuse people when they haven't done anything yet. So when the fifth round was over, Sonny came back to the corner and said, "Jesus I hate to hit this guy anymore."

Now for a guy like Sonny to say this was an event in itself. I told Sonny the fight is fixed against us. Sonny replied, "You're kidding?" I then replied, "No I am not. Go and knock him out this round," and Sonny sure did. My third would be Muhammad Ali. He was the perfect gentleman.

What is the greatest fight you have ever seen and why?

I would say Tommy Hearns vs Marvin Hagler. That had to be the best three rounds I have ever seen in boxing. They went all out that night and made it one heck of a fight.

Do you have any funny stories about boxing you were involved in, or around?

Well, it may not be that funny but I will tell you one. A guy from this area, named Bill Miller used to put on shows every Wednesday for 20 plus years. He goes and gets a pilot's license and than flies down to Mexico to pick up fighters. He would get two guys for a fight who may have been brothers or cousins, who he knew back then. He would fly them in for the fight and then fly them back. I was the ref for that fight and I could see I was going to have problems.

I am doing the sign language thing with them and the one guy would throw a punch while the other made believe he was dizzy from the punch that never landed. So I warned them and warned them. Finally, in the second round I went to the corner and told them, "NO PUNCH, NO PAY!" Those were the magic words. The one guy comes out and throws one punch and just taps the guy on the chin. He falls and I start counting.

7, 8, 9, the guy is laying there like he is dead and I am saying to myself, there is no way I could miss this hard of a punch. On 10, the guy jumps up and says, "10". He starts dancing around the ring and singing. He surprised me so much that he made me jump up too. So the moral to the story is, DON'T JUMP!, which Davey said with such a great laugh.

I recall that you did commentary, but always wondered why you didn't stick with it?

I was starting to get a lot of work commentating and a guy comes to me from the TV station one day and tells me that, "You just said that was one of the best rounds you have ever seen. Why did you not say it stronger?" He is picking on me about some crap and I told the guy to take a hike. That was the end of the commentating for me.

Do you favor a mandatory retirement fund for all boxers and if so, how would you like to see it accomplished?

Yes I do! If you can find honest people to do it, then it would be great.

What was the most brutal knockout you have ever seen?

I saw one the other night, that was pretty brutal. David Tua knocking out Obed Sullivan in only seconds of the first round.

Did you ever score a fight and when the decision was announced, you were surprised at how the other two judges had the fight scored?

I had the first Ali vs. Spinks scored for Leon Spinks. One judge had it for Ali and I thought before I heard the final judge's card, that he was going to rob Leon Spinks of the fight.

What do you want your many fans to remember you for?

Respect the little guy and that I was twice as fast as those big guys.

Finally, what is the saying you live your life by?

"NO PAY"! (This is famous for me).

In closing, Davey told me the following:

I loved the reputation I got with the fighters. They respect me so much, you would not believe it. I respect them back just as much and never give any of them garbage. I would also like to mention that I got put in the World Boxing Hall of Fame. My last statement to the whole crowd of over a 1,000 people was, "Everybody here is connected with boxing and for that, I love all of you."

Finally, Brad I want to tell you one other story about my friend Sonny Liston. I picked him up in my car one time and we are riding down the main street in Las Vegas. The cars are bumper to bumper. Sonny, out of nowhere, says "Stop the car!" I asked him, 'What are you nuts? I can't stop the car. We are bumper-to-bumper.' He yelled again, "Pull over!"

Well, I pulled over because this was unusual for him to holler at me, since he never had before. I pulled up to the curb and there is a little old white lady selling pencils on a rolling table. Sonny reached in his pocket and emptied it out. I mean, he did not have 10 cents left in his pocket, Brad. This is one of the reasons they can never say a bad thing to me about Sonny Liston.

As always fight fans, keep reaching for the stars, and all your dreams can be fulfilled.

Interview conducted June 2000

(L) Pettway mixes it up with WBC Junior Middleweight Champion Terry Norris

The Return of the Ambassador...

Up Close and Personal with Former IBF Junior Middleweight Champion Vincent Pettway

On March 3, 2001, former IBF JR Middleweight Champion Vincent "The Ambassador" Pettway makes his comeback when he takes on Jose Antonio Rivera for the vacant NABA Welterweight Title. The fight will be held at the Worchester's Centrum Centre in Worchester, Mass. and promoted by BoxAmerica.

Pettway, is a local legend in the Virginia, Washington, DC and Maryland areas, and rightfully so. He is yet another one of those fighters who always takes the time for his fans. Countless times I have seen Vince signing autographs and taking pictures with every fan, especially the children who ask him.

Not only does he do that, but he makes it a point to get out and support the other local upcoming boxers in the area. Vince is the type of fighter, and more importantly, person, that boxing needs, and to whom not enough spotlight is given.

I was able to catch up with Vincent in between his grueling training schedule, and from what I saw, he is in the shape of his life.

How has training been going for your upcoming fight?
Training is really coming along very well. I am very focused on this fight.

Are there any things you do differently in training now that you're a little older?
Not necessarily different, but I learned to relax a lot more and be a little more cagey. I used to do a lot of bouncing and excess movement which I don't do anymore. Instead, I give more angles and conserve my energy.

What should we expect from you on March 3, 2001?
Brad, I am in top notch shape and I may have a little ring rust because of inactivity beyond my control, but I still expect to look very sharp. My main goal is to make Rivera miss and make him pay when he misses.

In the Simon Brown fight did you ever imagine when you threw the punch that your knockdown would end up like that?
I really didn't think I threw that hard of punch, but it was more timing and throwing the punch that I had been shown over many years of fighting. (**If you have not seen the Vincent Pettway VS Simon Brown fight, get the tape. I would say it is in the top five greatest knockouts of all-time.)

Who are your three favorite fighters of all-time and why?

First of all, Vincent Pettway. I truly believe in myself and dedicate 100% to the sport of boxing. Second, Sugar Ray Robinson. He could do everything in the ring, and case in point, backup and still be able to knock a person out. Robinson had a lot of charisma and seemed very at ease with himself outside of the ring. Finally, Muhammad Ali. Ali backed up everything he talked about and really was able to reach the fans who loved him.

What is the greatest fight you have ever seen and why?

The Thrilla in Manilla. It was a true war of attrition and whoever wanted it the most was going to get it. Ali was just landing huge bombs on Frazier and the corner had no other choice but to stop the fight.

Do you favor a mandatory retirement fund for all boxers and if so, how would you like to see it accomplished?

I definitely support a retirement fund for all boxers. For one, we are not guaranteed to go out the same way we came into boxing. Our life's are constantly on the line for the sheer entertainment of the fans as well as the promoters.

With that said, if a retirement fund was in place, many fighters would not have to come back to make a buck or two. The way it should be done is like the IBF is currently doing it. They take a certain amount off a championship fight and put it in a pension plan. Only thing with that is, they need to show what they are doing with it and how they are earning interest for us off that money.

I have no problem with that as long as fighters have constant awareness of the money they have put in it.

On your pound for pound list today, who would you rank in your top three?
Ricardo Lopez; 2. Mark "Too Sharp" Johnson; 3. Roy Jones, JR

Finally, what is the saying you live your life by?
"What would Jesus do?"
In addition to our interview, I received the following quotes about Vince:
10Kount Productions, Vince's promoters: Arnie, Casey, Sam, and Pops Dansicker) "Vince is in the top shape of his life. We are very happy to have Vince part of our family and the boxing world is in for a big surprise when he steps into the ring."
Ken Kosla (BoxAmerica Productions) "We expect a great show at the Worchester's Centrum Centre on March 3, 2001 with a great mainevent and outstanding undercard.")
Isra Girgrah (IBF & UBA Female Lightweight Champion of the World) "Vince is more determined than ever to come back and win a world title for the second time."
Paul Vaden (Former IBF Junior Middleweight Champion) "Vincent's knockout of Simon Brown has to be one of the greatest knockouts of all-time. In our fight, I tasted the power that Vince has, and Rivera better be ready. Finally, Vince is a true gentleman and I wish him the best in his upcoming fight."

Vincent PETTWAY
Nickname: "The Ambassador"

Weight class: Junior Middleweight/154 lbs

Amateur record: 200 fights; 189+, 11-
Professional record: 51 fights; 43+ (32 KO), 1=, 7-
1992-1993: United States Junior Middleweight
1994-1995: I.B.F. Junior Middleweight

- **1984** -
+ (Feb-27-1984, Atlantic City) Ali Muhammad ko 3
+ (Apr-18-1984, Richmond) Ernest Perry ko 2
+ (May-10-1984, Baltimore) Vincent Bailey ko 2
+ (May-23-1984, Pikesville) Reggie Watkins ko 4
+ (Jun-14-1984, Richmond) Ric Graves ko 2
+ (Aug-29-1984, Atlantic City) Joey Soler 6
+ (Sep-6-1984, Baltimore) Charles Robinson ko 2
+ (Oct-16-1984, Baltimore) James Keir ko 3
+ (Nov-14-1984, Pikesville) Thomas Baker disq.8

- **1985** -
+ (Apr-8-1985, Atlantic City) Steve Mitchell kot 6
+ (Jun-20-1985, Baltimore) Antoine Lark ko 2
+ (Aug-21-1985, Baltimore) Marvin Ladson ko 3
+ (Sep-14-1985, Atlantic City) Keith Corbett ko 5
+ (Nov-7-1985, Pikesville) Mike Hutchinson ko 3
+ (Dec-3-1985, Atlantic City) Jose Luis Alejandro ko 2

- 1986 -
+ (Feb-27-1986, Pikesville) Donald Gwynn ko 1
+ (Mar-22-1986, Atlantic City) Hector Figueroa ko 1
- (Apr-15-1986, Baltimore) George Leach ko 4
+ (Jun-11-1986, Baltimore) Leland Hart kot 8
+ (Aug-28-1986, Mechanicsville) Pete Seward ko 3
+ (Nov-29-1986, Richmond) Marvin Ladson ko 2

- 1987 -
+ (Jan-10-1987, Richmond) Jerome Artis ko 1
+ (Mar-21-1987, Richmond) Lopez Mc Gee ko 1
+ (Aug-11-1987, Chicago) Miguel Narvaez ko 6

- 1988 -
+ (Jan-6-1988, Baltimore) Horace Shufford 10
+ (Mar-4-1988, Richmond) Tim Knight kot 9
- (Apr-9-1988, Las Vegas) Javier Suazo ko 6
+ (Oct-6-1988, Philadelphia) Hugh Kearney ko 2

- 1989 -
+ (Feb-5-1989, Atlantic City) Dexter Smith 10
+ (Apr-13-1989, Philadelphia) Sammy Brooks ko 1
+ (Jun-5-1989, Philadelphia) Luis Santana 10
- (Aug-14-1989, Baltimore) Agustin Caballero ko 4

- 1990 -
+ (Feb-13-1990, Baltimore) James Hugues ko 3
- (Apr-3-1990, Philadelphia) Victor Davis kot 9
- (Nov-13-1990, Baltimore) Stephen Johnson kot 6

347

- 1991 -

+ (Mar-4-1991, Baltimore) Eddie Van Kirk kot 6

+ (Oct-9-1991, Pikesville) Juan Rondon kot 8

+ (Dec-4-1991, Pikesville) Frank Montgomery 10

- 1992 -

+ (Feb-19-1992, Baltimore) Gilbert Baptist 12 (United States, Junior Middleweight)

+ (Oct-1-1992, Pikesville) Aaron Smith ko 6

- 1993 -

+ (May-12-1993, Baltimore) Dan Sherry kot 11 (United States, Junior Middleweight)

- 1994 -

= (Mar-4-1994, Las Vegas) Gianfranco Rosi 6 (I.B.F., Junior Middleweight)

+ (Sep-17-1994, Las Vegas) Gianfranco Rosi ko 4 (I.B.F., Junior Middleweight)

- 1995 -

+ (Apr-29-1995, Landover) Simon Brown ko 6 (I.B.F., Junior Middleweight)

- (Aug-12-1995, Las Vegas) Paul Vaden kot 12 (I.B.F., Juniormiddleweights)

- 1996 -

- (Feb-24-1996, Richmond) Terry Norris kot 8 (World, Junior Middleweights)

+ (May-30-1996, Baltimore) Benji Singleton 10

+ (Oct-23-1996, Baltimore) Harold Bennett kot 3

- 1997 -

+ (Dec-13-1997, Pompano Beach) Gerald Reed 10

- **1998: inactive** -

- **1999** -
+ (Feb-6-1999, Washington) Gerald Reed 10
+ (Sep-15-1999, Woodlawn) Anthony Ivory 8

As always fight fans, keep reaching for the stars, and all your dreams can be fulfilled.

Interview conducted March 2001

Magical Powers...

Up Close and Personal with Former WBA & IBF JR. Welterweight Champion Aaron "The Hawk" Pryor

Many of my readers and people who know me well will say two things without a doubt. One, is that my favorite singer of all-time is Frank Sinatra. The other, that my all-time favorite boxer is Aaron Pryor. Both come up in our conversations frequently.

Pryor's story is one of mountain highs and valley lows. He went to the mountain in 1980 when he won the WBA JR. Welterweight Title against then champion, Antonio Cervantes. He would defend it successfully 8 times. In a total of 10 world title fights, he was victorious in each one with two of those as the IBF JR. Welterweight Champion. His battles outside the ring would not be as successful.

Pryor had a well documented battle with cocaine, which had him down for years. He finally went the distance in 1994 and won the decision over his addiction. To this day, he remains a truly loved boxing figure amongst hardcore boxing fans.

In boxing today, who reminds you of yourself in your heyday and why?

Shane Mosley! The reason is that he is very clever and busy in the ring. He can fight in two weight divisions like I did. As I was in my days, he is up for the challenge.

What did you consider your best weapon in the ring?

My best weapons were my body blows.

What big fights were you approached with, but never materialized?

Ray "Boom Boom" Mancini and Sugar Ray Leonard. I called Ray out a few times on TV and knew he could punch. He wanted that fight to get the recognition in my division, which I sought.

What do you think of the state of boxing today?

I think it's as exciting as the days of Jack Johnson. Even though it's not on TV like in my day when you fought on CBS, ABC, and NBC. Today, the big fights are on Pay Per View yet, boxing is very much in demand and one of the highest paid sports out there. A fighter is a very special person who endures a lot and deserves any financial compensation he or she gets.

Do you favor a mandatory retirement fund for all boxers and if so, how would you personally like to see it accomplished?

That's very debatable. It's hard for a fighter when they're first starting out to pay in. Say they only make a small amount in their fights, which would make it hard to pay in after they have paid all their expenses and have little left over. I do favor a mandatory retirement fund when they start making big money. I would like to see it tax-free and through boxing not a corporation.

What are you doing with yourself today?

I am working with young amateur fighters who I am so proud of. I am very deep into the church and currently am a Deacon. I am waiting to see which direction I am going to go in the ministry. I think I may be called into the ministry a little bit deeper. In addition, I am traveling around a lot and doing speaking engagements stressing to people that if you get messed up, you can get straight.

To the young fighter who laces up the gloves as an amateur, what are your words of wisdom to them?

If you come to the gym every day and hit that bag for example, you are going to really learn the proper way to hit it. If you're only going to come on Monday and Thursday, you are not going to learn how to hit that bag.

I had 220 amateur fights and was totally dedicated to the sport. Bottom line to the young fighters, sacrifice and dedication!

Who are your favorite fighters of all-time?

I have so much respect for fighters now that I have met so many in boxing. I just don't admire a fighter inside of the ring but out as well. I look at the whole person concept. A great favorite of mine is Muhammad Ali. He was great in the ring and out. I really admire Oscar Delahoya as well.

What do you think of females in boxing?
I think it's good for boxing and they fight just as hard as the men do.

Do you feel that in your day you got the credit you deserved?
No. I should have gotten more even before I fought Alexis Arguello. I was undefeated for ten years.

If you could have chosen a profession other than boxing, what would it have been?
Martial arts. I held a black belt and was pretty good on my feet. (I have to give my buddy John Lee credit on knowing something I did not about Aaron. John had told me that he thought Aaron was into martial arts and I said I didn't think so).

If you had a time machine and could go back to that magical night in 1982 when you faced Alexis Arguello in the Orange Bowl, which made so many true believers of your greatness, who would you take from today's time back with you to face instead of Alexis?
That's a tough one. I would take Oscar Delahoya. I think I would have tested Oscar's abilities. He seems to be in great shape and can throw a punch. He appears not to be able to take a big punch.

What would be the outcome of the fight?

I would stop him in about the sixth or seventh round. I am not taking anything away from him, but feel he could not stand up under the pressure I carry.

What would your advice be to the young amateur who is on the verge of going pro?

Concentrate on getting a nice undefeated record of about 15-0. Then you're allowed to ask for some bigger money. Don't start out asking for big money. So many fighters do that and I am here to tell you, that's not going to happen.

With all the hype and big bucks the fighters are getting today, how do you feel they would fare against the fighters of your era?

Well, first of all, I think any fighter who steps into the ring today deserves any amount of money they can get because they put themselves at risk. I think the fighters of my era would beat the fighters of today because we were hungrier.

On June 9, 1996, you were inducted into the Boxing Hall of Fame in Canastota, New York. It was a well-deserved honor bestowed upon you. In addition to this and being the WBA and IBF Junior Welterweight Champion of the world, what would you like your legions of fans to remember you for?

I would really like my fans to remember me for all the things that happened to me. Even though I got in trouble, I was lifted up and released by the Father. I feel that was the greatest thing in my entire life when HE picked me up, turned me around, and put my feet back on solid ground. This allowed me the chance to give back to the community, and I am so thankful for it.

Finally, what is the saying you live your life by?
"God is the answer to all your prayers".

Writer's closing remarks:
We all have those special moments in life that are cherished and when I hung up with Aaron, I knew we had done something special in our interview. It was a moment that this writer will always cherish.

Aaron PRYOR
Nickname: "The Hawk"

Weight class: Junior Welterweight/140 lbs

Amateur record: 220 fights; 204+ (100 KO), 16-
1973: United States Lightweight:
1975: Golden Gloves Lightweight:
+ Harris points
1975: Pan-American Games Mexico Lightweight:
+ Michael Reid (Guy)
+ Clive Ellis (Jam)
+ Luis A. Echaide (Cub)
- Chris Clarke (Can) disq.2
1976: Golden Gloves Lightweight:
+ Gary Hinton
+ Thomas Hearns points
1976: Olympic Trials Cincinnati Lightweight:
+ Hilmer Kenty points
- Howard Davis points
1976: Olympic Box-Offs Burlington Lightweight:
- Howard Davis points

Professional record: 40 fights; 39+ (35 KO), 1-
   1980-1983: W.B.A. Junior Welterweight
   1984-1985: I.B.F. Junior Welterweight

- **1976** -
+ (Nov-12-1976, Cincinnati) Larry Smith ko 2

- **1977** -
+ (Feb-1-1977, Cincinnati) Larry Moore ko 4
+ (Feb-24-1977, Cincinnati) Harvey Wilson ko 1
+ (Mar-12-1977, Lincoln) Nick Wills ko 1
+ (Mar-26-1977, Cincinnati) Isaac Vega ko 2
+ (May-7-1977, Cincinnati) Jose Resto 8
+ (Sep-3-1977, Covington) Melvin Young ko 4
+ (Oct-7-1977, Cincinnati) Johnny Summerhayes 8
+ (Nov-11-1977, Cincinnati) Angel Cintron ko 3

- **1978** -
+ (Jan-6-1978, Cincinnati) Robert Tijerina kot 2
+ (Mar-1-1978, Dayton) Ron Pettigrew kot 5
+ (Mar-10-1978, Cincinnati) Al Franklin ko 3
+ (May-3-1978, Miami Beach) Scotty Foreman ko 6
+ (Jul-18-1978, Dayton) Marion Thomas ko 8

- **1979** -
+ (Mar-16-1979, Cincinnati) Johnny Copeland kot 7
+ (Apr-13-1979, Cincinnati) Norman Goins kot 9
+ (Apr-27-1979, Dayton) Fred Harris kot 3
+ (May-11-1979, Cincinnati) Al Ford kot 3
+ (Jun-23-1979, Cincinnati) Jose Fernandez ko 1

+ (Oct-20-1979, Cincinnati) Alfonso FRAZIER kot 5

- 1980 -
+ (Feb-24-1980, Las Vegas) Juan Garcia ko 1
+ (Mar-15-1980, Miami Beach) Julio Valdez kot 4
+ (Apr-13-1980, Kansas City) Leonidas Asprilla kot 10
+ (Jun-20-1980, Cincinnati) Carl Crowley ko 1
+ (Aug-2-1980, Cincinnati) Antonio CERVANTES ko 4 (W.B.A., Junior Welterweight)
+ (Nov-1-1980, Dayton) Danny Myers kot 3
+ (Nov-22-1980, Cincinnati) Gaetan HART kot 6 (W.B.A., Junior Welterweight)

- 1981 -
+ (Jun-27-1981, Las Vegas) Lennox Black Moore kot 3 (W.B.A., Junior Welterweight)
+ (Nov-14-1981, Cleveland) Dujuan JOHNSON kot 7 (W.B.A., Junior Welterweight)

- 1982 -
+ (Mar-21-1982, Atlantic City) Miguel Montilla kot 12 (W.B.A., Junior Welterweight)
+ (Jul-4-1982, Cincinnati) Akio Kameda kot 6 (W.B.A., Junior Welterweight)
+ (Nov-12-1982, Miami) Alexis ARGUELLO kot 14 (W.B.A., Junior Welterweight)

- 1983 -
+ (Apr-2-1983, Atlantic City) Sang-Hyun KIM kot 3 (W.B.A., Junior Welterweight)
+ (Sep-9-1983, Las Vegas) Alexis ARGUELLO ko 10 (W.B.A., Junior Welterweight)
9.1983: Pryor announces retirement.

- 1984 -

+ (Jun-22-1984, Toronto) Nick Furlano 15 (I.B.F., Junior Welterweight)

- 1985 -
+ (Mar-2-1985, Atlantic City) <u>Gary HINTON</u> 15 (I.B.F., Junior Welterweight)

- 1986 inactive -

- 1987 -
- (Aug-8-1987, Sunrise) Bobby Joe Young ko 7

- 1988 -
+ (Dec-15-1988, Rochester) Herminio Morales ko 3

- 1989 inactive -

- 1990 -
+ (May-16-1990, Madison) <u>Darryl JONES</u> ko 3
+ (Dec-4-1990, Norman) Roger Choate ko 7

As always fight fans, keep reaching for the stars, and all your dreams can be fulfilled.

Interview conducted February 2000

(L) Pete Rademacher mixes it up with Heavyweight Champion Floyd Patterson

One for the Records Books...

Up Close and Personal with Former Heavyweight Title Challenger Pete Rademacher

When a true boxing historian starts talking about the sport, the name Pete Rademacher will always come up. Pete has secured his place in boxing history as the only amateur fighter to ever step in the ring in his first professional fight and challenge for the Heavyweight Championship of the World.

The fight took place on August 22, 1957. The Champion at the time was Floyd Patterson. Pete put the champion down in the second round, but was unable to finish him off. He eventually was stopped in the sixth round of a gutsy performance by a young man fighting for the title in his first ever fight as a professional.

I recently had the pleasure to interview this legendary former amateur and professional star, while he took time away from the state cancer benefit he was working at. Pete was a true gentleman and one of those people who I have much respect for because of their true affection for the sport of boxing.

For the many readers who followed your career, what have you been doing since you hung up the gloves?

I went to work for a living, and developed some products because I have a little bit of an inventing nature to me. My job with McNeil Corporation placed me in Ohio, and I headed up one of their divisions for about 22 ½ years. At that time, I had about nine products that were patented. Most of them are in the swimming field.

Your name is forever linked in boxing history as the first man to ever challenge for the Heavyweight Title in your first professional fight. How were you able to do that?

Before I went to Australia, I knew that Marciano had retired and that Cus D' Amato along with Doc Kearns were going to get together to match Archie Moore with Floyd Patterson for the vacant title. I was really daydreaming about that title and knew if I could go over and win the Olympic Gold with a good showing, I would come back and challenge the winner to fight me.

If I won, it probably would have set a record that may never be equaled. When I finally did win the Gold Medal, I started thinking you're almost there. When I came back to the states, I started talking with Jack Dempsey, Joe Louis, Rocky Marciano, Charley Goldman and Al Weill. I kept hearing that you just can't do it.

I finally, through an intermediary friend, got a message to Cus D' Amato. Cus was not happy at that time with Jim Norris and his tactics. We went in to see Cus and he said "sure we can do it, but you guys have to give me $250,000."

We also were told that we had to put the show on and that Cus felt that no Commission would allow it. Since I had gained some popularity in Washington State, we figured it could be done there. We contacted Jack Hurley and asked him if he wanted to be part of it? Jack did, and the rest is history.

In your first two fights as a professional, coming off such a successful amateur career, you were knocked out. Many fighters would have called it quits, but you did not. What made you go on?

Brad, I just loved boxing. It was deep within me and I really had a lot of knowledge on the sport.

How would you rate the current heavyweight division compared to when you were in it?

I think they are not as well schooled, but they are stronger, bigger, and just have more endurance. I think the size and the training methods they have today, would make them better over all.

What changes in boxing since the days when you fought, do you feel have made the sport of boxing better today?

I think world title fights going twelve rounds is better for the safety of the fighters.

Now the flip side, what changes have you seen that you don't think have improved the sport of boxing?

I think some of the promoter stuff is not good. For example, a promoter can control a fighter, when it used to be he could not have anything to do with the control of a fighter. Today, it seems that promoters can control the action of a fighter for five years and make all the decisions for him.

I think that goes against the grain of boxing. I understand that they are working on a law to drop the five years to one year for the fighter to be tied up with the promoter. That would be much better.

If you could pick two fighters in the last 50 years that you felt brought the sport of boxing forward the most, who would they be and why?

I would say Rocky Marciano. He was a gentleman, good fighter and really moved the sport forward during his time in the spotlight. Secondly, Muhammad Ali. Ali could have beaten most of the fighters out there because of his elusiveness, punching ability and all around skills that really changed the complexity of boxing.

I do however think that Ali could not have gotten to Marciano, and Rocky would have caved his ribs in, eventually knocking him out.

Do you favor a mandatory retirement fund for all boxers and if so, how would you like to see it accomplished?

I think every Commission should force a federal law that every purse should have a percentage taken from it and set up in some type of fund. There will be some fighters who are making the millions who already have the big time financial advisers, and don't need it.

However, that is only a small percentage, so it would really help the guys who go out there and fight their hearts out, but are never heard about. (Take notice of this answer. I have always wanted to see something set up for the fighters who don't make the big time money, but give fans everything they have in the ring. This is who the pension helps out the most!)

What made you finally hang up the gloves?

I was 33 and had completed my BS in Animal Science. My skills starting slipping a bit and thought, if I start losing, it would tarnish my name. We put together my last fight in Hawaii and I went out on top, beating Carl "Bobo" Olson.

Funny thing about that fight Brad, was I went over there with no corner. Angelo Dundee was supposed to work it, but was unable too. My wife went along. When we got off the plane, the promoter was upset because Angelo did not come. I'm now working in the gym and have no one with me. I meet this kid who had one amateur fight and hired him on.

I am walking down the street and run into Babe Hollingberry, who was the coach at that time for the football team up at Washington State University, when they went to the Rose Bowl that year. He was there recovering from a heart attack and I asked him if he wanted to work the fight with me? He said, "I could not stand the excitement."

I replied, "There won't be any!" I am going to beat him easily, and we all can have fun working this fight. He did it. I then finally called my wife's classmate's husband, Monte Richards. Monte owned a 350,000 acre cattle ranch on the big island. He told me, "Pete, I have never seen a boxing match." I told him, "fine come on down."

So Brad, this was my corner for the last fight of my career and we had a ball.

What is the greatest fight you have ever seen and why?

I would have to say Evander Holyfield in a couple of his fights, but the one with Riddick Bowe the second time they fought. I have always found Evander exciting.

Finally, what is the saying you live your life by?

"Do unto others, as you would have them do unto you."

Pete would like to add the following to our interview:

I really think boxing is one of the greatest things in the world for youngsters to learn the skills which cause them to have a strong belief in themselves. Many times it helps them take a chip off their shoulders.

From my heart, I feel that boxing can turn more kids around more than any other sport from the standpoint of troubled children to well behaved youngsters. It's just a shame that the YMCA and the schools don't do it anymore. I still feel it's one of the finest training places in all of humanity.

****I would like to thank Mr. Joel Foose for making this interview possible.

Pete RADEMACHER
Weight class: Heavyweight/Unlimited

Amateur record: 79 fights; 72+, 7-
1953: America Heavyweight:
1956: Olympic Games Melbourne Heavyweight:
+ Joszef Nemec (Tch) ko 2
+ Daan Bekker (Afr.S) ko 3
+ Lev Moukhine (URSS) ko 1
Professional record: 23 fights; 15+ (8 KO),
1=, 7-

- **1957** -
- (Aug-22-1957, Seattle) Floyd PATTERSON kot 6 (World, Heavyweight)

- **1958** -
- (Jul-25-1958, Los Angeles) Zora FOLLEY ko 4

- **1959** -
+ (Aug-13-1959, Columbus) Tommy Thompson ko 5
+ (Sep-13-1959, Greenville) Ralph Schneider ko 3
+ (Sep-29-1959, Miami Beach) Cal Butler 10
+ (Nov-12-1959, Columbus) Buddy Keener ko 1
+ (Dec-9-1959, Cleveland) Johnny Yorke 8

- **1960** -
+ (Feb-6-1960, Francfort) Ulli Nitschke ko 7
= (Apr-8-1960, Berlin) Ulli Ritter 10
- (Apr-26-1960, London) Brian LONDON ko 7
+ (Jun-29-1960, Salt Lake City) Lamar CLARK ko 10
+ (Jul-19-1960, Toronto) George CHUVALO 10
+ (Dec-8-1960, Spokane) Kirk Barrow 10

+ (Dec-13-1960, Cleveland) <u>Willi BESMANOFF</u> 10

- 1961 -
+ (Jan-23-1961, Seattle) Donnie Fleeman 10
+ (Feb-22-1961, Yakima) Harvey Taylor ko 1
+ (Apr-14-1961, Gastonia) Dan Vanderford ko 12
- (Apr-29-1961, New York) <u>Doug JONES</u> ko 5
- (Aug-17-1961, Boise) George Logan ko 2
- (Oct-23-1961, Baltimore) <u>Archie MOORE</u> kot 6
+ (Nov-30-1961, Dallas) Buddy Turman ko 9

- 1962 -
- (Jan-20-1962, Dortmund) <u>Karl MILDENBERGER</u> 10
+ (Apr-3-1962, Honolulu) <u>Carl Bobo OLSON</u> 10

As always fight fans, keep reaching for the stars, and all your dreams can be fulfilled.

Interview conducted May 2000

In Memory of a Fallen Warrior...

Beethavean "Bee" Scottland

The death of Super Middleweight Beethavean "Bee" Scottland has been felt throughout the boxing world. But nowhere has it hit harder than in the boxing community of Scottland's home area, the Washington-Baltimore corridor. Both Gary and I expressed our feelings in the following memorial.

"Bad" Brad Berkwitt:
On March 23rd 2000, I covered my first boxing show at Michael's Eighth Avenue in Glen Burnie, Maryland. On that card, was a main event between number two ranked super middleweight Thomas Tate who took on tough local Beethavean Scottland. Tate went on to win the 10 round decision, but Scottland as always, had great moments, and was tough throughout. What I saw that night in "Bee" and also in subsequent fights, was a huge heart and desire to give everything he had in his skill bag. Scottland was a "Fighter's Fighter"

meaning he always came in shape, fought, and gave the crowd their money's worth.

Just one week ago today, "Bee" fought his last fight on ESPN2 against tough George Khalid Jones. Scottland took punishment throughout the fight, but as he always did, Scottland showed heart and actually pulled out rounds 8 and 9 before he was knocked out in the tenth round. "Bee" would lapse into a coma shortly after and never recover from the two brain operations he endured.

This tragedy, one that hits home even harder because I knew "Bee" from covering his fights, is why, until my last breath on earth, I will fight for a mandatory retirement fund and medical coverage for each and every boxer out there. Every other sport has it, and it's about time we did something to get it installed for boxers like "Bee", who should have a pension that could have gone to his wife and three kids to help them, now that he is gone.

Finally, I want to say to Beethavean's family, "What is loved can never be lost and as long as we have hearts, Beethavean will always be with us."

Gary "Digital" Williams:

I first met Bee in February of 1995. He was getting ready to make his pro debut after a solid amateur career. I remember, there was a serious buzz about him, and everyone thought he would be a pro champion. He was indeed a boxer who everyone, because of his style, paid to see. He was a true warrior. How ironic it seems now that in his pro debut he fought Stan Braxton, whose brother, Dwight Muhammad Qawi was one of the boxers who represented the meaning of being a ring warrior.

In December of 1995, after a 6-0-1 record, Bee fought another D.C. warrior in Alan "Boogaloo" Watts. Scottland took a lot of punishment and he gave a lot as well. But he really faltered in the latter part of the sixth and into the seventh round. Midway through the round, "Bee" took a wicked combination and he collapsed onto the floor, unconscious. I remember the pandemonium that flooded the ring that night as friends and family tried to rush the ring to help "Bee." How surprised we all were when Scottland got up and eventually walked out of the ring and did postfight interviews afterwards.

Beethavean Scottland's win-loss record (20-7-2, nine knockouts) says that he was not a championship caliber super middleweight at the time of his passing. When he fought against tougher competition like Eric Harding or Thomas Tate, he came out on the losing end. But he always, ALWAYS gave the fans their money's worth. He fought like a champion each and every time. He was only stopped twice in his career, the first Watts fight and in his final bout.

And, what's more, Bee never, EVER, lost hope of being a champion. In the last fight of his I covered in August of 2000 in D.C., he beat trialhorse Roosevelt Walker by an eighth round TKO. He told me afterwards that he wanted to be considered one of the elite in the super middleweight division. How sad it is that he never again will have the opportunity to reach that goal.

Even when I saw and talked to him for what turned out to be the last time, June 21, five days prior to his final fight, he looked and sounded ready to move to the next level.

One thing about the Washington-Baltimore boxing community, it is a tight-knit group. You may have seen newly-crowned WBO Junior Welterweight champ DeMarcus "Chop Chop" Corley's corner wearing "Bee" Scottland headbands last Saturday. Clarence Vinson dedicated his bout in D.C. last Friday to Scottland. Believe me, this has rocked our boxing community because everyone knew, respected and loved him.

"Bad" Brad and I are writing this because, to many people in the press, Beethavean "Bee" Scottland was just another club fighter who suffered a tragic fate. We wanted to relay the feelings of the Washington-Baltimore boxing community and say that he was a lot more than that to us.

I join my partner in not only sending condolences to Bee's wife, Denise and his family, but also calling for a mandatory retirement fund for fighters. Maybe a part of Bee's legacy will be that this tragedy will help our great sport get closer to achieving that goal.

Bee, we won't forget you. Thanks for everything.

Originally published in July 2001

Showing the Way...

Up Close and Personal with Former Light Heavyweight Title Challenger John "Ice Man" Scully

Throughout boxing, you have those tough fighters who may not be discussed in everyday boxing circles, but when their name is mentioned, people automatically recognize it. Scully is one of those fighters. He challenged for the IBF Light Heavyweight Championship against then Champion, Henry Maske, on May 25, 1996. He fought a very competitive fight, but dropped a decision to the Champion.

I have become friendly with John over the last couple of months and wanted to conduct an interview with him to get out all the great things he is doing for the Youth of America. Boxing fans all over the world take notice,

371

that there are many positive role models in boxing who continue to do great things in our communities throughout the world.

What inspired you to get into boxing?

Basically I would say Muhammad Ali. When I was a kid, my father had a book by Howard Cosell that talked a lot about Ali. He also had "The Greatest" which, as you know, was about Ali too. Finally, he had Sugar Ray Robinson's autobiography. When I use to stay with him on the weekends around the age of 6 or 7, I use to read these three books every single time I visited.

Ali really captured my young imagination. I used to start boxing on my bed. I would set the timer and fight Jimmy Young. I did this about three times every weekend for, like 15 rounds. My hands would be wrapped in toilet paper with tape over them. I would fight three minute rounds and at the end of each round, I would score it.

When the fight was over, I would be very dramatic and announce the scores. Finally I would pause and say, "And the New……." (I really enjoyed this honest answer because I am sure many fighters out there, like actors and singers, have done this before in their childhood. It shows the innocence of our youth which is a wonderful thing.)

What was it like being in the ring fighting for the Light Heavyweight Championship of the World against then champ, Henry Maske?

Brad, that was a very unique experience because things over there in his own country, which is Germany, are quite different from fighting in the United States. Over there, they consider him as big as Michael Jordan is here, in our country.

I can remember being in the ring first and surrounded by 14,000 plus people. Then, all of sudden, this real weird music starting playing like in the Wizard of OZ with the little munchkins. Out of nowhere, smoke appears, and here comes Henry walking down this long aisle.

I can remember watching this whole thing and thinking this is really cool for him. It seemed like I was watching two other guys fighting. I have to give him credit; he was a tough champion, and even back in the amateurs when I knew him, he was very tough.

Being friendly with you, I am well aware of all the wonderful work you are doing on behalf of the constant fight for AIDS awareness and a cure. What information would you like to get out to the readers who want to help in this fight, as well?

Basically I go around to the schools and youth groups always talking about the prevention of AIDS. When I was younger, it was so far off from me and I never really thought about it. Most people don't. When you finally have it hit someone that you are close to, it then really opens your eyes to this terrible disease.

It hit home for me when my buddy, former world rated number one contender, Lamar Parks, contracted the virus. Lamar and I fought each other twice in the amateurs and became very close over the years.

I use Lamar as an example when I'm talking to these young kids out there because we are close. I really just want people to open their eyes and realize that someone you know, may know, or they may not know they have the virus, are around you right now and we need to help them out.

I heard a rumor that you were making a comeback. Is it true? If so, give us the details.

Yes, Brad it's true. Currently, I have been training for about two months and have a fight up in Hartford, CT on the 21st of October. I am doing some things different this time around that I feel will help me out. I would like to get a rematch with Sammy Ahmad who just fought Julian Letterlough to a draw last night on ESPN2.

Our fight was very close, and I feel even though I only fought with one hand because of an injury I sustained in the first round of our bout, I still won it, but wasn't given the nod. The Light Heavyweight division is going to open up because I really feel Roy is going to move down, so that will open up three belts.

Who are your three favorite fighters of all-time and why?

Number one has to be Muhammad Ali. He was an inspiration to thousands of guys who became fighters, including me, as I said earlier. I love his way in and out of the ring. He always stood by his convictions and continues to this day. When I tell kids about sacrifice, I use Ali as an example - when he would not go into the Army and was stripped of his belt, which at that time, was his whole world.

He gave up the three best years (at least I think they would have been), to stand by his convictions. That is seldom seen in life, and I totally respect him for it.

Second, would be Archie Moore. I was a really good friends with him and I started writing to him through the mail when I was around 15 years old. He would always write me back. He became an advisor to me. This allowed me to watch a lot of his fights.

Finally, Willie Pep. In his day, he was an amazing boxer. He was an elusive master and if he didn't want you to hitn him, you didn't. He always gave me good advice.

What is your all-time favorite fight and why?

Aaron Pryor vs. Alexis Arguello I. It was amazing the heart Aaron showed because Alexis really tagged him with some huge shots. He really proved what a great boxer he was.

If you could have fought in any era, which one would you pick and why?

I would go with the one I was in. When I was at 160, there were a lot of fights that fell through, or ones that I should have not lost.

Where did the "Iceman" nickname come from?

Kids always ask me where does the nickname come from? I reply, "I have that name because I'm the coolest guy you are ever going to meet." I really got it from when I was in JR. High School. One kid use to call me Block Head, so when the kids would come to my amateur fights, they would yell out, Ice block which evolved into ICEMAN. So there you have it.

Do you favor a mandatory retirement fund for all boxers and if so, how would you like to see it accomplished?

It's very difficult in boxing to do. I think that you could use the money from these mega fights, such as, any fight over 5 million. Bottom line: It's going to be a tough thing to implement, but it's truly needed. I just want to see it done correctly from the start.

When you finally do retire from boxing, how would you like the fans that followed you from day one to remember you?
When they look back at me, I hope they remember that I gave it my all when I stepped in the ring.

Finally, what is the saying you live your life by?
It's not really a saying, but something I stress to the kids I work with. I always tell them do the best you can and live your life like a decent person.

John would like to add the following to our interview:
I really want to get a couple wins under my belt and hope the promoters will take notice. By taking notice, I hope to get a TV shot and if I look good, maybe one last title fight.

John SCULLY
Nickname: "Ice Man"

Weight class: Light Heavyweight/175 lbs

Professional record: 47 fights; 37+ (21 KO),
10-

- **1988** -
+ (Sep-16-1988, Hartford) Paulino Falcone kot 1

+ (Oct-22-1988, Salem) Steve Jefferson kot 1
+ (Oct-28-1988, Hartford) John Wilkinson kot 4
+ (Nov-25-1988, Hartford) Frank Ambrose kot 4
+ (Dec-2-1988, Poughkeespie) Jerry Fleming kot 4
+ (Dec-10-1988, Salem) Vic Ferrer kot 4
+ (Dec-15-1988, Rochester) Rahim Muhammad kot 4

- 1989 -
+ (Jan-6-1989, Hartford) John Berkins ko 1
+ (Feb-17-1989, Poughkeespie) Charlie Johnson kot 1
+ (Mar-17-1989, Hartford) Mike Bonislawski 6
+ (May-1-1989, Rochester) Jerry Fleming kot 3
+ (May-5-1989, Hartford) Mike Bonislawski kot 5
+ (Jun-16-1989, Hartford) Mike Caminitti kot 6
- (Jul-11-1989, Atlantic City) Brett Lally 10
+ (Aug-25-1989, Bridgeport) Victor King 6
+ (Sep-8-1989, Taunton) Victor King kot 4
+ (Sep-29-1989, Hartford) Tony Daley 10
+ (Nov-9-1989, Springfield) Alphonso Bailey 8
+ (Dec-12-1989, Atlantic City) Billy Bridges 10

- 1990 -
- (Mar-18-1990, Atlantic City) Kevin Watts 10
+ (Oct-23-1990, Worcester) Jose Vera 8

- 1991 -
+ (Sep-27-1991, Springfield) Randy Smith 10

+ (Nov-22-1991, Springfield) Willie Kemp 10

- 1992 -
+ (Feb-27-1992, Agawan) Jose Vera 6
+ (May-22-1992, Agawan) Melvin Wynn 12
+ (Jun-30-1992, Pensacola) David Mc Cluskey 6
+ (Aug-6-1992, Hartford) Danny Chapman kot 3
+ (Aug-20-1992, Milford) Herman Farrar kot 6
+ (Sep-24-1992, Randolph) Jose Vera 6
- (Nov-13-1992, Las Vegas) Tim Littles 12 (United States, Supermiddleweight)

- 1993 -
- (Mar-16-1993, Philadelphia) Tony Thornton 10
+ (Nov-6-1993, Foxboro Park) Jose Vera kot 4

- 1994 -
+ (Mar-12-1994, Hartford) David Mc Cluskey kot 4
+ (Jun-25-1994, Revere) Willie Kemp 8
+ (Aug-18-1994, Ledyard) Tim Cooper 8
+ (Oct-20-1994, Ledyard) Art Bayliss 10

- 1995 -
+ (Mar-14-1995, Boston) Luis Oliveira kot 1
+ (May-17-1995, Ledyard) Willie Kemp 8
+ (Sep-20-1995, Ledyard) Willie Ball ko 2
- (Dec-8-1995, Ledyard) Michael Nunn 12

- 1996 -
+ (Mar-15-1996, Revere) Jose Luis Feliciano ko 1
- (May-25-1996, Leipzig) Henry Maske 12 (I.B.F., Lightheavyweight)

- 1997 -

- (Mar-22-1997, Berlin) Graciano Rocchigiani 10
- (Jun-29-1997, Hartford) Ernest Mateen 10
+ (Dec-18-1997, Hartford) Scott Lopeck kot 6

- **1998** -
- (Aug-2-1998, Boston) Drake Thadzi ko 7

- **1999** -
- (Jun-4-1999, Philadelphia) Sam Ahmad 8

As always fight fans, keep reaching for the stars, and all your dreams can be fulfilled.

Interview conducted September 2000

(R) Earnie Shavers drops a bomb on WBC
Heavyweight Champion Larry Holmes

Power Punch...

Up Close and Personal with Former Heavyweight Title Challenger Earnie "The Acorn" Shavers

When a true boxing fan mentions the name Earnie Shavers the first thing out of his mouth is, hands down, the hardest heavyweight puncher in boxing history. I totally agree with this statement. However, I wish to tell readers a little bit about Earnie, the man I consider a friend.

Earnie has always been among my top three favorite fighters of all-time along with other greats as: first, Aaron Pryor and then, Alexis Arguello.

Over the years, I had spoken to Earnie many times on the phone and we really clicked. But finally, in November 2000, we met in person in

Washington, DC at the charity event, "Fightnight for the Children." Earnie and his wife, and my wife Gwen and I, met and shared laughs and our life stories, securing the bonds of our friendship.

Oh yeah, there was one other gentleman who joined us and that was Kenny Norton. Kenny is one of the funniest men I have ever met.

You would never have thought these two warriors met in the ring because they acted as if they were brothers, not former adversaries. Should you ever have the chance to meet Earnie, you will find out for yourself that he is one of the warmest, most interesting and decent men you could ever want to meet.

I can't tell you how many of my readers and fans of boxing I know who always bring your name up when we talk about boxing. They are always talking about your power, and the question most asked of me is, "What is he doing today?"

Currently I am a guest speaker at many events and travel all over the world making these types of appearances. People like to see a lot of the heavyweights from my era and we enjoy speaking to them.

How did you wind up in England?

I had a young fan here who I came to see and met his Aunt. Brad, the day I met her I knew I was going to marry this woman. I did, and now enjoy living in England. I travel back and forth to the states about twice a month.

I have always been a fan of yours and I am so happy to see you getting the credit you have deserved since your heyday in the ring.

381

Do you feel you got the proper credit you deserved when you were fighting?

No, not really. I am getting it now. I was chosen as the hardest puncher of the 20th Century. I think induction to the Hall of Fame will come soon.

I have followed boxing since 1975, but the fight that sticks in my mind the most up until 1980 in the heavyweight ranks, is your 1979 first round destruction of Kenny Norton. Going into that fight, what did you think would happen?

Well Brad, I knew Kenny was afraid of my punching power. I really beat Kenny six weeks before the fight. We had a press conference in California with Don King. Don King and Kenny Norton were talking about the return match with Larry Holmes. I turned to Don King and said you forgot about me. Don said, "oh yeah" and brought me up on the stage.

I turned to Kenny and said, "Kenny I am going to destroy you!" Kenny said, "Earnie we are going to both make a lot of money." I told Kenny I am the only guy who is going to remember that. I put the fear of GOD into him and he never got over it. I figured in three rounds I would have him out of there. My corner told me to go to him because he can't fight going backwards. I did just that - backed him up and knocked him out.

In your second attempt at the Heavyweight Title vs. Larry Holmes you had him down and what many thought, out. Somehow he was able to get up from that murderous punch and pull out the win. In hindsight, what would you have done to pull out the win?

Well one problem for me was in the third round. I got thumbed. I really couldn't see Larry properly. In fact, I saw three Larry Holmes and swung at the wrong one. Larry told me that out of all the guys he ever fought, that I was the greatest puncher. He said, "You hit me so hard in the seventh round that all I saw was like a flash from a camera."

Next thing I know I was hitting the floor, which woke me up. Larry ended by saying, "If you had cut back on your punching power, I would still be there today!" I didn't realize at the time that I was punching so hard and wearing down. I must tell you Brad, that Larry Holmes had the best recovery time I have ever seen. I must also say that Muhammad Ali did, as well. You know Brad, the fight game has been very good to me. Those two fights with Holmes and Ali have opened up so many doors for me, especially now. I am getting calls everyday and getting paid about $5,000 minimum, for personal appearances.

Who was your toughest challenger and why?

My toughest challenger was a guy named Roy "Tiger" Williams out of Philadelphia. When I first turned pro back on November 6, 1969, I trained upstate New York with some of the Philadelphia fighters. They would tell me all about this guy and say, "Earnie this guy is tough. You guys will meet and it will be a life and death fight. So get all the money you possibly can for the fight because it is going to be a tough one." From then on, I never forgot that name.

So what happened was, when I was trying to get a fight with Muhammad Ali, who at the time had Roy Williams as a sparring partner and fired him because he was so tough. Ali then told me, "If you beat Roy, I will give you a title fight." Brad, I didn't want nothing to do with Roy. In fact I didn't even want to go past Philly because I might run into him. I really had no other choice, but to fight him so I could get my first title fight. See, I had Roy as a sparring partner too, and after a week, my trainer fired him because every day in sparring was a war. My trainer told me, "You can't have these kinds of wars every day because you're leaving the fight in the gym."

What was the outcome of the Roy "Tiger" Williams" fight?

I knocked him out in the 10th round. The first eight rounds were very close. I was ahead on points and Roy decided to come back in the 9th and 10th rounds to make up for the first eight. He literally had me out in those two rounds. Brad, I watch the fight now and still get afraid.

I feel that the current heavyweight division today lacks the excitement and the characters of your era. What do you think of the current heavyweight ranks?

I feel the same way. During the 1970s, it was the toughest era in the history of the heavyweight division. In fact, it was known as the Golden Era for heavyweights. There were so many great guys out there and great trainers too. We were so competitive back then. We did not want any fighter to get an edge on us, so we did whatever we had to do to stay on top.

I have always heard a rumor, but want to clear it up. True or false? You use to knock the heavybag off the chain?

True! I use to break the speedbag too. Earnie then said, "I had a little punching power." I replied to his statement by saying, "a little?" That's like saying Donald Trump has a little bit of money.

Talking about your power. Where did it come from?

Well Brad, I grew up on a farm and used to throw bales of hay, carried bags of wheat, and chopped down big trees. This gave me power in the back of my leg muscles. So when I turned professional, Archie Moore and those other guys would have me chop down trees to keep my punching power going. Every time I chopped for a fight, I could tell the difference. In fact, when I chopped, I punched 25% harder than when I didn't for a fight.

What do you think of females in boxing?

I really don't care for it. Boxing is a tough sport and in the long run they are going to get hurt. Women's bodies are not built to take punches and a man's body is not built to take punches either. Look at us guys and see what it has done. I just don't like to see that for women.

Do you favor a mandatory retirement fund for all boxers to pay into once they turn professional?

I totally agree with you 100% from day one you should start putting something away. Take me for example, I did not make that much money in the ring, but boxing gave me a name that now has allowed me to make and put money away, that I wish I would have done when I was fighting.

If you could have chosen any other profession besides boxing, what would it have been?

First of all, I am an outdoors person, so it would have to be an outdoors job. Probably something like construction, because I enjoy hard work and because it keeps you in shape and makes you stronger. Like I said, construction or maybe a builder.

How did you get into boxing?

Since the age of 12, I knew I wanted to be an athlete. So I started taking care of myself. My brother's friend, who was a high school football player, told me what I had to do and other guys did as well, growing up. I never smoked, drank or did drugs my whole entire life. I dedicated my whole life to being an athlete. I got into the fight game at 22 and thank God for me starting late, because I was more mature, stronger than most guys and well-conditioned.

What would your advice be to the young man who is just turning professional?

You must eat, sleep and live boxing 24 hours a day. Listen to fighters who came before you and the trainers who can tell you good, bad, and what not to do.

With all the hype and big bucks the fighters are getting today, how do you feel they would fair against the boxers of your era?

I am glad the guys today are getting big money, but they would not fare well against the guys from my day. We just had better competition back then.

Do you have any funny stories of things you were involved in that happened before a fight, or after?

I sure do. I used to tell guys about doing something I learned a long time ago. You start to tell an opponent a little story, but you don't finish it. By doing this, you get the guy's mind messed up. You find out something bad about your opponent, but you wouldn't tell him the whole story. You tell him just enough to make him think and worry.

I did this when I fought Howard Smith. See, Howard used to be one of my sparring partners. I used to knock him out in the gym everyday with the big gloves on. At the weigh-in, I said, "Howard remember the old times." He turned to his trainer and told him, "I am not ready for this guy."

I will tell you another story about Jimmy Ellis. Ali told me how to fight Jimmy. Ali knew Jimmy, who, by the way, is a wonderful guy. Ali told me "If Jimmy boxes you, he is going to beat you because he has more experience than you. You have to make him try and out punch you." So Archie Moore went to Jimmy and told him about a week before our fight, that he cannot punch. Jimmy and Angelo Dundee had the plan to outbox me. Well after hearing that, Jimmy tried to out punch me.

He hit me with a good right-hand in the first round, but forgot to move. I threw a right uppercut and caught him. Bingo, ballgame is over. If he would have just boxed me, he would have probably beaten me. The whole key to the fight game is to be in good condition and learn how to con your opponent. I had a problem with Ali and Larry Holmes. I tried to con those guys and they just stared right back at me. I said to myself it's going to be a long night.

Brad I have to tell you one more funny story about when I fought Jeff Sims in Nassau. Well, before I fought him they called me and I was in retirement at the time. They offered me $50,000 to fight my grandmother, meaning basically an opponent I could beat. My people told me "You know that they are going to switch opponents on you before the fight."

So, fight time, naturally he got hurt. So, when I got to Nassau some guy asked me who I was going to fight and I said, "Jeff Sims." He said, "Oh my God he punches almost as hard as you and that's him over there". I looked over him and he looked like a gorilla. I went over to him and said "Jeff, is so and so your manager"? He said "Yes". My reply was "You are nothing, but one of his Negroes. He isn't even here. I bet he will be here in time to cut up the money though." Jeff said, "That's right". See I got him going. I then said "Look Jeff, don't get hurt". So in the first round, he had me down.

I got up and said, "Hey Jeff, slow it down we have ten rounds to go." He said, "ok." So, I went to work on him in about the third or fourth round and knocked him out in like the 5th or 6th round. Jeff told me, "Man, you told me to slow it down. You tricked me!" I told him, "You bought it, welcome to the BIGTIME!"

Why did Ali nickname you "The Acorn"?
Because I had a shaved head that looked like an acorn. When the fight was over, he said, "Earnie, you're a hard nut to crack!"

Have you stayed friendly with any of the fighters from your generation?

Every last one of them. There is not one guy in the fight game I do not like. There is not one of them who has turned me down for any request I have ever asked of them.

I have reviewed your fight record and it's quite impressive at give or take, 73 wins, 14 losses, and one draw. I noticed that if it went to a decision, you came up on the short end of the stick almost every time. Why do you think that is so?

I usually tensed up in a fight and it took me a long time to learn to relax in there. If you don't relax in there you burn yourself out. So, if the fight went more than five rounds, I would burn myself out from being so tense. I learned to relax at the end of my career. They told me, "You never learn the fight game till your fight game is over."

I have many of your tapes and noticed you were interviewed by the legendary Howard Cosell. What was it like be interviewed by him?

Howard was ok. He was your friend as long as you were there in front of him. When you turned and walked away he got you. I guess that was part of his job.

Finally, what would you like your fans to remember you for when they mention the name Earnie Shavers?

That I gave them their money's worth when I fought, win, lose, or draw. People paid their hard-earned cash and they want to see a good fight, which I think I gave them.

Earnie SHAVERS
Nickname: "The Acorn"

Weight class: Heavyweight/Unlimited

Amateur record: 1969: America Heavyweight
Professional record: 88 fights; 73+ (67 KO),
1=, 14-

- 1969 -
+ (Nov-6-1969, Akron) Red Howell ko 2
+ (Nov-11-1969, Orlando) George Holden ko 1
- (Nov-14-1969, Seattle) Stanley Johnson 6
+ (Nov-21-1969, Rapid City) Lee Roy ko 3
+ (Dec-4-1969, Akron) J.D. Mc Cauley ko 2
+ (Dec-18-1969, Canton) Chico Froncano ko 1
+ (Dec-26-1969, Orlando) Gene Idolette ko 2

- 1970 -
+ (Jan-7-1970, Akron) Tiger Brown ko 1
+ (Jan-24-1970, Canton) Joe Byrd ko 3
+ (Jan-27-1970, Orlando) Tiger Brown ko 5
+ (Mar-6-1970, Canton) Arthur Miller ko 1
+ (Mar-23-1970, Youngstown) Ray Asher ko 1
+ (Apr-14-1970, Canton) Frank Smith ko 4
- (May-11-1970, Omaha) Ron Stander ko 5
+ (Aug-29-1970, Youngstown) Jim Daniels ko 1
+ (Sep-12-1970, Columbus) Don Branch ko 1
+ (Oct-14-1970, Canton) Johnny Hudgins ko 1
+ (Nov-18-1970, Youngstown) Johnny Mac ko 4
+ (Dec-7-1970, New York) Bunky Akins ko 1

- 1971 -
+ (Jan-6-1971, Akron) Lee Estes ko 2
+ (Jan-15-1971, Miami Beach) Nat Shaver ko 1
+ (Feb-3-1971, Las Vegas) Johnny Mac ko 3
+ (Feb-17-1971, Akron) Richard Gosha ko 5
+ (Mar-3-1971, Las Vegas) Steve Carter ko 1
+ (Mar-24-1971, Las Vegas) Young Agabab ko 1

+ (Apr-21-1971, Akron) Mac Harrison ko 2
+ (Apr-24-1971, Tampa) Willie Johnson ko 4
+ (May-14-1971, Las Vegas) Jimmy Brown ko 1
+ (Jun-1-1971, Stateline) Chuck Leslie ko 10
+ (Jun-30-1971, Warren) Bill Hardney ko 1
+ (Jul-13-1971, Stateline) Bill Mc Murray ko 1

+ (Sep-28-1971, Reno) Pat Duncan ko 5
+ (Oct-17-1971, Akron) Charlie Boston ko 2
+ (Oct-29-1971, Stateline) Elmo Henderson ko 4

+ (Nov-23-1971, Warren) Cleo Daniels ko 2
+ (Nov-30-1971, Bryant) Del Morris ko 3

- **1972** -
+ (Feb-1-1972, Warren) Ted Gullick ko 6
+ (Feb-15-1972, Beaumont) Elgie Walters ko 2
+ (Apr-6-1972, Warren) Charlie Polite ko 3
+ (Apr-22-1972, Akron) Bob Felstein ko 5
+ (May-5-1972, Akron) Lou Bailey ko 2
+ (Aug-26-1972, Canton) Vicente Rondon 10
+ (Sep-22-1972, Canton) A.J. Staples ko 1
+ (Oct-25-1972, New York) Leroy Caldwell ko 2

- **1973** -
+ (Feb-19-1973, Philadelphia) Jimmy Young kot 1
+ (May-12-1973, Windsor) Harold Carter ko 1
+ (Jun-18-1973, New York) Jimmy Ellis ko 1
- (Dec-14-1973, New York) Jerry Quarry ko 1

- **1974** -
+ (May-16-1974) Cookie Wallace ko 1
- (Nov-4-1974) Bob Stallings 10
= (Nov-26-1974) Jimmy Young 10

- **1975** -
+ (Feb-11-1975) Leon Shaw ko 1

+ (Apr-9-1975) Rochelle Norris ko 10
+ (May-8-1975) Oliver Wright ko 3
- (Sep-8-1975, Denver) Ron Lyle ko 6
+ (Nov-13-1975) Tommy Howard ko 3

- **1976** -
+ (Mar-28-1976) Henry Clark 10
+ (Sep-28-1976) Henry Clark ko 2
+ (Dec-11-1976) Roy Williams kot 10

- **1977** -
+ (Apr-16-1977, Las Vegas) Howard Smith ko 2
- (Sep-29-1977, New York) Muhammad Ali 15 (World, Heavyweight)

- **1978** -
- (Mar-25-1978, Las Vegas) Larry Holmes 12
+ (Jul-20-1978, Virginia Beach) Harry Terrell ko 1
+ (Oct-9-1978, Hampston) John Girowski kot 4
+ (Dec-4-1978, Saginaw) Harold Carter ko 3

- **1979** -
+ (Mar-23-1979, Las Vegas) Ken Norton ko 1
+ (May-25-1979, Richfield) Eddie Porette ko 3
- (Sep-28-1979, Las Vegas) Larry Holmes kot 11 (W.B.C., Heavyweight)

- **1980** -
- (Mar-8-1980, Mc Afee) Bernardo Mercado ko 7
+ (Jun-14-1980, Cincinnati) Leroy Boone 10
- (Aug-2-1980, Detroit) Randy Cobb kot 8
+ (Oct-17-1980, Palm Beach) Ted Hamilton ko 2

- **1981** -

+ (Jul-29-1981, Saginaw) Terrell Williams ko 2

+ (Sep-9-1981, Michigan) Mike Rodger kot 2
+ (Dec-11-1981, Nassau) Jeff Sims kot 5

- **1982** -
+ (Apr-21-1982, Traverse City) Ali Haakim 10
+ (May-8-1982, Dallas) Joe Bugner kot 2
+ (May-15-1982, Yorktown) Danny Sutton kot 7
- (Jun-11-1982, Las Vegas) James Tillis 10
+ (Jun-22-1982, Houston) Billy Joe Thomas ko 5

- (Aug-17-1982, Lafayette) Walter Santemore 10
+ (Sep-5-1982, Wales) Chuck Gardner kot 2
+ (Nov-5-1982, El Paso) Tony Perea kot 7

- **1983** -
+ (Jan-29-1983, El Paso) Robin Griffin 10
- (Mar-1-1983, Baltimore) George Chaplin disq.9

- **1984-1986: inactive** -

- **1987** -
+ (May-16-1987) Larry Sims ko 1

- **1988-1994: inactive** -

- **1995** -
+ (Sep-19-1995, Omaha) Brian Morgan 8
- (Nov-24-1995, Wisconsin Dells) Brian Yates kot 2

As always fight fans, keep reaching for the stars, and all your dreams can be fulfilled.

Interview conducted April 2000

393

** One update to this interview is Earnie just released his autobiography WELCOME TO THE BIG TIME. I think readers will truly enjoy it as I did. It offers the reader a great insight into not only Earnie's life, but his great sense of humor. The book can be purchased at: www.sagamorepub.com

Picture © by Mary Ann Owen

Moving Forward...

Up Close and Personal with Three Time Women's World Champion Marischa Sjauw

As many of the readers know, I enjoy interviewing ladies who really add to the sport of female boxing. Well, here is a special interview with one lady who exemplifies that by more than just words, but by actions. Those actions take place in the square circle where they belong, by taking on stiff competition, which only makes one a better fighter.

What inspired you to get into boxing?
I wanted to get in shape and I just love sports. Two of my brothers were boxing, so I decided to try it. After a while, I really started loving it, so I stuck with it. Later,

I started to play soccer and trained in the martial art of "Kun Tauo".

What are you words of wisdom to a young female that want's to lace up the gloves?
Make sure that you really, really love it, because it's a lot of hard work just for conditioning, as well as competing. Besides the bad side of it, politics, it's a great sport. It's worth it. Never do it for the money.

If you could emulate any fighter, who would it be and why?
Roy Jones, JR. He is a great role model, brilliant fighter and very smart person.

How long have you followed boxing?
Since 1990, when I started training.

Who are your top three favorite fighters of all-time and why?
First Henry Armstrong. He managed to win titles in a number of different divisions simultaneously. Second, Julio Ceasar Chavez, who was a true legend. I try to remember him only in his prime. It's a shame he keeps on coming back for way too long. Finally, Bernard Hopkins. I believe he will break the middleweight title-defense record. Great fighter, great spokes-person and a very intelligent person.

What is the greatest fight you have ever seen and why?
Julio Ceasar Chavez Vs Meldrick Taylor I. A great action packed fight with Taylor leading comfortably on the cards, and then Chavez

knocking him out with a few seconds left in the last round.

Do you favor a mandatory retirement fund for all boxers and if so, how would you like to see it accomplished?

I don't think it should be mandatory. You can't force people to do something if they don't want it. I see it no different from a regular retirement plan in that context. I would love to see fighters join one though, but it has to be run by trustworthy people.

I understood things went terribly wrong with the retirement plan of the California State Athletic Commission and that's something that needs to be avoided at all costs. I would like to see the Retired Boxers Foundation be involved in a plan like that, because I know Alex Ramos and Jacquie Richardson are incredible and very trustworthy people who work very hard for the sport.

What do you think of the female ranking systems and if you had control of them, what changes would you make?

I feel that it needs to be changed, dramatically. I respect the IWBF rankings and way of working a lot, but there are major mistakes in other ones. They should take in consideration WHO you fought, HOW LONG you have been inactive and HOW you lost your previous fight(s). All too often, you will see people entering in title fights who just came off 2 losses or even more, or people who "build" a 10-0 record by fighting very weak competition.

Everybody should have to make a mandatory and DECENT step up in class (and WIN of course) before they can fight for a title. If you think male boxing is bad regarding politics and incompetent sanctioning bodies/people, female boxing is catching up really fast. We had a chance to make something good out of it since the sport is young, but we are going the wrong way now.

I received a very raw and ridiculous deal after my fight from Patrick Ortiz in Oregon, and I will try to battle this kind of misconduct of sanctioning bodies, like the WIBF displayed there. It has to change if you want this sport taken seriously.

What went through your mind the first time you stepped in the ring as a professional?

I was very excited and pumped up. I couldn't wait for the bell to ring. It was just great.

Even though you don't have the chance to fight in 15 rounds today, would you like to see it reinstated?

No, I wouldn't. There are too many accidents already fighting 12 rounds. With all the politics and mismatches occurring these days, I think it would be a very bad move.

Being a female fighter, what is your take on the age-old complaint that female fighters are only for entertainment purposes and not equal to their male counter parts?

I can't stand it, but I know where it's coming from. Look at Mia St. John. The girl can't fight and yet she is on TV all the time. For what reason? Only because she's a T&A act. As long as those girls get the chance to appear in this exciting sport instead of the talented girls, this old complaint will not change.

A nice show around a fight is great, and there is nothing wrong with that, but sometimes it goes just a little too far. I can't wait for her and a few others to retire.

Who do feel was you toughest opponent to date, and why?

Britt VanBuskirk. She hits extremely hard and is a very tall person with a huge reach. On top of that, she will grab and hold to offset one's boxing skills.

When you finally hang up the gloves for good, what would you like your fans to remember you for?

That I took on the strongest competition possible in order to make the sport look good, and as a good person.

Finally, what is the saying that you live your life by?

"What comes around goes around."

Marischa wanted to add the following to our interview.

I would like thank everybody I had the pleasure to meet, work with, and for the support they gave me; all my fans that send me great fan mail and make all that I do worth it. My list would be too long to mention, but the people involved know who I'm thanking.

Finally, Christy Martin I sent you a pen and a picture, so you can see who I am, and you can write me on your list.

Thanks guys!

Marischa SJAUW
Weight Class: Lightweight/135 lbs

Professional Record: 20 fights; 15+ (3 KO), 5-

- 1995 -
+ (1995) Anne-Sophie Mathis

- 1996-1997: inactive -

- 1998 -
- (Mar-21-1998, Atlantic City) Lisa ESTED 6
- (May-24-1998, Atlantic City) Kathy COLLINS 10
- (Nov-7-1998, Palm Beach) Daisy OCASIO 4
+ (Dec-30-1998) Carla WITHERSPOON 4

- 1999 -
+ (Jan-15-1999, Lake Worth) Lisa CUEVAS 6
- (Feb-20-1999, Teesside) Jane COUCH 10
+ (Aug-9-1999, Anaheim) Blaire ROBINSON kot 4
+ (Aug-30-1999, Delmar) Jennifer MC CARTNEY ko 2
+ (Sep-10-1999) Beverly SZYMANSKI 6
+ (Oct-7-1999, Victoria) Snodene BLAKENEY 4
+ (Oct-23-1999, Las Vegas) Isra GIRGRAH 4

- 2000 -
+ (Feb-11-2000, Kenner) Zulfia KOUTDOUSSOVA 10
+ (Apr-22-2000, Auckland) Weana KARAKA 10
+ (May-13-2000, Cologne) Heike Noller injury 3
+ (Oct-7-2000, Ignacio) Britt VAN BUSKIRK 10
+ (Dec-22-2000, Ledyard) Liz MUELLER 8

- 2001 -
- (Apr-21-2001, Lincoln City) <u>Lisa HOLEWYNE</u>
10
+ (Jun-16-2001, Anchorage) <u>Kelly WHALEY</u> 8
+ (Oct-12-2001, Pala) <u>Summer DE LEON</u> 6

As always fight fans, keep reaching for the stars, and all your dreams can be fulfilled.

Interview conducted April 2001

(L) Murray Sutherland with Legendary boxing trainer Angelo Dundee

Leaving a Mark...

Up Close and Personal with Former IBF Super Middleweight Champion Murray Sutherland

When you mention the name Murray Sutherland, a knowledgeable boxing fan will automatically say, he comes from that golden era of Light Heavyweights of the mid 1970's early 80's. It was an era that not only had exciting champions but worthy challengers throughout the top ten of each division which, at that time, only consisted of the WBA and WBC.

Murray Sutherland along with Alvaro "Yaqui" Lopez were always two worthy title challengers who I would always make sure I watched. Each time they stepped into that ring, the fans ALWAYS got their monies worth. In fact, if any of the readers out there can get me in touch with Yaqui, I would be honored to do an interview with him just like this one with Murray.

If you do not know this boxing fact, Murray was the very first crowned IBF Super

Middleweight Champion of the World. He earned this part of history on March 28, 1984, when he won a decision over Ernie Singletary over 15 rounds.

For the readers that always mention your name, what are you doing today?

I am a full-time promoter for the regional Toughman contests that you see on the FX Channel every Friday night. Currently, the Toughman contests keep me traveling and busy all the time.

You came from the magical era when the Light Heavyweight division was just loaded with great talent. Two particular contenders that I always enjoyed were you and Alvaro "Yaqui" Lopez. Without taking anything away from some of the great fighters of today, I still feel that on the whole, we just don't see as many memorable fighters like in your day. Why do you think that is?

Brad, I just don't think we are talking about the Light Heavyweight division on this. Back in the 70's and early 80's, no matter what division you looked at, you had at least 4 – 6 stars in the rankings in each weight division. Any of them could, at any time, win a world title. To name just a few, Danny "Little Red" Lopez, Salvador Sanchez and then you move up in weight, and you had Wilfred Benitez, and fighters like Pipino Cuevas, along with countless others.

When I look back on my division you had Eddie Mustafa Muhammad, Marvin Johnson, Matthew Saad Muhammad, Michael Spinks, and Victor Galindez along with so many other greats that on any night, they could win the belt. It's not the same now and I blame the amateur programs. I currently have two nephews over in Canada who box and when I talk to their dad, he is always saying they got robbed in a fight because of this terrible scoring system we have that was highlighted in the Olympics this year.

There are so few venues for amateurs to work on their skills. In my day, you had just loads of places for amateur fighters to work on the badly needed skills in venues throughout the United States. I think this really hurts a lot of the professional fighters today, and is the main reason you saw so many greats in my day, because of our amateur experience.

You fought Michael Spinks twice. The first time you went the distance and the second time around you were stopped. You gave a great effort and in your opinion, what was the difference in Michael the second time around?

The second time around Michael improved 400% since the first time we met about a year and half earlier. The first time he was a good fighter and the second time he was a great fighter. When he won his title, he just improved so much. I have always felt when a fighter wins a title, he improves 100%. Michael was a harder puncher, and his confidence level had truly increased.

One fighter on your record I have always talked about was Dwight Davidson. What do you remember about him, and just how good was he?

He was one hard-punching fighter. He knocked me out in the fourth round. I dropped him in the first round of our fight. He was very tall, rangy, and a great straight right hand. In the fourth, he caught me with a body shot and that was it for me. I haven't seen Dwight in years. Funny story. I was on an airplane not long ago, sitting beside this gentleman and he asked me if I used to box? I told him yes, and he said, "My cousin used to box." He then told me he was Dwight Davidson. I gave him my business card, but never heard from Dwight.

Your fight with Matthew Saad Muhammad was truly an exciting fight and gave the fans all they could handle. How would you rate Matthew?

He was a good puncher and had just amazing endurance. I hit on him like crazy and he just kept coming. In the fight, I had him all busted up with his eyes badly cut. In fact, Angelo Dundee and I were in Las Vegas about a year ago and we were reminiscing about that fight since he commentated it. Angelo told me if that fight had taken place today, you would have been the champion because they would have stopped it because of the shape Matthew was in.

Who do you feel was your toughest opponent and why?

Jean Marie Emebe was my toughest opponent. I fought him on May 27, 1983 on the undercard of the Marvin Hagler vs. Wilfred Scypion. The reason he was so tough was, that on May 21st, my wife had to go in the hospital to give birth to my son, and he was born premature. He immediately had to go to a Neo-Natal clinic about 20 miles away from the town.

I would get up in the morning and go running very early, then go with my mother, who was staying with us, to the hospital to visit my wife. From there, I would then go to other hospital where my son was at, and then later on that same day go to the gym. I did that every single day up until the fight.

There were some nights we would stay in the hospital till the wee hours just praying for my son's recovery. I was really drained mentally and spiritually because of what was going on. The first seven rounds of that fight, he just beat the crap out of me. I can remember coming back to the corner and my corner man asked me, "Are you going to fight at all tonight?" I went out in the ninth knowing I needed a knockout to win because I was way behind on the scorecards. I stopped him in that round. That by far, was the hardest match I ever had. (** Take notice to this answer because you hear all these excuses in boxing and here is a man that had tragedy in his life at that time and still got in the ring and fought. I totally respect Murray for this because having a son, I can imagine what he went through.)

Who are your three favorite fighters of all-time and why?

First, Salvador Sanchez. He was a terrific little workhorse. I trained with him in Texas one time when I was working with Earnie Shavers. Salvador just did everything so well. Second, Carlos Palomino. He was a tough fighter and truly exciting to watch. I really learned so much from them on TV. I used to record them on the old Beta and just watch their fights over constantly. Finally, Alexis Arguello. Alexis was just a warrior in the ring and had lots of heart. He really defines the word, CLASS!

What is the greatest fight you have ever seen and why?

The first one that comes to mind Brad when you ask is, Alexis Arguello vs Alfredo Escalera when they fought back in Rimini, Italy for the WBC Junior Lightweight Belt held by Alfredo. They were both cut real bad and fought their hearts out. Alexis went on to stop him in the 13th round.

If you could take an opponent from any era in your weight class to fight who would it be, and what would the outcome be?

I would like to have fought Matthew Saad Muhammad in my prime. I needed to have a couple of more years to truly season, and if I would have fought him when I fought Ernie Singletary, I think I would have beat him. My confidence was so much stronger and I had a little more age on me, as well.

Do you favor a mandatory retirement fund for all boxers and if so, how would you like to see it accomplished?

This is a difficult thing Brad because, if someone would have come to me back when I was fighting and said, "Murray you're making $15,000 on this fight. We want to take out $2,000 to go into a retirement fund." At that time, I would have been dead against it.

Now that was back then. Of course, I am retired from boxing and older, I think it's a very good idea. I would not like to see it done by the Government. I would like to see someone like Marc Ratner handling it like a unified thing across boxing that is not associated with the Government. Then I would fully support it.

On July 22, 1984, you reached the pinnacle of an exciting career when you won a decision

against Ernie Singletary over 15 rounds for the first ever IBF Super Middleweight Belt. Share with the readers your feelings on that special night.

It was like training for the Olympics for three or four years. Finally going there, and winning the Gold. When I won, it took a little while for it to sink in. The sad part was the IBF was a fledging organization at that time and it took people a long time to recognize it. I was just floating on air for weeks after winning my belt.

Do you think boxing has moved forward since the days you turned professional in 1977?

I don't think it's moved forward or backwards and ten years from now, it will be the same.

Since you fought in the days of 15 round championship bouts, why do you feel they shortened them?

First of all, TV controls boxing just like any other sport. The reason, in my opinion, that the rounds got reduced has nothing to do with the safety of the boxers. It has everything to do with TV. If you have a championship fight that goes the 12 round distance, they can package that into a one hour program with commercials. You can't do that with 15 rounds. That is the reason I feel they were reduced.

Now that you are retired from boxing, how would you like your fans to remember you?

Never losing a fight for any other reason than the guy I was in there with was better than me. I had 13 losses in my career and I can't cry foul about any one of them. I never lost a fight because I was not in condition. It was like I said, the other man was better than me on that night. (** Here is another answer that I really enjoyed hearing because Murray makes no excuses, something that has become a standard procedure in boxing today for a loss.)

Finally, what is the saying you live your life by?
"Do unto others as you would have done unto you."

Murray would like to add the following to our interview:
In my career I had a pretty good defense and an ok punch. The real reason I did so well in boxing was because of my conditioning. My dad instilled in me, at a young age back in Scotland, that you must train religiously. Back then, I didn't want to hear that and wanted to go and goof off with my buddies. He instilled hard training and values such as the saying, "Do unto others as you would have done unto you."
When times got tough in that ring, I would think of all the values my father instilled in me at a young age which always helped me persevere.

Murray SUTHERLAND

Weight class: Light Heavyweight/175 lbs and Super Middleweight/168 lbs

Professional record: 63 fights; 49+ (39 KO), 1=, 13-
   1980: United States Light Heavyweight
   1981-1982: United States Light Heavyweight

    1984: I.B.F. Super Middleweight
    1984-1986: United States Super Middleweight

    - 1977 -
    + (Aug-18-1977, Hamilton) Kevin Downey 6

    - 1978 -
    - (Jan-17-1978, Toronto) Willie Featherstone
kot 3
    + (Feb-1-1978, Cleveland) Tony Curovic ko 3
    + (Apr-6-1978, Cleveland) Gus Turner ko 4
    - (Apr-21-1978) Dwight Davison ko 4
    + (5.1978, Flint) Ivy Cory ko 2
    + (May-27-1978, Brantford) Harold Riggins ko
6
    + (Sep-29-1978, Hamilton) Zack Page ko 3
    + (10.1978, Canton) Gary Alexander 8
    + (Dec-4-1978, Saginaw) Bill Hollis ko 3

    - 1979 -
    + (Jan-31-1979, Saginaw) Rick Jester ko 1
    + (Mar-4-1979, Saginaw) Harold Riggins ko 2
    - (Jul-21-1979, Pontiac) Richie Kates 10
    + (Nov-9-1979, Saginaw) Karl Zurheide kot 2
    + (Dec-9-1979, Columbus) Al Bolden 10

    - 1980 -
    + (Jan-2-1980, Bay City) Jose Gutierrez ko 2
    + (Jan-15-1980, Pensacola) Alex Bell ko 2
    + (Jan-26-1980, Lansing) Gus Turner ko 5
    + (Feb-1-1980, Chicago) Julius Noble kot 4
    + (Mar-8-1980, Detroit) Don Addison kot 4
    + (Apr-13-1980, Huntington) Ed Smith ko 4
    - (May-4-1980, Kiamesha Lake) Michael Spinks
10
    + (Jul-8-1980, Tampa) Greg Payne ko 6
    + (Aug-1-1980, Council Bluffs) Johnny
Townsend kot 6

+ (Aug-11-1980, Grand Rapids) Benny Mitchell kot 3
+ (Aug-15-1980, Muskegon) Stanley Scott kot 2
+ (Sep-12-1980, Milwaukee) John Cox ko 2
+ (Sep-13-1980, Milwaukee) Joey Butcher ko 1
+ (Oct-4-1980, Des Moines) Paul Wade ko 3
+ (Oct-25-1980, Pontiac) Pablo Ramos 12 (United States, Light Heavyweight)
+ (Dec-5-1980, Columbus) John Beveridge ko 1

- 1981 -
+ (Feb-13-1981, Iowa) Rocky Mack ko 3
+ (Feb-27-1981, Lansing) Fred Brown kot 6
- (Apr-25-1981, Atlantic City) Matthew Franklin ko 9 (W.B.C., Light Heavyweight)
+ (Jul-29-1981, Saginaw) James Williams 12 (United States, Light Heavyweight)
+ (Sep-9-1981, Lansing) Darnell Hayes ko 1
+ (Dec-15-1981, Chicago) Henry Sims kot 9

- 1982 -
+ (Feb-13-1982, Atlantic City) Chris Wells ko 1
- (Apr-11-1982, Atlantic City) Michael Spinks ko 8 (W.B.A., Light Heavyweight)
- (Jun-11-1982, Las Vegas) Eddie Davis ko 6 (United States, Light Heavyweight)
+ (Jul-14-1982, Houston) Gonzalo Montes kot 7
+ (Aug-12-1982, Bay City) Ron Ayers ko 2
+ (Sep-6-1982, Sydney) Tony Mundine 10
+ (Oct-21-1982, Saginaw) Fred Reed ko 1
+ (Nov-23-1982, Atlantic City) Mario Maldonado 10
- (Dec-10-1982, Las Vegas) J.B. Williamson 10

- 1983 -

411

= (Feb-4-1983, Worcester) Robbie Sims 10
+ (Mar-5-1983, Bay City) Johnny Heard ko 5
+ (May-27-1983, Providence) Jean Marie Emebe ko 9
- (Jul-10-1983, Atlantic City) Thomas Hearns 10
+ (Sep-13-1983, Atlantic City) Alex Ramos 10
- (Nov-19-1983, Saint-Joseph) James Kinchen 10

- 1984 -
+ (Feb-24-1984, Wichita) Joe Brewer ko 2
+ (Mar-28-1984, Atlantic City) Ernie Singletary 15 (I.B.F., Super Middleweight)
- (Jul-22-1984, Seoul) Chong-Pal Park kot 11 (I.B.F., Super Middleweight)
+ (Oct-24-1984, Saginaw) Joe Byrd ko 3
+ (Dec-8-1984, Phoenix) Wilford Scypion kot 12 (United States, Super Middleweight)

- 1985 -
+ (Feb-9-1985, Port Huron) Len Edwards ko 3
+ (Mar-1-1985, Atlantic City) Robert Pew 12 (United States, Super Middleweight)
+ (May-31-1985, Wheeling) Lloyd Richardson ko 3 (United States, Super Middleweight)
- (Jul-26-1985, Atlantic City) Bobby Czyz 10
+ (Nov-15-1985, Greensboro) Mike Hyman ko 2

- 1986 -
(Feb-25-1986, Sterling Heights) Lindell Holmes kot 3 (United States, Super Middleweight)

As always fight fans, keep reaching for the stars, and all your dreams can be fulfilled.

Interview conducted August 2000

(L) WBA Heavyweight Champion Mike Weaver mixes it up with "Quick" Tillis

So Close...

Up Close and Personal with Former Heavyweight Title Challenger James "Quick" Tillis

October 3, 1981, the words, "Son do you want to be a bum all your life?" rang out in the Rosemont Horizon in Chicago, Illinois. Angelo Dundee was hollering at his young protégé James "Quick" Tillis who was facing then WBA Heavyweight Champion, Mike Weaver. "Quick" was ahead on points, but seemed to burn out in the later rounds dropping a 15 round split decision to Weaver.

I remember "Quick" well, since he trained for that fight at the same gym where I was training in North Miami Beach, Florida called Allen Park. At that time, he was working with Johnny Lira, Young Joe Louis, and of course the legend, Angelo Dundee. Tillis would go on to have several big fights, but never reached the same success he had early in his career.

413

However, all these years later, he still remains just as funny and outgoing as he was to a young amateur fighter named Brad Berkwitt.

For the readers, what are you doing today?

Well my autobiography is just out called "THINKING BIG". I am looking into doing a feature film on it. I am still a cowboy and into the rodeo, very deep.

What inspired you to get into boxing?

Cassius Clay in 1964 when he fought Sonny Liston. I got into boxing nine years later. But he left a mark on me that I still have to this day.

What was it like being in the ring challenging for the Heavyweight Championship of the World?

Brad, it was amazing to be there. My dear sweet mother was there along with Muhammad Ali, Sugar Ray Robinson, Don King, Larry Holmes and many others. I felt like a million dollars having my idols watching me. I was on top of the world.

In your hey day, you faced many tough opponents. Who do you feel was your toughest opponent and why?

Hands down, Earnie Shavers. Earnie hit so hard, that he could turn goat piss into gasoline. Brad, it was a 120 degrees in the ring and he dropped me like a brick in the ninth round. I am still amazed I was able to get up. In the tenth, I had him out on his feet, but the bell saved him. I took the decision.

Were there any matches that you really wanted, but were unable to get the opponent to the table?

Gerry Cooney was someone I really wanted to fight.

You and I trained at the same gym in the early 80's called Allen Park in North Miami Beach, Florida. Angelo Dundee was your trainer at that time. Give me your observations about Angelo.

I really liked Angelo, but he was better as a businessman than as my trainer. He really moved me along, but I needed Drew Bundini Brown who was with Muhammad Ali.

Being the first opponent to go the distance with Mike Tyson, could you tell that night that Mike had the potential to go on and clean out the heavyweight division?

I thought he had great potential, but with that said, if you boxed him, you could beat him. So many of his opponents stood right in front of him and he will beat you to death when you do that.

I always heard you had a breathing problem which was at the root of your getting so tired in many fights where you were ahead. Can you clarify this?

Brad it wasn't a breathing problem, but a problem I had with citric acid that was making me very tired in the majority of my fights. I went to a doctor and he diagnosed me, and I didn't believe it. However, I changed my diet and it sure worked.

What are your thoughts about the current heavyweight division?

Lennox Lewis is a bad boy. My hat is off to him. I still believe that a true championship fight was back in the days when you fought 15 rounds and, since they don't fight that today, they are not getting the real deal.

If you could pick a heavyweight from any era to face in the ring at your prime, who would it be and what would the outcome be?
Floyd Patterson. I would have outboxed him.

Do you favor a mandatory retirement fund for all boxers and if so, how would you like to see it accomplished?
Brad, I love the idea. They should put money away from day one along with the promoters. Right now, I am actively involved at looking at avenues to help out fellow boxers who are in dire need of assistance. I am looking at setting up a foundation for ex-fighters.

When you finally hang up the boxing gloves, how do you want your fans to remember you?
As the "Fighting Cowboy", who is still riding to this day!

Finally, what is the saying you live your life by?
"I live my life by Jesus Christ".

"Quick" wanted to add the following to our interview:
I am actively being called to fight in the Legends series where you just saw Larry Holmes knock out Mike Weaver this past month.
So look forward to me cleaning out the old guys.

James TILLIS
Nickname: "Quick"

Weight class: Heavyweight/Unlimited

Professional record: 65 fights; 42+ (31 KO), 1=, 21-, 1 N.C.

- 1978 -
+ (Nov-18-1978, Chicago) Ron Stephany ko 1
+ (Dec-15-1978, Chicago) Al Bell kot 1

- 1979 -
+ (Feb-2-1979, Chicago) Dave Watkins ko 1
+ (Feb-28-1979, Chicago) Sylvester Wilder kot 3
+ (Mar-31-1979, Chicago) Rocky Lane ko 1
+ (Jun-11-1979, Chicago) George Goforth kot 5
+ (Jul-20-1979, Chicago) Henry Porter kot 6
+ (Jul-30-1979, Chicago) Charles Atlas kot 2
+ (Sep-7-1979, Chicago) Jimmy Cross ko 2
+ (Oct-19-1979, Chicago) Bob Whaley ko 1
+ (Nov-20-1979, Chicago) Harry Terrell ko 1
+ (Dec-13-1979, Tulsa) Memphis Al Jones ko 4

- 1980 -
+ (Feb-1-1980, Chicago) Cookie Wallace 10
+ (Mar-3-1980, Chicago) Ron Stander kot 7
+ (Apr-17-1980, Chicago) Frank Schramm kot 2
+ (May-15-1980, Chicago) Walter Santemore 10
+ (Jun-12-1980, Chicago) Eric Sedillo retiring 4
+ (Aug-14-1980, Chicago) Mike Koranicki 10
+ (Nov-13-1980, Chicago) Domingo D'Elia kot 4

- 1981 -
+ (Mar-9-1981, Chicago) Tom Fisher 10

\- (Oct-3-1981, Rosemont) Mike Weaver 15 (W.B.A., Heavyweight)

- 1982 -
+ (Mar-13-1982, Las Vegas) Jerry Williams ko 3
+ (Jun-11-1982, Las Vegas) Earnie Shavers 10
\- (Aug-14-1982, Cleveland) Pinklon Thomas kot 8
\- (Nov-26-1982, Houston) Greg Page kot 8 (United States, Heavyweight)

- 1983 -
+ (Mar-28-1983, Chicago) Leroy Boone 10
+ (Apr-25-1983, Chicago) Grady Daniels kot 4
+ (May-22-1983, Chicago) Larry Givens kot 2
+ (Jul-9-1983, Chicago) Lynwood Jones ko 4
\- (Sep-23-1983, Richfield) Tim Witherspoon kot 1 (North America, Heavyweight)

- 1984 -
+ (Feb-9-1984, Tulsa) Otis Bates ko 2
+ (Apr-26-1984, Tulsa) Bobby Crabtree ko 3
+ (Jul-10-1984, Tulsa) Billy Joe Thomas ko 3
+ (Aug-20-1984, Miami Beach) Michael Bennett ko 1
\- (Oct-23-1984, Atlantic City) Carl "The Truth" Williams 10
+ (Dec-15-1984, Waukegan) Bashir Wadud 10

- 1985 -
\- (May-20-1985, Reno) Marvis Frazier 10
\- (Sep-7-1985, Johannesburg) Gerrie Coetzee 10

- 1986 -
\- (Jan-25-1986, Lancaster) Tyrrell Biggs 8
\- (May-3-1986, Glenn Falls) Mike Tyson 10
+ (Jun-17-1986, Tulsa) Mark Young ko 8

+ (Jul-29-1986, Lexington) Art Terry 8
- (Sep-15-1986, Sydney) Joe Bugner 10
+ (Oct-18-1986, Mesquite) Eddie Richardson 10
+ (Oct-28-1986, Pittsburgh) Lorenzo Boyd ko 3
= (Nov-11-1986, Las Vegas) Avery Rawls 10
- 1987 -
- (Jan-8-1987, Houston) Mike Williams kot 8
+ (Mar-6-1987, Fort Smith) Ronnie Douglas kot 5
- (Mar-24-1987, London) Frank Bruno kot 5
- (Jun-23-1987, Johannesburg) Johnny Du Plooy kot 10
+ (Oct-16-1987, Atlantic City) Dennis Jackson ko 5

- **1988 -**
+ (Apr-9-1988, Las Vegas) Rodney Smith ko 2
- (Jul-16-1988, Stateline) Evander Holyfield retiring 5
- (Nov-30-1988, Southwark) Gary Mason kot 5

- **1989 -**
- (Jan-14-1989, Auburn Hills) Arthel Lawhorne 10
- (Mar-20-1989, Toledo) Adilson Rodrigues 10

- **1990 -**
+ (Dec-7-1990, Crystal City) Carlton West kot 3

- **1991 -**
- (Jan-11-1991, Atlantic City) Tommy Morrison kot 1
+ (Nov-22-1991, Peoria) Danny Blake 10

- **1992 -**

+   (Feb-28-1992, Countryside) Jack Jackson kot 3
-   (Oct-8-1992, Columbus) Alexander Zolkin 10
-   1993-1994: inactive -

- 1995 -
N.C. (Dec-7-1995, Denver) Will Hinton 3

- 1996 -
+   (Jun-21-1996, Vancouver) Craig Payne 8
-   (Aug-31-1996, Vancouver) Cliff Couser kot 6

- 1997-1998: inactive -

- 1999 -
(Oct-16-1999, Issaquah) Tim Puller 10

As always fight fans, keep reaching for the stars, and all your dreams can be fulfilled.

Interview conducted August 2000

Dreams Fulfilled...

Up Close and Personal with Former IBF Junior Middleweight Champion Paul "THE ULTIMATE" Vaden

In boxing, I have always felt that a boxer should be remembered for his greatest accomplishments and not his worse showing, or a tragedy that he has become forever part of, even though he is not at fault. As the boxing world knows, Paul was the last fighter to step into the ring with the late, Stephan Johnson, who died shortly after their fight.

Instead of tragedy, I wish to remember Paul's greatest night, when he won the IBF JR. Middleweight Title in a spectacular knockout of then champion, Vincent Pettway. Paul's place in boxing history was cemented in the 12th round of that fight, when he knocked out Pettway for the IBF Junior Middleweight Belt.

Common sense would dictate that Paul is, and probably will always be, affected by the death of a fellow fighter who he faced in the ring. However, like I said earlier, a boxer cannot be held responsible for something that happens in a clean fight.

This is one of the main reasons I am an advocate of a retirement fund for boxers, so if they maybe fight on longer than they should in order to receive the financial compensation, this might deter them, as they will have money put away.

After speaking with Paul, I found him to be yet another example of a fighter having class in and out of the ring. We spoke for almost two hours and considering how passionate we are that all fighters be safe and succeed, I feel we will somehow cross paths in the near future.

I recently received a wonderful e-mail from Paul commenting on my recent interview with former IBF Light Heavyweight Champion, William Guthrie. He commented on the quality of the questions and the fact that it was a very positive interview. That e-mail led to this interview.

Is it safe to say you are retired and if so, what are you doing now since you retired from boxing?

It's very safe to say I am retired from boxing. I really should have never come back. Right before my fight with Keith Holmes, I started up my Executive Boxing Program. My corporation is called MultiPaul Productions and I run it with my business mentor, Robert Firtel, who basically helps me designate what the next business venture is that we are going into.

I currently have on the market what is called, "The Ultimate Workout" which is an alternative form of working out. It is a true boxing workout and I am right out front there doing it on tape. In addition, I am a part owner in a gym that is named, "The Boxing Club." It's located in the northern part of San Diego, California. What I want to stress about this particular gym is that it is a multi-purpose gym which includes aerobics, boxing, and kickboxing. We our also getting one together for the Los Angeles area. The current business ventures that I am involved in are really doing well and I could not be happier.

I want to ask this question as delicately as I can. So before I ask, I know that you, as well as boxing fans all over the world, still hold Stephan Johnson's family in our prayers and wish them the best. There have been many deaths of boxers over the years and I know that the fighter who faced them has to in some way, blame himself.

However, a true boxing fan knows that this is a brutal sport and a death in the ring is by circumstance, not intentionally by a fighter. If possible, for the readers who I know have wondered, how did it affect your desire to continue to fight and is this the reason you retired?

Brad, it is the reason I retired from boxing. Whatever I had left in boxing, ended that night in the ring and throughout that tragedy. I had always read about these tragedies, never thinking I would be involved in it. I have been criticized over the years for not being an aggressive fighter and more of a superior boxer.

With that being said, this type of thing was totally something that I was not used to. It messed me up emotionally and mentally. I had to assess my own self by thinking, this can happen to me too. My training was affected as well, from that tragedy.

To be honest Brad, I should have not even come back to have that fight. I was really doing well in business and I think it was more for my ego to get back into boxing. I think that fight was a sign from God that I should have not come back. After that fight, I fought one other time and knew it was over for me.

Currently, I have a team investigating the entire incident which I feel was shaky from the start. Several items will come out with the conclusion of the investigation from my team. I talk with Stephan's fiancé every other month. She is a beautiful person. There were so many people who wanted to be in the newspaper about this tragedy, and they really couldn't care less about Stephan. As I said earlier, when this investigation comes out, these so called people are going to be put out there.

Brad, I never want anyone to get into a boxing ring who should not be there because of medical reasons, or other reasons, which should have been detected from the start. (**I would like to add to this question by saying, remember, until you walk in a mans shoes, never judge him by a circumstance, especially one as tragic as this one was. Paul has a sincere heartfelt desire to get answers on this event and to continue to comfort the loved ones of Stephan Johnson. For that reason alone, among many, Paul has my utmost respect.)

You had a very impressive amateur career with an amazing 337 wins against only 10 losses. What do you think of the current crop of amateur fighters turning pro in the years since you did?

I think there is a lot of talent coming out of the amateurs today. The boxers all came to my gym in August and worked out for the last days before they went to Sydney. Ricardo Williams and Ricardo Juarez really impressed me. The scoring system currently is a terrible system and really needs to be changed, because you see fighter's getting bad decisions.

That being said, there is going to be someone who received less press, but will go on to really shock the boxing world and make a big mark winning a world title. Finally, their work ethic was very hard when I watched them and that, I admire.

For the fighters who are trying to get to the level of winning a world title like you did on August 12, 1995 when you knocked out then IBF Champion Vincent Pettway in the 12ᵗʰ round, give the fighters a brief summary on what one feels on that special night from the walk-in to the ring to the moment your hand was raised.

Well, first of all, I proposed to my wife two weeks before the fight because I just felt so confident that I was going to win. I was the underdog and Vincent had just come off of that stunning knockout of Simon Brown which had Brown punching up from the canvas.

Everything was going great in camp and my entire team was sharp. I can remember thinking on the ring walk that I had dreamed about this from the age of eight years old. My father had passed away back in 1992 and he was a big part of my boxing career, so his spirit was there. My mother and my late Uncle Ron, were in attendance. It took a lot to get there because my manager, Arnie Rosenthal and I, were not with a big promoter, so we had to take the tough road.

During the fight and up to the point where they raised my hand in victory was absolute magic. I am even more reflective now than I was back then.

I commend you in your first defense of your title. You picked a tough fighter in Terry Norris for a unification bout. Why would you take a fight like that in only your first defense of your title?

First off, I have to be honest, I did not like Terry. This was funny because I like everyone. I really was fighting up in weight and when he said some messed up things about me, I moved down in weight, so I could fight him. I wanted to fight the best out there and at that time, Terry was the best. I could have taken some easier fights, but I wanted to find out how good I was. I make no excuses, Terry was better than me on that night.

Who do you feel was your toughest opponent and why?

Hands down, Keith Holmes. Keith is the only fighter I continuously felt the power of throughout the match. Holmes did to me what I was able to do to many of the fighters I fought and that was, to use the size advantage over them. Although I was not a power puncher, my size and boxing ability allowed me to have the edge and Keith had that over me, for sure.

Holmes is the only guy to ever drop me and eventually stop me. He is the most underrated fighter out there. I have mad love for him because he really is a great guy.

Being in boxing as a professional for the last nine years, do you feel it's moving in the right direction?

I think boxing as a whole is moving ahead. I would like to see some of the boxers go with some promotion people who are up and coming, so they can dedicate quality time to their careers. When they sign with these promoters who already have big names on their roster, these younger fighter's careers are put on the back burner. I don't agree with this.

I had a manager named Arnie Rosenthal who really cared about me and to this day, we still talk on the phone all the time, because he wants to make sure I am doing well. Brad, I have made five mistakes in my boxing career. First was fighting, Terry Norris. Second, Keith Holmes. Third, fighting Shibata Flores when my mind was totally messed up. Fourth, was coming back to boxing and finally fifth, when I did, without Arnie Rosenthal, who cared about me more than I can describe.

I have nothing to do with Arnie's income anymore and we still have a true bond. This is what I wish for the young fighters coming into this sport to look for. (**This is one of those answers that comes from the heart, and I feel all young boxers need to take notice of it).

Who are your three favorite fighters of all-time and why?

Muhammad Ali. He just recently was honored by President Clinton with a Lifetime Achievement Award for work in and out of the ring. I admire his love for people and feel the same way. His skills were amazing. Second, would be Sugar Ray Leonard. He had an aura and charisma that transcended boxing and of course the skills. Finally, Sugar Ray Robinson. He was slick in and out of the ring and I loved the way he carried himself.

Do you favor a mandatory retirement fund for all boxers and if so, how would you like to see it accomplished?

Brad, I totally agree with you that all fighters need a retirement fund. As my buddy William Guthrie said in your column, "It's unbelievable that all the other major sports have one, but boxing." Bottom Line: I think all the sanctioning bodies should pay in, along with promoters and finally, fighters should pay in and we need one now.

In your prime, if you could have fought any fighter in your weight class from any era, who would it have been? What would the outcome of the fight be?

Brad, I can only answer that question like this. I was an 8 year old kid who always had dreams of being a world champion in boxing, who idolized Muhammad Ali and Sugar Ray Leonard. I never said to myself that I would want a dream match with so and so. I just wanted to be as I said, a world champion, if only for a minute, hour, or one day. I wanted to be in the record books and when you looked up my era, it would say, Paul Vaden, World Champion.

Also, that I won my belt, and not by some phony injury, like the opponent was faking he was knocked out. I wanted to win it with honor. My point is this Brad, I came along at the right time in boxing. If I was around when

Sugar Ray Leonard, Roberto Duran, Tommy Hearns or Sugar Ray Robinson were in the sport, I am honest enough to say, I would have not beat them and would not have had the chance to become a world champion.

Brad, I have three belts downstairs in my home and I am very proud of each one. When my son grows up and realizes his dad was a champion and also reads it in books, he will be able to say my dad was a World Champion. That is what is dear to my heart.

Now that you are retired, what do you want your fans to remember you for?

That I was always a nice guy to all the fans and always took the time for them, because they are what make a fighter. Boxing has allowed me to forge some really special friendships. My love for people transcends all boundaries.

Finally, what is the saying you live your life by?

"I can do all things through Christ, who strengthens me".

Paul would like to add the following to our interview:

Brad, I want the fans to know that I am very happy since I have retired and have the same determination that I had in boxing, just now it's in my businesses. I have some really good people behind me who fully support me, and that is really a good feeling to have.

As you read in my original e-mail about your interview with my friend William Guthrie, I sent you Brad, I really admire your quality interviews and thank you for your continuous efforts to be so positive in them. Finally, I would like to also mention Julianna Nikolic who heads all my public relations charities, advertising, etc.

With Robert Firtel as my partner and business mentor along with Julianna's creative ideas, I compare this team's depth to my affiliation with Arnie Rosenthal 1994-97, which were my most productive years.

Writer's closing comments:
It was a true pleasure to interview Paul. We both share some common threads in the arena of caring for the boxers of this sport I truly love, called BOXING. Sincerity is a trait, that in my opinion, cannot be faked. Paul has that and much more. If you ever get the chance to meet him, take the time to go up and say hello. You will be delighted in your meeting. One other side note I found out while doing research on Paul, he is the only true San Diego native boxer, to ever win a world title.

Paul VADEN
Nickname: "The ULTIMATE"

Weight class: Junior Middleweight/154 lbs

Amateur record: 337 fights; 327+, 10-
1988 United States Welterweight
1988: Olympic Trials Welterweight:
- Kenny Gould points
1989: United States Junior Middleweight
1989: W.C. Moscow
1990: United States Junior Middleweight
Professional record: 32 fights; 29+ (16 KO), 3-
1995: I.B.F. Junior Middleweight
1999-2000: United States Junior Middleweight

- 1991 -
+ (Apr-5-1991, Albuquerque) Quirino Garcia 4
+ (Jun-10-1991, Tijuana) Venustiano Paredes 4
+ (Jul-5-1991, Del Mar) Jesus Lopez ko 1
+ (Jul-22-1991, Tijuana) Rigoberto Garcia 4
+ (Aug-29-1991, Lake Side) Armando Higuera ko 1
+ (Oct-7-1991, Inglewood) William Krijnen 6
+ (Nov-11-1991, Tijuana) Heriberto Valdez ko 3

- 1992 -
+ (Feb-22-1992, San Diego) Richard Evans 6
+ (Mar-25-1992, San Diego) James Rivas 6
+ (Apr-29-1992, San Diego) Fred Thomas ko 8
+ (May-27-1992, San Diego) John Armijo 8
+ (Aug-27-1992, San Diego) Malcolm Shaw ko 6
+ (Nov-11-1992, San Diego) Sergio Medina kot 3

- 1993 -
+ (Feb-24-1993, Las Vegas) Brian Isbell kot 3
+ (May-6-1993, Las Vegas) Greg Lonon 6
+ (Jul-23-1993, Lansing) Mohammed Moka kot 5
+ (Oct-5-1993, Las Vegas) Greg Lonon kot 4
+ (Dec-18-1993, Las Vegas) Randy Smith 6

- 1994 -
+ (Mar-25-1994, Las Vegas) John Montes 12
+ (Jun-30-1994, Atlantic City) Jason Papillion 12
+ (Dec-16-1994, Las Vegas) Heriberto Valdez kot 6

- 1995 -
+ (Mar-14-1995, Kenner) Andreas Arellana kot 6

431

+ (May-16-1995, Atlantic City) Ruben Bell 10
+ (Aug-12-1995, Las Vegas) Vincent Pettway kot 12 (I.B.F., Junior Middleweight)
- (Dec-16-1995, Philadelphia) Terry Norris 12 (World, Junior Middleweight)

- 1996 -
+ (May-18-1996, Las Vegas) Clem Tucker kot 6
+ (Oct-19-1996, Upper Marlboro) Bernice Barber 10

- 1997 -
+ (Apr-19-1997, Shreveport) Wayne Powell kot 8
- (Dec-5-1997, Pompano Beach) Keith Holmes kot 11 (W.B.C., Middleweight)

- 1998: inactive -

- 1999 -
+ (Jun-19-1999, New York) Jorge Luis Vado kot 6
+ (Nov-20-1999, Atlantic City) Stephan Johnson ko 10 (United States, Junior Middleweight)

- 2000 -
- (Apr-15-2000, Las Vegas) Shibata Flores 12 (United States, Junior Middleweight)

As always fight fans, keep reaching for the stars, and all your dreams can be fulfilled.

Interview conducted November 2000

In With the Crowd...

Up Close and Personal with Singing Legend Jerry Vale

Once again, I have the unique pleasure to bring to you another celebrity interview. This time with one of the top Italian-American singers of the last 45 years, Jerry Vale.

Jerry, as you will read is a diehard boxing fan and truly a nice man. We both in fact, share some of the same views, as you will see in the following interview.

How long have you followed boxing?
Most of my life. I really learned to appreciate it, as I got older.

Who do you feel is the greatest fighter of all-time?
I would have to go with Rocky Marciano. He retired undefeated and was a very big puncher. I was friendly with Rocky and I remember when he fought Joe Louis. Rocky felt really bad about beating Joe up.

What era do you think had the best fighters and why?

I think back in the era when Rocky Graziano fought Tony Zale. The late 40's had some very exciting fights. I was friendly with Rocky and can remember when Jake, Rocky and I, were eating dinner over my house in the Bronx. Rocky said he felt really good and was in great shape. He turned to Jake and said, "We should fight." Rocky really meant it. Jake really wasn't interested in the proposal. That would have been some exciting fight if they fought. I saw many of Jake fights over the years and even remember being there when he fought Irish Bob Murphy at Madison Square Garden and lost by a knockout.

Who are your top three favorite fighters of all-time and why?

Rocky Marciano for his huge punching power. Wille Pep for his great boxing ability. I remember when he fought Sandy Saddler and just gave him a boxing lesson. Finally, Muhammad Ali. I have met Ali many times and he is a lot of fun. He always made me laugh when he used to show me magic tricks all the time.

In today's boxing, do you feel there are any throwback fighters?

I would say Oscar Delahoya. His style and whole personality have traits of the fighters of old. We share the same doctor.

Do you prefer 15 rounds vs. 12 in championship fights?

I like the 12 rounds better because it makes the fighter do earlier, and is probably safer for them too.

What is the greatest fight you have ever seen and why?

The Thrilla in Manilla. That was some fight with all the action in it.

Where did you watch The Thrilla in Manilla?

I think a big screening PPV in Las Vegas.

Who did you want to win it?

Well, I like the underdog, so it would be Joe Frazier.

What do you think of boxing today vs. when you first starting watching it?

I liked it better when you had one champion instead of all these belts. Today, I couldn't tell you who the Lightweight Champion is because there are so many. You have all these organizations like the WBA, WBC and IBF. There are just too many belts. There should be one world champion in each weight class.

Finally, in all the years you have been a boxing fan, what was the most brutal knockout you have ever seen?

Well Brad, I was at the Emile Griffith vs Benny "The Kid" Paret fight. I knew if they did not stop it sooner, Benny was going to be seriously hurt. In fact, I can remember screaming for them to stop the fight. It was stopped too late and Benny lapsed into a coma, which he never recovered from and eventually died. Very Sad!

As always fight fans, keep reaching for the stars, and all your dreams can be fulfilled.

Interview conducted May 2000

Good Investment...

Up Close and Personal with Former IBF Junior Middleweight Champion "Ferocious" Fernando Vargas

In all sports today, I don't think that there is one such as boxing which allows a professional athlete great acclaim in the face of defeat. As the stock market plummets, there is one stock that you will not hear about on the New York Stock Exchange (NYSE). That stock is "Ferocious" Fernando Vargas.

In his recent, gallant effort against Felix "Tito" Trinidad, he showed his heart where other, lesser fighters would have quit, after being dropped in the first round with huge shots, that clearly hurt him.

Vargas didn't quit right there, and went on to put Trinidad down and give us, what I consider, the Fight of the Year for 2000, before being stopped by Felix in the 12th and final round. For this effort, his stock rose double digits, and I feel, would be a very good buy for future investors in the sport of boxing, because he will be a champion again, very soon.

First of all, how is training going for your upcoming bout with Wilfredo Rivera?
Training is going great. I definitely needed to work on some things that I caught in my last fight and we are making adjustments.

Are we going to see any changes to your style from the Trinidad fight?
I made a lot of mistakes in that fight. For instance, being a brawler with him, trying to only go out there and knock him out, when that is not my type of fight. Fernando Vargas is more of an intelligent fighter than I showed that night and should have been more like the Fernando who fought Raul Marquez, Yori Boy Campos and Ike Quartey.
In those fights, you saw me do me intelligent things and when the knockout came, it came without me just going for it. I really beat myself that night. In training now, my mind is set that I can't go out and knock out everyone I fight. Bottom line: You are going to see a much more intelligent Fernando Vargas on my new quest to gain back a world title.(I really admire this answer because Fernando pointed only to himself and didn't put any blame on anyone else for his loss to Trinidad).

Having an extensive amateur career and impressive record, do you see major changes if any, in the amateur programs today vs. when you first entered?
To be honest Brad, I never really enjoyed being an amateur. Even though I did well and eventually went on to the Olympic Games, my

style was not suited for the amateurs, but more for the professional ranks. When I fought, I would wait and pick my punches, which would cost me the first round and maybe the second, but I would go on to stop my opponent in the third.

I really don't follow the amateur programs today, but when I am in Oxnard, my trainer is always working with amateur fighters who have a pro style similar to mine. What my trainer does is recognize this quickly and works on their speed and ability to throw lots of punches which is needed in the amateur ranks.

If you had to pick one fight to date, which do you feel the fans saw Fernando Vargas at his very best?

It's hard to pick just one because I think the fans saw me at my best against Yori Boy Campos, Raul Marquez and Ike Quartey. I fought very intelligent in those fights.

What was it like when you first won your world title and heard the announcer say, "And the new IBF Junior Middleweight Champion of the World"?

It was the most beautiful feeling in the world next to my two baby boy's birth. Its' something, that as long as we have history, can never be taken away from me. All the goosebumps, pain, sweat and tears went into my winning the championship. It was worth every bit of it.

I have noticed that you have a huge following of young children that root you on. To the young man or woman who wants to lace up the gloves for the very first time, what are your words of wisdom to them?

First of all, this sport is very hard and if you're not into it 110%, I would seriously advise you not to get into it. This sport is no different from medieval times, when you had only those two gladiators in there fighting to the death. There is no teamwork when the bell rings and you must know that it's only you out there.

Although a small percentage of fighters become a world champion, never ever think that you won't be a world champion. Have that dream in your heart to help you on those days when this sport gets very hard.

Does the Vargas style emulate any fighters you have watched from days gone by in boxing?

I don't think so.

Who are your three favorite fighters of all-time and why?

First, Julio Cesar Chavez. I grew up on him and loving him. As I got older, I was able to talk with him and that just reinforced why he is my idol. When I talk about his great career, I look back, and not at what he is doing now, or continues to do. No Mexican fighter ever had the Mexican people in his pocket like him. He truly defines Mexican pride. Each time I step into the ring, I have that same pride.

Second, Salvador Sanchez. He died before his time. We know he was great, but imagine what he could have done if his career was longer. Finally, Muhammad Ali. I loved when he called someone out, or if someone called him out, he always stepped up to the plate. He brought more to the public, where they didn't think all fighters were dumb, and he really was a huge icon.

What is the greatest fight you have ever seen and why?

Julio Cesar Chavez vs Meldrick Taylor I. Chavez was down on points and going into the last round with nothing to lose; he went for it all which led to him knocking out Taylor.

I can remember, as a small kid, praying for him to pull it out and when he did, everyone in my house was jumping up to celebrate his win.

Do you favor a mandatory retirement fund for all boxers and if so, how would you like to see it accomplished?

Brad, I support it 110%. If you analyze all the fighters who win big championship fights, you would not believe how much we pay in taxes. Yet, there is no social security for all the money you give, or a pension to fall back on. If you put your money away that's great, but there are fighters out there who need help with the money they make.

Every sport has a retirement fund, but boxing. I would make the fund unified across the states and we probably need Government help to regulate it. Finally, promoters need to pay into this fund to help the boxers because they are always making money and never taking punches.

We really need to clean boxing up and I would fully support anyone who has extensive knowledge on boxing that could clean it up.

Do you feel rules should be unified in boxing across the world?

I fully support a unified system where all participants in boxing know that anywhere we fight, will be the same.

When you finally retire from boxing, what would you like your fans to remember you for?

I want them to remember me as a fighter who fought everyone out there and was not afraid of anyone. That I always stepped up to the plate, even when people said I was nuts for taking such a tough opponent. Finally, a Mexican Warrior who always gave his fans everything he had in the ring.

Finally, what is the saying you live your life by?

"Mess up once, shame on you. Mess up twice, shame on me. But I never let it get to twice".

Fernando would like to add the following to our interview:

I want to send a huge shout out to all my fans who have supported me through everything. From the bottom of my heart, I thank all my Mexican fans and all my other fans in general. I have a very neat website that all my fans can checkout and if you want to email, feel free. www.fernandovargas.com Please don't miss my fight May 5, 2001 in EL Paso, Texas.

Fernando VARGAS
Nickname: "Ferocious"

Weight class: Junior Middleweight/154 lbs

Amateur record: 105 fights; 100+, 5-
1994: United States Lightweight:
+ Terrance Cauthen points
1994: W.C. Juniors Istanbul Lightweight:
+ Danny Happe (Angl disq.3
+ Oleg Buts (Mol) points
- Talgat Kalimov (Kaz) points

1995: Panamerican Games Mar del Plata:
- Luis Perez (P-R) points
1996: Olympic Trials Welterweight:
+ Thomas Davis points
+ Fareed Samad points
+ Gary Jones points
1996:   Barrages   Olympics   Augusta
Welterweight:
+ Brandon Mitchum points
1996: Olympic Games Atlanta Welterweight:
+ Tengiz Meskhadze (Geo) points
- Marian Simion (Rou) points
Professional record: 21 fights; 20+ (18 KO),
1-
1998-2000: I.B.F. Junior Middleweight

- **1997** -
+ (Mar-25-1997, Oxnard) Jorge Morales ko 1
+ (Apr-26-1997, Atlantic City) Claude Staten
kot 2
+ (Jun-7-1997, Sacramento) Bill Burden ko 2
+ (Jun-20-1997, Atlantic City) Jim Maloney
ko 1
+ (Jul-12-1997, Lake Tahoe) Eugene Lopez ko
1
+ (Aug-19-1997, Austin) Kevin Payne ko 1
+ (Oct-4-1997, Atlantic City) Alex Quiroga
kot 6
+   (Nov-22-1997,   Atlantic   City)   Jose
Fernandez ko 1
+ (Dec-13-1997, Ledyard) Eduardo Martinez ko
2

- **1998** -
+ (Mar-13-1998, Miami) Dan Connolly kot 2
+ (Apr-14-1998, Ledyard) Romallis Ellis ko 2
+ (May-9-1998, Sacramento) Ron Johnson kot 4
+   (Jun-23-1998,   Philadelphia)   Anthony
Stephens kot 5

+ (Aug-22-1998, Atlantic City) Darren Maciunski kot 6

+ (Dec-12-1998, Atlantic City) Luis Ramon Campas retiring 8 (I.B.F., Junior Middleweight)

- 1999 -

+ (Mar-13-1999, New York) Howard Clarke kot 4 (I.B.F., Junior Middleweight)

+ (Jul-17-1999, Stateline) Raul Marquez kot 11 (I.B.F., Junior Middleweight)

+ (Dec-4-1999, Lincoln City) Ronald Wright 12 (I.B.F., Junior Middleweight)

- 2000 -

+ (Apr-15-2000, Las Vegas) Ike Quartey 12 (I.B.F., Junior Middleweight)

+ (Aug-26-2000, Las Vegas) Ross Thompson kot 4 (I.B.F., Junior Middleweight)

- (Dec-2-2000, Las Vegas) Felix Trinidad kot 12 (World, Junior Middleweight)

As always fight fans, keep reaching for the stars, and all your dreams can be fulfilled.

Interview conducted April 2001

Time of our interview

New Champion

A Champion in the Making...

Up Close and Personal with Female Fighter Brenda Vickers-Dudney

Throughout the United States there are pockets of ladies who can fight, but for some reason, the press goes to the new wave of daughters-of-former-boxers, who can't necessarily fight.

Vickers is one of these tough ladies who get in the ring and fight their hearts out, giving credibility to the rising popularity of women's boxing.

How long have you followed boxing?
I have followed it very closely for the last four years.

444

Do you feel that, since you first turned professional in women's boxing, the sport has moved forward?

I feel it has moved forward, but hope it would move a little faster. There a lot of former boxer's daughters who are coming into the sport that have given it tons of press, and I hope that women such as myself and others, will get some of the same prestige as they do.

What inspired you to get into boxing?

One night my husband and I were out, and we stopped by a gym where they had a two for one deal. I started working out there with my husband and a trainer, who worked there, who thought I had some potential. That led to my getting involved in boxing.

What are your words of wisdom to the young ladies out there who want to pursue a professional boxing career?

First of all, go to a good gym. You need to be very careful because there are lot's of people who want to lead you in the wrong direction just to make a buck off of you.

If it doesn't feel right, it's not! Finally, make sure you have a good trainer, which is the foundation to success.

If you could emulate any fighter who would it be and why?

I would like to emulate Prince Naseem Hamed. He is just so flamboyant, and skilled, and gives the fans a great show. If you look at him closely, and I have, he is very at ease with himself in the ring. That is always to a fighter's advantage.

445

Who are your three favorite fighters of all-time and why?

First of all, Muhammad Ali. He took the sport of boxing very seriously and raised the stakes for all boxers. Second, Evander Holyfield. When Tyson bit him in the ring, he handled the whole incident with class, which I appreciate. Finally, I like Prince Naseem Hamed for the reasons I mentioned earlier.

What is the greatest fight you have ever seen and why?

Evander Holyfield vs Mike Tyson I. I was there sitting ringside and it made me want to get in the ring and fight.

What do you consider your best weapon in the ring?

My straight left hand.

What went through your mind the very first time you stepped in the ring as a professional fighter?

I was saying to myself, do what you know you came to do. Tune out everything outside of the ring and take care of business inside it!

Do you favor a mandatory retirement fund for all boxers and if so, how would you like it accomplished?

I never really thought about it before and just don't want to give an answer without hearing more about how it would be done?

Being a female fighter, what is your opinion of some of the female fighters coming into the sport of boxing using their father's last names who really can't fight, but get all the press?

Brad, let me explain it like this. I take this sport very seriously and work very hard to constantly get in shape while continuing to learn the skills of boxing. They come in with a name and make the big bucks, while there are plenty of ladies out there such as myself, who are not making that kind of money, but have the skills and love boxing.

We should be getting the money fights because it's only fair

When you finally hang up the gloves, how do you want your fans to remember you?

I would like to be remembered for being good in the ring and humble outside of it.

Finally, what is the saying you live your life by?

"Treat everyone the way you want to be treated".

Brenda wanted to add the following to our interview:

I just want the readers to know I am very focused on my boxing career. Along with my wonderful husband and daughter who, through my success in boxing, I will be able to do great things for.

Brenda VICKERS-DUDNEY

Weight class: Lightweight/130 lbs

Professional record: 5 fights; 4+ (1 KO), 1-

- **1999** -
+ (Apr-30-1999, Hialeah) Marcela Guido kot 4
- (Jun-19-1999, Miami) Snodene Blakeney 4
+ (Aug-28-1999, Biloxi) Pamela Opdyke 4

447

+ (Oct-1-1999, Bossier City) Demetrius Steel 4

- 2000 -
+ (Mar-25-2000, Bay Saint-Louis) Mary Haik 4
- (Nov-24-2000, Pugwash, Nova Scotia) Doris Hackl 10

As always fight fans, keep reaching for the stars, and all your dreams can be fulfilled.

Interview conducted October 2000

*** One side note of importance since this interview originally was conducted. Brenda did in deed win a World Title. On March 28th, 2002, she defeated Doris Hackl over ten rounds to win the International Female Boxers Association (IFBA) Lightweight Title.

WEPNER KNOCKS DOWN ALI

Lots of Heart...

Up Close and Personal with Former Heavyweight Title Challenger Chuck Wepner

Many readers will associate the name Chuck Wepner with blood from his many cuts, that poured out in the ring. Be that as it may, he not only poured out blood, he also poured out sweat and tears each time he stepped into that coveted square circle, where he showed the boxing fans what true heart is all about.

On March 24, 1975, he secured his place in history by fighting the legendary Heavyweight Champion, Muhammad Ali in Cleveland Ohio. Wepner did what many thought he couldn't do and that was, going 15 rounds with the champion. In the 9th round, Wepner had Ali down to the canvas, which shocked the then champion. The fight would end in the 15th when Wepner was knocked down and unable to regain himself.

This fight would inspire a young movie actor on the verge of super stardom. The actor of

449

course, was Sylvester Stallone, who based his character Rocky Balboa on Wepner, who showed tremendous heart in his title attempt.

During our interview, I found Wepner to be a sheer delight, with a great sense of humor and candor, which shows why so many fans are still endeared to him today.

First of all, for all the readers who bring up your name when the Golden Era of Heavyweights is mentioned, what are you doing today?

I've been in sales and public relations with a company here in New Jersey for the last 34 years. Also, I work for a pharmaceutical company doing the same type of work.

In one of your biggest wins, you beat former WBA Heavyweight Champion, Ernie Terrell. What do you remember about that fight?

It was a very tough fight. I won the fight by a very close 12 round decision, with me, not being sure if I won until they announced the decision.

Who do you feel was your toughest opponent in your boxing career and why?

The opponent was Sonny Liston. He was a tremendous puncher and as you know, I could always take a great punch. Sonny banged me up pretty good in that fight. I had a broken nose, left cheekbone and my face needed 72 stitches. Brad, every time he hit me, I could feel something crack." With a chuckle, he said, "I was to stubborn to fall down."

In hindsight, what, if anything, would you have done differently in your attempt for the Heavyweight Championship against Muhammad Ali?

It really was the first fight in my 20 plus year career, that I trained full-time for. I was allowed to go to camp and I lived there. In all my other fights, I would get up early in the morning, do my roadwork, and then go to work. When I got off work, I would go to the gym. I think the only thing I would have done differently would be to get better sparring partners. I had some good ones, but probably could have gotten a couple more that really emulated the way Ali boxed.

What secured your shot at the coveted Heavyweight Championship of the World?
Well, I was ranked in the top ten for 48 months straight, anywhere from five to eight in the rankings. Don King had just gotten out of jail and became Muhammad Ali's promoter. King and my manager, Al Braverman, had known each other for many years. King was looking for a young white guy to fight George Foreman. As you know, Foreman was supposed to be unbeatable and he went to Zaire Africa and Ali knocked him out. King said to me, "I promised you that shot and you're going to get it." I didn't believe him, but three months and a day later, he broke the news in Cleveland Ohio (where he was from), that I would get the shot.

I was one of the few guys in the top ten who Ali had not beaten, and they thought I wouldn't give him that much trouble, and it didn't hurt that I was white.

How true to the legendary story is it that Rocky was made based on your boxing career?
The fight with Ali inspired the movie. Stallone got the idea from seeing me, the 30-1 underdog Chuck Wepner, the white, heavyweight

451

- basically a club fighter, (even though I was ranked in the top ten), going the distance with the great black champion. There was a lot of stuff in the movie, such as the way he dressed down and out, which was never me. I always dressed well, drove big cars and lived well.

I questioned Stallone about this and he thought making Rocky the underdog in so many ways, would really sell better. He was absolutely right. Stallone had me as a consultant on some of the fight scenes.

You fought Sonny Liston in a very action packed fight. What do you recollect about this fight and what was Sonny Liston really like?

He really was a mean, nasty guy. We trained at the same gym, with me working out in the afternoon, and he would go in at night to workout. The first time I met him, he was coming down the stairs and I was going up. I said, "Hello Sonny" and he didn't even look or acknowledge me.

You fought former heavyweight contender and now boxing referee, Randy Neumann three times. You went 2-1 in those matches. What do you remember about him as a fighter?

Brad, a funny story about our fight in Madison Square Garden, which was the main event fight. We came out of clinch in the third round with blood all over the place. I turned to Arthur Mercante and said, "Arthur don't stop the fight, I always get cut and I don't want you to stop it." Arthur than turned to me and said, "Chuck, you're not bleeding, Neumann is." I then said, "oh my God, that cut is awful. You better stop this fight." It was eventually stopped a couple of rounds later.

(Chuck and I, both laughed hard when he got done telling this story, which was very funny, especially the way he tells it). Randy was a tough kid and very good boxer. All three fights were tough.

Who are your three favorite fighters of all-time and why?

Number one, Muhammad Ali. I thought, in his prime that no one could beat him. As a personality, he was great and we still meet with each other today. Second, Joe Louis. He was a great fighter. I met him in Las Vegas years after his career was over. He was a very quiet and unassuming gentleman, who never bothered anyone. I really think he was a great man and a credit to the sport of boxing.

Finally, Rocky Marciano. I knew Rocky and he came to a couple of my fights in Secaucus New Jersey because he was a friend of Al Certo's. He was another guy who was quiet and unassuming. He really was a great fighter.

What is the greatest fight you have ever seen and why?

The one with my friend Bernard Hopkins, just last week.

I had told people he would win and they basically all felt he would get killed. He proved them wrong and I hope now, he gets the credit he deserves.

What big fights were you approached for, but never materialized?

I was supposed to fight Floyd Patterson. For three months, it was on and off again. I had knocked out his brother Ray Patterson in Sunnyside Gardens, in New York. Everyone said that Ray, who I had put down seven times, had a better chin than Floyd, which I think caused him not to want to take the fight.

Do you favor a mandatory retirement fund for all boxers and if so, how would you like to see it accomplished?

Brad, I would definitely support a mandatory retirement fund. Boxing as you know, is the only professional sport that has no retirement fund, hospitalization or insurance for the athletes involved. In fact, I have been to the Senate twice in New Jersey lobbying for it. Both times, Governor's Hughes and Caine, were for it. Naturally, the promoters were against it for kicking in the money, but it was the fighters who were more against it. They felt the promoters should pay. What I wanted, was the promoters to put in like, ten percent and the fighters say, a two percent cut into a fund.

How do you match the current heavyweights to your group?

I hate to sound like an old guy, but when I was ranked in the top ten, at that time there was only one ranking. In those rankings, were fighters like Sonny Liston, George Foreman, Muhammad Ali, Joe Frazier, Ernie Terrell, Jerry Quarry, and Oscar Bonavena. Anyone of us could have been a world champion today. Today, they have really diluted the sport with so many champions, which is crazy.

In today's boxing, I really feel the lower weight divisions are terrific and could compete with boxing from yesteryear.

Bottom Line: I think the Heavyweight and Light Heavyweight divisions today are poor compared to my era.

Now that you are retired from boxing, how do you want your many fans to remember you?
That I was a tough, blue collar guy who always gave 100% in the ring.

Finally, what is the saying you live your life by?
"Treat others like how you would want to be treated".
Chuck has a neat website where you can find out more information about him. His site can be reached at:
http://wepner.homestead.com/

Chuck WEPNER
Nickname: "Bayonne Bleeder"

Weight class: Heavyweight/Unlimited

Professional record: 51 fights; 35+ (17 KO), 2=, 14-
1973: United States Heavyweight

- 1964 -
+ (Aug-5-1964, Bayonne) George Cooper ko 3
+ (Aug-14-1964, New York) Rudy Pavesi 4
= (Oct-27-1964, New York) Everett Copeland 6
+ (Dec-18-1964, New York) Jerry Tomasetti 4

- 1965 -
+ (Jan-19-1965, New York) Ray Patterson ko 6
= (Mar-23-1965, New York) Everett Copeland 6
- (Oct-19-1965, New York) Bob Stallings 6

- 1966 -
- (Jan-7-1966, New York) Buster Mathis ko 3
+ (Feb-22-1966, New York) Jerry Tomasetti 6
+ (Apr-6-1966, White Plains) Cleo Daniels 6
+ (Aug-3-1966, Scranton) Johnny Deutsch ko 6

+ (Oct-21-1966, New York) Dave Centi 6

- **1967** -
+ (Apr-28-1967, Jersey City) Don Mc Ateer ko 7

- (Jul-19-1967, New York) Jerry Tomasetti ko 5

+ (Nov-27-1967, Secaucus) Charles Harris ko 6

- **1968** -
+ (Jan-22-1968, Secaucus) Clay Thomas ko 3
+ (Apr-30-1968, Walpole) Eddie Vick 10
+ (May-20-1968, Secaucus) Mike Bruce 8
+ (Sep-26-1968, New York) Forest Ward ko 7
+ (Nov-9-1968, Scranton) Mert Brownfield 10
+ (Dec-13-1968, New York) Jerry Tomasetti ko 1

- **1969** -
+ (Mar-14-1969, New York) Roberto Davila 10
+ (Apr-28-1969, Secaucus) Mike Bruce 8
- (Jun-22-1969, San Juan) Jose Roman 10
- (Aug-18-1969, New York) George Foreman kot 3

+ (Dec-19-1969, New York) Pedro Agosto 10

- **1970** -
+ (Jan-26-1970, New York) Manuel Ramos 10
- (Jun-29-1970, Jersey City) Sonny Liston kot 10
- (Sep-8-1970, London) Joe Bugner injury 3

- **1971** -
- (Jan-16-1971, Scranton) Jerry Judge ko 5
+ (Sep-16-1971, North Bergen) Jesse Crown ko 4

+ (Oct-14-1971, North Bergen) Mike Boswell ko 10

- (Dec-9-1971, North Bergen) Randy Neumann 12

- 1972 -
+ (Apr-15-1972, Jersey City) Randy Neumann 12
+ (Dec-7-1972, Bayonne) John Clohessy 10

- 1973 -
+ (Mar-15-1973, North Bergen) Billy Narquart 12
+ (Jun-23-1973, Atlantic City) Ernie Terrell 12 (United States, Heavyweight)

- 1974 -
+ (Jan-17-1974, North Bergen) Billy Williams 10
+ (Mar-8-1974, New York) Randy Neumann ko 7
+ (May-23-1974, North Bergen) Charley Polite ko 4
+ (Sep-3-1974, Salt Lake City) Terry Hinki ko 11

- 1975 -
- (Mar-24-1975, Cleveland) Muhammad Ali ko 15 (World, Heavyweight)
+ (Nov-13-1975, Portland) Jimmy Evans ko 4
+ (Nov-29-1975, Fort Lauderdale) Johnny Dolan ko 3

- 1976 -
+ (May-7-1976, Kearny) Tommy Sheehan ko 2
- (Oct-2-1976, Utica) Duane Bobick ko 6

- 1977 -
- (Feb-19-1977, Johanesburg) Mike Schutte 10
- (May-20-1977, Binghampton) Horst Giesler ko 10

- 1978 -

+ (Apr-7-1978, North Bergen) John Blaine ko 3

+ (Jun-2-1978, Jersey City) Tom Healy ko 5

- (Sep-26-1978, Totowa) Scott Frank 12

(***Chuck informed me that he actually had more fights than listed above at smaller club venues which were not documented. With these fights, his actual record would stand at 58-14-2 unconfirmed.)

As always fight fans, keep reaching for the stars, and all your dreams can be fulfilled.

Interview conducted October 2001

About the Author

"Bad" Brad Berkwitt came into this world in the year that saw "The Greatest", Muhammad Ali, in exile. The year was 1968, and very early in his life, a passion would begin to form for a sport that this young, native New Yorker, would get involved in as a fighter, and eventually as a writer, becoming one of its greatest supporters. Of course, that sport is Boxing.

As a young man in the early 1970's, Brad would watch all the televised fights with his late father, Alvin, who had a deep passion for boxing, stretching as far back as the early 1940's.

A number of years later, in August of 1980, Brad ventured into the local community center to sign up for football, when he heard a noise that stopped him in his tracks, captivating him from then on, till this day. That noise was the sound of a boxing gym. Goodbye Pigskins-Hello Gloves! Brad would go on to fight as an amateur boxer for the next three years, winning more than he lost. His last fight, which came against a young man named Ronnie Williams, would come in the summer of 1983. As Brad recalls, "It was my greatest triumph in the ring when, in the second round, I dropped him with an overhand right." Williams would rise and finish out the fight on his feet, but Brad would win the decision and this would be his last fight in his amateur career.

Some years later, he became involved in another fight where this time he took on his opponent with a determination that may be unmatched by anyone in the sport of boxing. That fight was for the betterment of boxing and for the creation of a mandatory retirement fund for all boxers who have fought their hearts out and, where after a career, have nothing to show for it. To this day, Brad continues to pursue implementation of a retirement fund for boxers.

"Bad" Brad Berkwitt graduated from Mahopac High School located in Mahopac, New York in 1986. Shortly thereafter, he enlisted in the United States Navy on September 2, 1986. He attended Boot Camp in Great Lakes, Illinois. Upon completion, he was stationed in Pensacola, Florida. His tours of duty also include, Sigonella, Sicily, Alexandria, Virginia, Washington, DC (3 tours), Guantanamo Bay, Cuba and Seoul, Korea. This 16-year Navy veteran has also served in Desert Shield/Desert Storm.

"Bad" Brad has demonstrated in the Navy, the same passion he has for the sport of boxing. And, like in boxing, he has shown in the Navy, his deep concern for people and his deep desire to help make things better in the world. If his current successes are any indication, then his future in boxing is very bright.

Brad's success as a boxing interviewer is based on the strong principles he embraces: honesty and a positive approach to his interviews where he enables fighters to be heard in their own words.

The nickname "Bad" came from fellow author and ring announcer, Henry "Dis-com-bob-u-lating" Jones. In Henry's words, "I gave him that nickname because he always stands up for what he believes in, and the fighters truly respect him for being so positive in all of his interviews."

Brad constantly credits his late father, Alvin Frank Berkwitt, for his passions in life, most especially boxing. And, the sport could not be happier to have him.

"Bad" Brad's work has been featured on many boxing internet sites including the largest and most popular, "www.fightnews.com", where he has been employed as their feature writer since July, 2000. He has done TV and radio, being called upon many times for his expert analysis of the sport. He also has featured boxing interviews in the largest Italian American newspaper,"The Italian Tribune".

As of late, "Bad" Brad has been featured in many boxing publications and boxing books, while serving in Seoul, South Korea, where he was recently, in 2002, recognized by the Korean Boxing Commission along with the Korean boxing magazine "Cross Counter" as a "true star" in their words, who made a difference in boxing with all the positive coverage he brings that for the most part, died off many years ago.